I Wish I'd Known...
How Much I'd Love You

I Wish
I'd Known...

Copyright © 2013 I Wish I'd Known... (Julie Cwir)
Updated Edition 2018

ISBN-13: 978-1494736538
ISBN-10: 1494736535

Compiler and Editor: Julie Cwir
Photo Editor: Megan Rahn
Grammar Editors: Melanie Needham and Arlen Cwir
Book Cover and Logo Design: Rachelle Haines
Front Cover Photo: Ashley Gruber
Back Cover Photo: Meg Gallina
Foreword: Dr. Andrew P. Ordon, M.D., F.A.C.S.

Assistant Editors:
Shontina Caudle
Taryn Evans
Jo-Anne Osika King
Ashley Jackson
Erin Tisi

www.iwishidknown.yolasite.com
iwishidknown@hotmail.com

Presented To:

_____

By:

_____

Date:

_____

Dedication

To the global cleft community: this is your book,
these are your stories, this is your advice, and these are your children.

Table Of Contents

Read "Dear Pregnant Mom" letters on the following pages:

15
22
34
46
60
76
92
110
119
129
137
148
162
172
186
209

Acknowledgments

I Wish I'd Known… How Much I'd Love You has been an incredible journey in itself. Similar to each child's journey wrapped lovingly in the pages of this book, this project has had its ups and its downs with lots of love to carry it through. I have been incredibly blessed by the help I have received from people all over the world wanting to see this book come to fruition. This book would not have been completed without their generosity, hard work, and encouragement.

I'd like to thank Dr. Andrew Ordon for writing such a wonderful foreword and for supporting this book of cleft stories. His work with Smile Train, the Surgical Friends Foundation, and *The Doctors* TV show provides much value to the cleft and general medical community.

Thank you, Kate Ylst, for helping me get this project up and running. Your encouragement and support has pushed this book to be bigger than I had first imagined.

To Rachelle Haines, for creating the most beautiful logo and book cover ever. Her advice in web and graphic designs has been an invaluable asset to *I Wish I'd Known…*

Thank you to those in the media providing coverage about this book. Your work helps to spread cleft awareness and support for the cleft community.

To Transforming Faces, for their passion in spreading cleft awareness and for their support in the making of this book. The care they provide through their organization is top notch and their featured story proves to be a wonderful addition to this book.

My co-editors deserve many thanks. Their amazing help and support has put the pieces of this book together. Shontina Caudle for her tireless effort, reliability, and friendliness. Megan Rahn for her awesome work in photo editing. Erin Tisi, Taryn Evans, Jo-Anne Osika King, and Ashley Jackson for all your work, help, and support.

Thank you, especially, to Melanie Needham and Arlen Cwir for their reliable and comprehensive efforts to amend the grammar of this book.

My Husband has been a wonderful support throughout this project. I am incredibly grateful for his help and reassurance along the way. He has pushed me when I needed to be pushed and comforted me when I needed comforting. Also, this book would not even be a reality if it weren't for my own cleft child. I am thankful for his smiles, laughter, and the joy he brings into our home. Thank you to my entire family; you have been incredibly supportive, loving, and helpful in the making of this book and beyond.

I would, personally, like to thank my Lord and Savior. He has given me strength and perseverance to see this book come to fruition. I have been extremely blessed to be a part of this book. God is good.

Finally, thank you to every single parent that has submitted a story, survey, advice, or photo for *I Wish I'd Known… How Much I'd Love You*. I cannot thank you enough for helping make this book into something absolutely, undeniably remarkable. It is you who has brought this book into existence. This is OUR book; a product of the global cleft community.

Foreword

Our children and our patients come first. What better way to enter the world of all those who deal with cleft lip and palate, than through the remarkable and enlightening stories that Julie Cwir has so masterfully collected. It is through these stories that all of us who are touched by the journey of the cleft patient (i.e. the patients themselves, other children, family, and health care providers), will better understand the physical, mental, and spiritual road to being whole once again.

The surgeon's task is to restore the structure and function of the divided facial parts to as near as normal as possible while causing no damage to the sensitive growing tissues. But, that is only part of the story. These are kids; children with delicate and sensitive issues. I, personally, now feel better equipped to treat my cleft patients having the benefit of better comprehension of our patients as a whole and not just an operation.

I remember well, doing my first cleft lip and palate repair in 1983, and being so intent on doing that perfect operation. Some thirty years later, reconstructive techniques and our knowledge of the physiology of clefting have evolved greatly. But, this remarkable evolution is only of value when we combine it with understanding the cleft patient as a human being, in need of help. *I Wish I'd Known... How Much I'd Love you* takes us to that place.

This is a must read for all of us committed to bettering the quality of life for our cleft children.

Dr. Andrew P. Ordon, M.D., F.A.C.S.

Dr. Andrew Ordon practices plastic and reconstructive surgery in California, USA. Ordon is one of the founders of the Surgical Friends Foundation. The Surgical Friends Foundation is a non-profit organization created to "provide reconstructive surgery and post-operative care to individuals living with physical deformities who do not have access to quality medical care."

Dr. Ordon has also had the opportunity to work with Smile Train. Ordon had wonderful things to say about his experience with Smile Train. "Working with Smile Train in India was the best experience I have had in my career! The whole trip left me inspired with a sense of accomplishment I have not felt before. It made me feel proud to be a plastic and reconstructive surgeon... utilizing my skills for such a noble cause. The Smile Train Organization is such a class act, changing lives with a purpose."

ANDREW P. ORDON , M.D., F.A.C.S.
Certified American Board of Plastic Surgery
Certified American Board of Head & Neck Surgery
Host, The EMMY AWARD winning, THE DOCTORS TV
Assistant Adjunct Professor of Surgery
DARTMOUTH MEDICAL SCHOOL

Roxbury Clinic and Surgery Center
465 North Roxbury Drive, Suite 1001
Beverly Hills, California 90210
(310) 248-6250
www.drordon.com
www.thedoctorstv.com
www.surgicalfriends.org

Introduction

It started out as an idea; an idea to put together a few stories between some online friends and package it in a neat little book. This small idea has grown to be so much more throughout the creation of *I Wish I'd Known... How Much I'd Love You*.

After first facing the news that their child has a cleft condition, many parents go through a grieving period. This first phase of the cleft journey can be sad, depressing, frightful, stressful, and leaves many heavy-hearted. It is a time consumed by pouring over the internet for information and trying to find the best care and support for their new babe. In that moment, it is hard to see what is on the other side of that mountain.

Once parents meet and bond with their precious and perfect child, they all come to the realization that love conquers fear. The love that a parent has for their child is so great that it surmounts any grief, stress, or sadness. This love calls a parent into action to fight for their child in the hardest of times, to be their best or only advocate and to do whatever they need to in order for their child to thrive. When a parent experiences this love for their child, when they climb every hurdle, then they can finally see what is on the other side of that mountain. It is beautiful. It is rewarding. It is a blessed journey.

If you are a new parent to a cleft affected child, fear not. You will probably feel every emotion possible, which is normal, but know that your child IS beautiful. Your child IS perfect. Your child was made just the way they were supposed to be and you were chosen specifically to be their parent. There will come a day, when you will look at your baby with the utmost love and realize there was and is no need to stress.

Our hope for this book is to bring encouragement and education to new parents of cleft affected children. They are not alone in their journey and there are many others that have walked the same path.

Our wish is that this book will provide cleft specialists and family medical doctors with new information, medical techniques, and theories as well as new resources.

This book is also for the everyday person. *I Wish I'd Known... How Much I'd Love You*, promotes cleft awareness. Our desire is to educate others in what parents of cleft children endure, find ways to support them, and be uplifted by following along in their journeys.

With each story, you will see the name of the child along with their cleft information and story. With most stories in the book, you will be able to see before and after surgery photos as well. Each story ends with a statement of what the parent wishes they would have known before their journey began.

What makes this book unique are the "Dear Pregnant Mom" letters found in-between the chapters of this book. These letters are written by parents of a cleft affected child and are written encouragements and advice to pregnant moms and/or new parents of a cleft child. The name for these letters is based on a discussion thread from the cleft lip and cleft palate group on BabyCenter.com. This online thread has proven to uplift many parents as they begin their cleft journey. The letters included in this book are a compilation of thoughts and encouragements from the stories submitted, the survey conducted for the book, and with permission from some of the writers of the online posts.

Take the time to educate yourself further by reading the frequently asked questions regarding clefts, the results of our cleft survey, checking out the lists of resources, and the answers parents gave to our questions about their cleft journey. While reading this book, if you ever come across a term you're not sure about, flip to the glossary at the back of the book to look it up.

I feel incredibly privileged to be a part of a community made up of individuals from all over the world. Stories for this book have been submitted from across the globe: the United States of America, Canada, United Kingdom, South Africa, Australia, and New Zealand.

As parents, we have a story to share. We have experiences and advice to pass on to others. This is our book. These are our stories. May you be uplifted, informed, and encouraged.

Frequently Asked Questions

What is a cleft lip and cleft palate?

Cleft lip and cleft palate are birth defects that occur during early pregnancy. A cleft occurs when the mouth or lip area does not form properly and does not fully join.

A cleft lip refers to a separation of the two sides of the upper lip. A cleft palate refers to a split or opening in the roof of the mouth. A cleft palate can involve the hard palate and/or the soft palate. Further, a microform cleft is a mild form of a cleft lip in which the lip is still intact, but a scar appears in place of a cleft gap.

What are the different types of clefts?

A cleft may be referred to as complete or incomplete. Complete means that the cleft reaches all the way to the nose in the case of the lip, or all the way to the back of the mouth in the case of a cleft palate. Incomplete refers to a cleft that does not reach the nose or back of the mouth.

Clefts can be unilateral, meaning affecting only one side of the lip. A cleft can also be bilateral, meaning that it affects both sides of the lip. More rarely, a cleft can be midline, meaning occurring in the middle of the top lip.

What causes a cleft?

In most cases, the cause of cleft lips and cleft palates is unknown. According to the Seattle Children's Hospital, 60% of cleft cases are not a result of any specific occurrence during or after pregnancy. It is believed that clefts are caused by a combination of genetic and environmental factors. Medications, drugs, or alcohol may also be a potential cause of clefts. Drugs such as anti-seizure/anti-convulsant medications, acne drugs, or SSRI's may cause clefts if taken by the mother during pregnancy. Exposure to viruses or chemicals while pregnant can also be a possible cause.

How common are clefts?

The Centers for Disease Control and Prevention (CDC) estimates approximately one in every 33 babies is born with a birth defect. Every year, an estimated 2,651 babies in the United States are born with a cleft palate and 4,437 babies are born with a cleft lip with or without a cleft palate. Clefts of the lip are more common than cleft palate. Isolated clefts are one of the most common birth defects in the United States. The CDC averages about 70% of all orofacial clefts are isolated and not alongside any other birth defects.

Can it be repaired?

Clefts are repaired by way of surgery. The severity of the cleft will determine the amount of surgeries needed. Most often, surgery to repair a cleft lip is performed by the time a baby is three to five months of age. Those with an alveolar ridge notch may need a bone graft at five to seven-years-old in order to create support for permanent teeth.

Repair of a cleft palate often requires multiple surgeries over the course of childhood and even teen years. A surgery at approximately one year of age initially closes the gap in the palate. Children with a cleft palate may also need ear tubes, fistula repairs, or other surgeries to help improve their speech and overall health.

Some surgeons chose to use a cleft device in order to reshape a cleft prior to surgery. Most often, the options are between a Nasoalveolar molding device (NAM) or the Latham device. Both devices are used to bring the cleft closer together. The NAM is a removable device, whereas the Latham device is surgically planted for a period of time.

Braces are often required to straighten teeth when cleft children are older. Additional surgeries may be performed to improve the appearance of the lip and nose, repair fistulas, aid in breathing, jaw realignment, and scar revision.

Please note that the age ranges given for procedures can vary greatly depending on surgeon recommendations and the health of the patient.

Who treats children with cleft lip and/or palate?

There are many different professionals that make up a cleft team. A cleft team refers to the many different professionals that provide cleft care. These medical professionals may be located in one facility or many.

The main provider of cleft care is the plastic surgeon. He or she will evaluate and perform necessary surgeries on the lip and/or palate.

At the very least, a dentist is seen to provide regular dental care. Further, an oral surgeon may be required for jaw reposition or reparation of the gum line. An orthodontist would be essential if braces are recommended. Also, a prosthodontist would make any needed artificial teeth and/or dental appliances.

An otolaryngologist (an ear, nose, and throat doctor) may be required to evaluate hearing problems and consider treatment options for hearing problems. As well, an audiologist, speech pathologist or speech therapist may be needed to evaluate any hearing or speaking issues.

Occasionally, parents are referred to a geneticist to examine possible causes of the cleft, the probability of having more children with a cleft, or any possible related health issues. A social worker or psychologist is available for support and assessment of any emotional and family difficulties along the journey.

What do cleft babies struggle with?

The most common setback among cleft babies is feeding. The separation or hole in the lip and/or palate creates a loss of suction. Only a select minority of cleft babies are able to breastfeed direct from the breast. Most often, a cleft baby is fed via a special cleft bottle. Occasionally, feeding tubes are required to provide cleft children with the nutrition they need. Further, a cleft palate may cause food to pass back up through the nose or even out the ears.

The second most common struggle of a cleft baby is dental problems. Children with a cleft may be at increased risk of cavities and may have missing, extra, malformed, or displaced teeth. These problems are repaired through oral surgery, dental, and/or orthodontic treatment.

A common complaint of cleft palate patients are ear infections. The ears may not be able to drain properly because of abnormal palatal muscles. Often ear tubes are placed to remedy this. If left untreated, ear infections can cause hearing loss.

Because of the gap in the lip or palate, speech problems may result. Surgery may fix these problems, or a speech pathologist may be required. It is interesting to note that it is momentous when a cleft child can suck through a straw, blow a balloon, or play through an instrument. This is because certain clefts and/or the presence of fistulas can make these things difficult to perform.

What types of scar treatment are used?
Please follow your surgeon's recommendations regarding post-surgery care. Depending on the type of surgery or technique the surgeon performs, he or she may have different suggestions.

A common recommendation is to keep the area moist (with Polysporin or petroleum jelly) while it is healing. A surgeon may recommend massaging the healed scar with a doctor approved cream to keep the skin pliable and reduce bumps. Some popular scar treatment creams include SCARprin, ScarFade, Emu Oil, Cimeosil, etc.

"I just found out my baby has a cleft. What do I do?"
First of all, be sure the cleft is confirmed by a doctor. Contact your health care provider to be put in contact with a cleft team. Find the resources in the back of this book and research clefts and cleft care. Join a local and/or online support group for parents of cleft affected children. Confirm how the surgeries and impending essential cleft care will be paid for. This might entail calling your insurance provider or your cleft team.

If you have found out during pregnancy, relax, enjoy the pregnancy, and begin to prepare for your baby. Cleft babies do not necessarily need extra baby gear compared to a non-clefted baby. It would be helpful to have special bottles available to try out when baby comes. Do not buy too many of one kind, as often it may take trial and error to find the perfect fit.

After having a cleft baby, what should I do if trying to conceive again?
If trying to conceive after having a cleft child, it is good to take into consideration a variety of things before becoming pregnant. First of all, an increase in folic acid is an important factor. The Cleft Lip and Palate Association (CLAPA) recommends a 4mg (4,000mcg) dose of folic acid per day for those who have previously had a child with a cleft. It is important to begin taking this at least two months before trying to conceive.

Consider any medications the mother or father may be taking, as certain medications can potentially have an effect on a growing fetus. It is important to refrain from smoking, drugs, alcohol, or toxic substances. If possible, it is best for the mother to be in good health, appropriate weight, and eating healthy.

How do I prepare my toddler or older child for surgery?
A surgery can be scary for a child. Therefore, it is good to prepare them and make them feel comfortable with the process. Ask the cleft team or hospital for a walk through of the areas the child would be going through and staying in. During this process, explain what will be happening. Ask if siblings are allowed to join as well so they can better understand and be a good helper. For older children, showing before and after pictures can help as well as walking through what will happen during the surgery.

Another idea is to perform pretend surgery on a stuffed animal with the child to explain the process. Begin with initial tests, checking Teddy's weight and heartbeat to make sure he is healthy enough for surgery. Teddy could be given a hospital gown, brought to the 'operation room,' and have a bandage on when he comes out. Of course, Teddy would get lots of cuddles when he's all done.

Featured Stories

Story of Dedication

A cleft story dedicated to those who have bereaved their cleft child:

She was diagnosed with Trisomy 13. She had a bilateral cleft lip and palate, six fingers on both hands, rocker bottom feet, a hole in her heart, and her brain was three weeks behind her body.

I was 25 weeks and five days when I miscarried. They hooked me up to a baby monitor and found no heartbeat. They hooked me up to a Doppler – still no heartbeat. They ordered an ultrasound. Our Jamie was not moving and she had no heartbeat. She had passed.

I got to hold her before they cleaned her off and after. She was incredibly adorable and I just wanted to keep her in my room with me. I miss my little girl so much. I wish I could just spend a couple more minutes with our beautiful, little Jamie!

Dear God,

Tell my baby girl that when I found out I was pregnant and had her body in mine,
I loved her from that very second.
I knew we would be inseparable for nine months.
Please tell her, that I would wait just to feel her kick,
that I would just wait to feel her move around in my stomach.
Tell her that I smiled every time I felt her kick once she started.
Please tell my little girl that the day I found out she was my little girl,
I fled to find the perfect things for her when she would come into the world.
I jumped to find the PERFECT name for her.
Please tell her as soon as I found 'Jamie Nicole' I knew it would fit
and never be changed.
Please tell my little Jamie that, yes, mommy and daddy had problems,
but it never changed the love we had for her.
Please tell my little Jamie, how I told her big brother Cameron
he would have another little sister come into this world.
Please tell her that the day I found out she had so many birth defects I was scared,
but I knew I would love her no matter what.
Please tell her the day I found out she had Trisomy 13 I started to look up what it was,
its possibilities, and how long she might be with Mommy.
Please tell her I cried every day,
thinking about how I may never get to spend time with her.
Please tell her that every day I felt her kick, I thanked You for keeping her alive.
Please tell her that the day I felt her stop moving
I was so scared and worried that she was no longer with me.
I cried like a big baby when I found out my little girl was now with You.
Please let her know that I think about her every day and she will never be forgotten.
God, please let my little girl know that I love her and will never stop.
Please let her know, I can't wait until I get to meet her face to face.
Please tell her to watch over Mommy and Daddy
And please let her know, that she is my sweet little angel, always and forever.

Transforming Faces

Transforming Faces is a Canadian charity that provides free multidisciplinary cleft care for children and adults in developing countries. They work in partnership with local cleft specialists and fund community-based medical teams. The Transforming Faces partner teams provide multi-disciplinary cleft care, so that children can be socially accepted and lead a productive life.
www.transformingfaces.org

Meet Sayuri, who was born with a cleft lip and recently celebrated her first birthday! Her parents, from the district of San Juan de Lurigancho in Lima, Peru were initially shocked when the doctor told them that Sayuri had been born with a cleft lip. Her mother had never seen a child with cleft lip. She was initially sad, scared, and desperate. Little by little, she turned that fear into action and armed herself with information.

Sayuri, as a result, had her first operation when she was eight-months-old. Then, they began to visit Kusi Rostros, a program which administers Community Rehabilitation Centres (CRCs) in four poor areas of Lima, for follow-up care such as speech stimulation support and dentistry advice. The family has also been seeing a psychologist. Sayuri's mother is grateful that she can access free cleft care close to home.

Children like Sayuri and her parents need help in the early stages of infancy to make sure that the child has the best possible future. Transforming Faces provides both the initial surgeries as well as comprehensive rehabilitation. That includes feeding and psychological support in developing nations. But, it's not just children who are being supported; it is teenagers and parents too!

In some countries, parents do not often have the ability or desire to photograph their babies due to the suspicions and shame associated with cleft. A photographic clinic was introduced to improve ties between parents and their children with cleft lip and palate. One dad commented, "I thought that no one wanted to see my child, so I hid those pictures."

The photographic clinic, where parents and newborns with cleft lip and palate are photographed through the years, works closely with psychologists who use it to work with the family. The hope is to achieve a healthy attachment between parents and children, so that the children can grow up a bit more confident and happy.

Since 1999, Transforming Faces has transformed the lives of 10,000 cleft lip and palate patients through 155,779 surgeries and interventions! A private charitable foundation covers the overhead costs of Transforming Faces, so 100% of donations are directed to cleft programs for children around the world.

Dear Pregnant Mom,

I know your heart feels like it is breaking. You may have received the news in your ultrasound or had a birthday surprise. I know you are probably on the internet, worrying about how you will handle this, what your child will look like, how your other kids will feel, if there will be anything else wrong, how bad the cleft is, if the palate is involved, and so on.

You are in a state of grief. You are mourning the loss of the child you expected. You might feel jealous of your friends who have healthy kids and pregnancies with nothing to worry about. You may consider whether to proceed with the pregnancy or be researching cleft teams who will help you get through this.

All of these feelings are normal. We have been there and we can promise you that you will get through it. Some of us immediately bond with our babies, not noticing the cleft at all. For others, it takes time to establish that bond. Either way, you are normal for feeling worried and sad right now. There is simply a lot of unknown.

My advice, for what it is worth, is to get your ducks in a row. Find that perfect cleft team, focus on feeding plans and equipment, and do your very best to enjoy your pregnancy. You will love that child. He will be unique in so many ways having nothing to do with his cleft. He will need you to be positive and strong. So, cry now, worry now, grieve now, and get it all out of your system.

You CAN do this, like many mothers before. I am the wife of a cleft affected man who never thought about his cleft a day in his life. Try not to fixate on how your child will feel when he is 15. In many ways, the way you handle this will dictate how he views himself. The way you approach surgeries, will be how he approaches the same event, and the way you focus on his cleft will be the way he focuses on it.

You will get through this and your baby will be a special part of your family - much loved, doted upon, and cared for.

With much love and many hugs.

It Only Takes One to Care

" *This little person is counting on you to be that person to*

help them get through this life. "

Reese

Country: United States of America
Type of Cleft: Bilateral Cleft Lip and Palate
Birthdate: April 13, 2001
Cleft Team: Dr. Glassman, MD, Dr. Allen, MD, and Dr. Smith, MD
Found Out About Cleft: At Birth
Cleft Device: Palate Expander
Surgery: 11 Surgeries to Date
Family History of Clefts: No

My son was born on April 13, 2001. He weighed in at nine pounds, 14 ounces and was 21 inches long. He was born with a bilateral cleft lip and palate. The first time I was able to hold him I thought to myself that people were staring. How could I show them I love him? I held him close and kissed him on the cheek. His smell was unlike anything I ever smelled. I can't describe it, because my second child didn't smell like that. But, his scent lasted three days. We had established a bond in those three days. It was a good thing because his own father left us because he couldn't handle the situation. We both carry his last name, but that is all he left us with. Yet, he gave me my son, who gave me hope. I had no one else. I was 21-years-old and terrified. But, we had each other and I couldn't give up. Reese was counting on me to help him through this life.

I'm not going to lie. It has been hard. There have been many nights where I have blamed myself for his condition, cried after they led him away to surgeries, and prayed that he would not be bullied again at school. I wish I had someone who had all the answers. But, I learned. The Mead Johnson squeezable bottle was our life safer in the beginning. I learned that Q-tips worked great for taking boogers out of his collapsed nostrils. I would microwave a Popsicle for 30 seconds with apple juice from the hospital to make the best slushy for post-op surgery.

There are perks for having a child so unique! You get to meet the most extraordinary staff that will provide medical care for your child. You will meet other kids that have similar problems and their families. You will experience joy when they overcome obstacles. You will feel contentment like no other because you care for this child that needs you.

It only takes one person in this world to care! This little person is counting on you to be that person to help them get through this life. It only takes one person to care for an infant and bring them up in this world today; only one. If there are hundreds or thousands of people that care, that's gravy. I hope that you care.

I Wish I'd Known… it only takes one person to care.

Chris

Country: United Kingdom
Type of Cleft: Incomplete Unilateral Cleft Lip and Palate
Birthdate: May 29, 1994
Cleft Team: Great Ormond Street Hospital
Found Out About Cleft: At Birth
Surgery Dates: At 11 weeks, six months, seven years, 10, 12, 16 and 18 years.
Family History of Clefts: Unknown

My son, Chris, was born with an incomplete cleft lip and palate. For me, it wasn't totally unexpected. I had been adopted, so there is no medical history available for my side of the family. I was very glad that it was something that could be 'fixed.'

Unfortunately, his father found it very hard and, to cut a long story short, left us just after Chris' third birthday. Life got easier in some aspects. I was always disappointed that his father was not more supportive, but I was determined to make sure that Chris did not miss out. Life as a working single parent, having to juggle work, childcare, and the demands of parenting was a struggle at times. Tiring, but then parenting is anyway.

It was nine years of one appointment per month to see the orthodontist. I'm not complaining though; all treatment in the UK was covered for us. We also get to use possibly the best Children's hospital in the world. Chris has had six operations so far. He is expected to have at least one more. So, we continue to juggle a bit more for a little bit longer.

What is the icing on the cake? Chris has achieved a place to study music at Oxford University. What an achievement. Together we did it!!

I Wish I'd Known... that the better times would always outweigh the tough times.

18

Azalea

Country: United States of America
Type of Cleft: Left Unilateral Cleft Lip, Notched Alveolar Ridge, Bone Defect and Submucous Cleft Palate
Birthdate: September 2, 2005
Cleft Team: Boston Children's Hospital; Dr. Richard Bartlett, MD (Reconstructive surgery), Dr. Bonnie Padwa, MD (Oral surgeon), and Dr. Stephen Schustermann, MD (Pediatric dentist)
Found Out About Cleft: At Birth
Surgery Dates: November 2005 (Lip repair), February 19, 2013 (Top teeth extracted in preparation for bone graft), May 1, 2013 (Bone graft)
Family History of Clefts: No

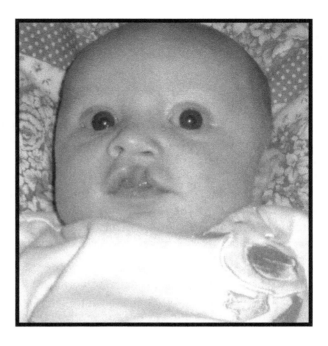

On September 2, 2005, an amazing little soul named Azalea Jo entered the world. I had spent nine months imagining who she would look like. Hopefully, she would have her Dad's chicken legs, my brown eyes, and a smile that could light up the room like her older brother's. Her arrival would be nothing short of momentous and I felt blessed to be given a daughter.

My pregnancy was riddled with minor complications. Hyperemisis Gravidium, placenta previa, and bleeding in my uterus all topped with a very hot summer. My husband and I had spent the majority of my pregnancy building a house on a little piece of land we had bought in the town we grew up in. Against countless suggestions to not bite off too much with a two-year-old and being pregnant, we kept going. We were determined to make a home for the four of us. Admittedly, it was exhausting as everyone suggested and may have evoked a few tears in the aisles of Home Depot while attempting to select bathroom fixtures with a two-year-old and a very pregnant belly. At the end of nine months, the house wasn't finished. Surprisingly, it didn't really matter to us. We felt more than grateful for our new beginning taking shape and the arrival of Azalea would be part of that.

Azalea would come to us via a scheduled C-section in the morning. We rose early and I spent the morning taking in every part of our son, Keegan, before the days of just "he and I" would end. I felt every emotion a mother-to-be of two feels: sadness, joy, fear, and a quiet calm that our lives were about to change. My husband and I headed to the hospital to embark on the routine that we had gone through three years ago. Of course, we were bumped by a woman who had been in labor all night and so our wait was longer than expected. My anxiety increased and by the time my husband attempted to depart at the operating room, I had decided I couldn't go in there. I cried hysterically and begged him not to leave. I wasn't ready. Every bit of readiness I had felt hours ago had vanished and I felt more scared than ever and so uneasy. Something just didn't feel right. I look back now and wonder if my "mother's intuition" had set in.

My pregnancy with Azalea brought several ultrasounds, none of which showed any sign of a cleft lip or palate to any technician or doctor. There was one small moment after my 20-week ultrasound that I looked at her squirming body on the screen and thought for just a fleeting second that her face looked somehow different. After questioning the technician and being assured that it was just her positioning for the most part, I let it go. Every now and then, I would catch a glimpse of that ultrasound image on the fridge and think, "Something looks weird." On the morning we met our daughter, I think those inklings had taken over and somehow she was telling my heart to be alert. I could feel it in every bone of my body that something was wrong.

The first words I heard were, "She has a cleft." I was in the operating room with my Mom and my husband and could see their faces after I heard the word. She wasn't held up for me to see like Keegan was and my husband quickly left my side to see her. I heard the pediatrician talking and, although it is hard to admit, my husband looked sad and my mother looked serious. I felt like everything inside me was going to burst. I prayed in my head for those first few minutes that the doctor would take back those words. I just wanted to change it. Those minutes before I saw Azalea for the first time were unbearable. And then, like any other baby, they wrapped her up and brought her to me. It was almost like I didn't even see it. I thought everyone in the room was crazy. I had only one thought, "She's perfect."

The following days were filled with mixed emotions. We live in a small town and were at a hospital that didn't frequently see babies born with a cleft. I felt angry that there was a lack of information and that we were not given a Haberman Feeder until 12 hours after she was born, at which point she was dehydrated and weak. I felt infuriated by the pediatrician who repeatedly kept talking about her "defect." To me, this little creature that lay nestled in my arms was anything but defective.

Like every mother in my position, I felt like it must have been something I did to her. I felt guilty, worried, mad, and alone. I wondered if a boy would love her someday and want to kiss her. I already thought about how harsh kids can be in school to someone who looks different. I just wanted everyone to see her like I saw her; without a cleft, perfect and complete. I worried about my son. We hadn't been able to prepare him for what she would look like. He was quiet when he looked at her and too little to articulate how confused I'm sure he was about why she didn't look like other babies he had seen. I felt so overwhelmed and every now and then thought, "I just can't do this." I left the hospital a day earlier than I should have. I signed a consent form saying that I was being discharged "against medical advice" and headed home to figure out our next step. I was sure that once we got home my head would be clearer and I could take this on.

When we arrived home, everything seemed a little better. I had some clarity and my husband went into work mode. We had received no information about where to go or a referral to anyone who could repair her lip. At that point, we didn't even know the term "cleft lip repair" existed. Family and friends researched cleft lips, the causes, and the repairs among other things.

Our first week home was filled with countless phone calls, seeking information about where the best surgeons were located, and how to assemble a "cleft care team." We knew that our small state of Maine would probably not be able to offer the resources we needed, so we started looking elsewhere. We did agree to go to a couple consult appointments in Maine to surgeons who supposedly had experience with clefts. Those consults were a nightmare. After measurements and profile pictures, at one consult we were told, "I'll never be able to make her look perfect. It just won't happen." I quietly looked at my husband, swaddled her back up in her car seat and left the room with parting words of "I'll meet you outside."

We quickly discovered that we were her only advocates. It had become our mission to be her voice. When people stared, we told them the correct term for what her lip looked like. It is safe to say that the pity party that I may have had for myself in that lonely hospital room on the day she was born, had all but disappeared. What remained was a new-found strength in myself, in my husband and in my two children to stand in the face of adversity and just keep walking forward.

Seven years later, we are still taking steps forward. We made it through Azalea's lip repair at three months. It is hard to admit, but every now and then when I am by myself wrapped up in my own thoughts, I wish that she would have never been born with a cleft. Just recently, when she had her top teeth pulled in preparation for an upcoming bone graft, I felt like seeing her in pain was unbearable. Then, as if she knows right when I need it most, she shows me her strength. She smiles bigger than anyone in the room and she laughs without caring that her teeth are gone. I am reminded of how resilient her spirit is. I am reminded that I wouldn't want anything about her to be different; that deep dark wish vanishes and I count my blessings.

Our lives are exactly how they are meant to be. Our purpose is always just a glimpse ahead and strength is as abundant as the love that supports it. I am grateful for Azalea and all she has taught me already about my purpose and about those around her. She is truly an amazing little creature who makes the world a little brighter because she's in it.

I Wish I'd Known...
that our lives are
exactly how they are
meant to be.

Dear Pregnant Mom,

To the parents about to embark upon this journey, it is okay to feel any and every emotion at your disposal. I wish someone had told me, that all my insecurities were perfectly normal and okay. If you are angry, be angry. If you feel cheated, feel cheated. If you are scared, be scared; cry, scream, or break something if you need to. If you supress such torrential sentiment it will manifest itself in other ways and you simply cannot become embittered toward, or jaded by, the injustice of it all.

You did nothing to cause this. Regardless of what people might say, there is nothing you could have done differently to keep it from happening and there is nothing you can do now to change what it is. This is your new reality; accept it, embrace it. Do not waste your precious time and energy on what might have been. There are far too many crossroads and obstacles to overcome in the days, weeks, months, and years to come. How you perceive your child's cleft and how you handle it day by day determines how your child perceives not only his or her cleft, but himself or herself. You cannot shield them from the world, but you can arm them. Your positivity, your creativity, and your proactivity are the catalyst for warmth and comfort in your child.

Be active in your child's care, be utterly involved, ask one hundred thousand questions and, when you feel as if you have asked enough, ask even more. Do your research, extensively and scholarly, and document everything. Above all, know that while there will be many times you have to relinquish authority and immense trust to your medical team, there are times when you must follow your heart. Even if you have the most fabulous and understanding team, your child is still another face in the crowd of many other cases. You are the world to your child and your child is the world to you.

Never forget that there are some things that cannot be explained by science in a textbook or learned in a classroom. A parent's intuition is one such phenomenon. When I look back on this long and incredible journey we have had, the only times I regret are the times I did not trust my instinct. You are your baby's best, and sadly, sometimes only, advocate.

Sending you love and support.

Pregnancy: The Long Wait

"The tech got quieter and quieter as she studied his face."

River

Country: United States of America
Type of Cleft: Left Complete Unilateral Cleft Lip and Palate
Birthdate: January 18, 2012
Cleft Team: Doernbecher Children's Hospital; Dr. Anna Kuang, MD
Found Out About Cleft: Elective 28-Week Ultrasound
Surgery Dates: August 23, 2012 (Lip repair), January 23, 2013 (Palate repair)
Family History of Clefts: No

After having two girls, we really wanted to try one more time for a boy. After a year of trying, we found out we were pregnant! The ultrasound confirmed we were going to get our little man! We were over the moon with the news that our girls would have a brother! At our 20-week scan, he was covering his face and we never did get a full on face shot. None-the-less, everything looked normal and I continued to have a healthy pregnancy. Since I knew this was going to be my last baby, I really wanted to go all out. We wanted to do a belly cast, have a 3-D/4-D ultrasound, and do other things I would never get to do again.

At 28 weeks, my husband and I took the girls with us to get a 3-D/4-D scan. Again, our little man was being stubborn and would not let us see his face! They told us to come back the next day so we could try again. The next day, we returned without the girls and tried again. This time we got a clear picture. As the technician was doing the scan and we were watching images of our baby on the screen, my husband said, "Looks kind of like he has a cleft lip." I was in disbelief. How could this be? The tech confirmed that it could possibly be a cleft, but she was no doctor and could not be 100% sure.

I left the office stunned. As soon as we got into the car, I started looking for "cleft lip ultrasound pictures" on Google. I desperately searched the Internet for something that looked like our picture. The next day I called my doctor to tell her what we were told and see what the next step was. She immediately called the hospital where I had my 20-week scan to have them go over my original scan and see if they would take a look at my new scan from 28 weeks. I drove our photo disc to the hospital and waited by my phone. It was only a matter of hours before they called to confirm that he indeed had a cleft lip and it looked like the palate was involved as well.

The next few months were filled with lots of sadness, grief, and a little joy, too. We were incredibly happy to a have our son on the way. Yet, all that happiness didn't seem to matter. I remember crying and saying, "Why me? Why us? Why my son?" I did so much crying and worrying that it really took over my life. On the outside, I was happy and fine, but in the inside my heart was broken. After doing lots of research and feeling prepared with the knowledge of clefts, we were ready for our baby boy to arrive.

It snowed the night before he was born. I love snow and we rarely get it where we live. Somehow, this snow was brought to me as a sign from a high power that everything would be okay, and it was. The next morning, my sweet son was born via C-section. When I saw him for the first time, I was in love and at peace!

Now, as my son is just turning one, I hardly think about his cleft anymore. Of course, we still have years to go on this journey, but we are okay and so is he! He is healthy, happy, and just as normal as any other one-year-old boy!

I Wish I'd Known...
that at one-year-old, my boy would be thriving and
healthy and I don't really think about the cleft that much.

Hughitt

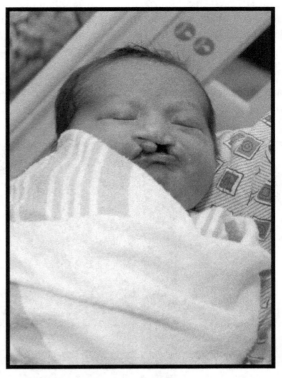

Country: United States of America
Type of Cleft: Bilateral Complete Lip and Palate
Birthdate: August 22, 2012
Cleft Team: Inova Fairfax Children's Hospital; Dr. Baker (Plastics), Dr. Maull (Orthodontics)
Found Out About Cleft: 21 Weeks Gestation
Cleft Device: NAM Device Pre-op
Surgery Date: November 26, 2012 (Lip and nose repair)
Family History of Clefts: No

"I see you declined the amnio as part of your prenatal screening. You may want to reconsider." Those were the first words out of the doctor's mouth when he walked into the room. This was a doctor we had never met and planned on never meeting again; a doctor who was supposed to walk into the room and tell us that the images captured by the radiologist at our routine 20-week anatomy ultrasound looked perfect and we could go home to enjoy the last half of our pregnancy.

Before I could even take a breath, he continued on about the risks and benefits involved with an amniocentesis and added that it could be done that day if we wanted to proceed. I nervously laughed at his seemingly rehearsed little speech and told him we would pass. That's when he sat down, looked me in the eye for the first time, and said, "There was a finding on your scan, so you may want to reconsider." At that moment, I stopped breathing and my heart may have stopped beating. I stared at him blankly, as if he had just told me a joke and left out the punch-line. By the time I found words, it seemed like an eternity had passed.

I'm not really sure how the conversation went over the next few minutes. My mind was racing at a pace too fast for my memory to keep up. I remember him saying, "Your baby, ("Our son," I interjected.), your son has a cleft lip and palate." It appeared complete on the left side and incomplete on the right. My knowledge of clefts at that time ran about as deep as the commercials; showcasing impoverished, grown children with severely malformed facial features. I could feel my heart beating in my stomach as he continued on about our increased risk of genetic syndromes, some of which are "not compatible with life." A vast majority of clefts are isolated birth defects, but he was encouraging us to move forward with the amnio to rule out the possibility that our child would be suffering from something more serious.

I couldn't. The risks associated with amniocentesis terrified me. I made up my mind that day that I wasn't going to dwell on the unknown. I would enjoy my pregnancy, deliver my child, and go from there. So, that's what we did.

Hughitt Richard came into our lives in August, on a beautiful summer morning. I heard his beautiful cry and for half a second I completely forgot about the cleft and the possible associated problems. I allowed myself to be completely and utterly joyous. They placed him on my chest and as I looked him in the eyes for the first time, any worry or concern I had over the previous several months evaporated. I knew we would be fine. He was my perfect, wide smiling, crazy haired, bouncing baby boy.

Life since his birth four months ago has been a whirlwind. He was fitted for his NAM device at three weeks of age, which he wore 23 hours a day until he had his lip and nose repair at three-months-old. Seeing him for the first time post lip repair was the most emotional moment of my life. I felt relief knowing he was physically okay. I mourned the loss of his adorable wide smile that I had grown to love so much. I felt elation seeing his beautiful new mouth and nose. My heart broke seeing him in pain. I've never experienced such a wide array of emotions all at once.

Currently, we are one month post-op and will soon be scheduling his palate repair to take place around six months of age. We are so thrilled with his cleft team and how well he has done. His resilience is astounding. I am so proud of my son, and I am proud to be his mommy.

I Wish I'd Known...
that raising my cleft
affected child would
not be any different
than raising my non
affected child.

Arvin

Country: United States of America
Type of Cleft: Bilateral Cleft Lip and Palate
Birthdate: January 31, 2013
Cleft Team: University of Oklahoma Health Science Center; Dr. Kevin Smith, MD
Found Out About Cleft: 20 Weeks Gestation
Surgery Date: April 17, 2013
Family History of Clefts: Yes

We were trying to get pregnant and not having any luck. I eventually had a HSG test done. It was a very painful test to go through, but it was worth the pain. I got pregnant in the first month after doing the test and we were so happy.

When we found out we would be expecting a baby, the happiness was unimaginable. It was an amazing time for us. We just bought our first home the same month; our first child and our first home. But I was scared too, as I have a severe bicornuate uterus and my OB-GYN said there was a chance our baby would be born premature. So, I was very cautious about everything.

At my 20-week ultrasound, we were very excited to find out if we would be having a boy or a girl. The tech went through all the details and we were so excited to find out that it was a boy. We saw his nice tiny feet and little hands, but for some reason, he wasn't showing his face. So, the tech was trying from different angles and finally got a profile picture. I noticed a change on her face and suddenly she was quiet. I asked her if everything was okay and she answered me, "Yeah, everything is all right. The doctor will talk to you about all the details." Then, she printed out the ultrasound picture and left the room, asking us to wait for the OB-GYN.

I looked at the profile picture and told my husband right at that moment that the picture looked like our baby boy had a cleft lip. He denied and said, "I don't see anything." While I was praying that my husband was right and I was wrong, my OB-GYN entered the room and started looking at my ultrasound again. She confirmed that our baby boy, in fact, did have a cleft lip. Then, she asked if I wanted to do an amniocentesis to check if there were any other problems, but stated that there was a 0.5% risk of miscarriage. We denied it right away. She suggested that we do a blood test to check for any genetic problems. I agreed. The blood test results came negative and we were relieved to know that our baby boy didn't have any other problems.

On our way home from the doctor's visit, I kept crying all the time. My husband kept telling me, "It is not a big problem. It is fixable, so, we should be thankful to God." I had gone for the ultrasound in the middle of the day from work and had to go back to work after that. One of my colleagues had even called me before I came back to work. I didn't pick up the phone as I was crying and my husband was driving, trying to calm me. I did not want to go back to work that day, but my husband suggested that I go back to work and tell my colleagues what happened.

He told me, "You have to go back tomorrow anyway and the fact will not change." He was super supportive. I wish I could have thought like him.

I came back to work and when my colleague saw me, she asked me if it was a boy or a girl and why I was looking so upset. I burst into tears and said, "It's a boy with cleft lip." She hugged me right away and was very supportive.

I used to not believe superstitions about solar and lunar eclipse. In our culture, people say if you do certain things on those days while you are pregnant, your baby will be born with birth defects. In 2012, solar and lunar eclipse both happened. I didn't know I was pregnant on the solar eclipse day and did not restrict my movement. On the lunar eclipse, I did whatever I was told to do. Then, my baby boy had been diagnosed with a bilateral cleft lip. I feel guilty at times that I didn't do a home pregnancy test before the Solar eclipse and didn't restrict my movement.

Whenever I would talk to my son in the womb, I made sure to tell him, "Mom and Dad will be there for you in any situation and we will pass through it together. You are a perfect little boy. Mom and Dad love you so much."

Finally, the day came and my labor started on January 30, 2013 in the evening. After 12 hours of labor, I noticed the baby had no heartbeat. I immediately called the nurse and she said everything was okay. After arguing with the nurse on the matter, I insisted the nurse call my OBGYN. My OB came and immediately put me on oxygen. She then turned Arvin's head and his heartbeat was back. Arvin's heartbeat slowed down again after two hours of strong contractions. I called the nurse again and she rudely stated, "Your baby is trying to give his nurse a heart attack." This time she did not argue anymore and called the OB immediately for suggestions. A C-section was suggested and, after a seemingly long wait, Arvin was born. I was so happy, excited, and relieved that he was finally here.

I am so much in love with Arvin since the first moment he came into this world. I cried with happiness at that moment. I didn't even notice his cleft. He is cute and he is absolutely perfect. He is such a handsome tough guy.

Arvin's smile is perfect with his bilateral cleft lip; I love it so much. I am nervous about the surgery day and all the pain he will have to endure. I love his present face so much that I know I will miss it. But, I am eagerly waiting to see his new face with a new smile. I wish I had not blamed myself for his cleft and did not believe any superstition. I am becoming a stronger and better person after finding out my baby boy had a cleft.

I Wish I'd Known... I would be a stronger and better person after knowing my baby boy had a cleft.

Brynleigh

Country: United States of America
Type of Cleft: Unilateral Cleft Lip
Birthdate: May 23, 2012
Cleft Team: Riley Hospital for Children;
Dr. Havlik, MD
Found Out About Cleft: 19 Weeks Gestation
Surgery Date: September 18, 2012 (Lip repair)
Family History of Clefts: No

Time moves fast. Life has given us a marriage. In our case, that meant a blending of two adults, plus five kids to equal lucky number seven. Little did we realize that our real lucky number was going to be eight.

A boy or a girl, that was the one question we were most concerned about. All parents want a healthy baby, though, regardless. As I remember it, my biggest worry was about having a boy. There was basically no doubt in my mind it would be. What I should have been wanting and wishing for all along was for our expected infant's good health and, boy (pun intended), did that become apparent on January 25th, 2012. That wasn't only the day we found out the baby's sex – that was the day the doctor's ultrasound reading revealed what I knew nothing and had thought nothing about: a cleft lip.

My wife, bravely battling the hard trials of what was actually her seventh pregnancy, immediately shattered. The news was one more head-on crash into what had seemingly been four months of struggle and frustration. Her tears were joined with my stunned shock.

My wife agonized over what she could have done wrong. I internally held tight my desire to panic, still not comprehending what the doctor was telling us. I'm not sure I really even acknowledged him because I was in such disbelief at the dramatic news.

A specialist spent extra time on a more thorough scan and eventually inundated us with information on what we were now facing: an 'imperfect' baby. Now, all babies are perfect in their own way as all five of ours had been, but this was new territory for both of us. The word 'defect' packs a punch. It nearly takes the life out of a person and, mentally, my wife was being swallowed by unwarranted guilt.

Mainly, guys like me can only be sources of support because, let's face facts, we aren't the ones who endure nine months of pregnancy. Granted, my kids jokingly remind me that I look several months "with child" as the reflection in the mirror seems to indicate too honestly. Frankly, there is not another human being relying on my blood, food, and health to survive. Truly, my wife is an amazing person to physically carry such precious cargo, while dealing with the unexpected trauma of a pending abnormality.

So, to do my small part, I tried to stay positive and keep a minimal complications belief in my head. Meanwhile, in the battlefield of my wife's mind, she was constantly fighting the worst-case scenario. The doctors felt that it just appeared to be only a unilateral cleft lip. That was certainly the vision and the focus I maintained when studying the monitor. However, my wife was concerned with the palate as well. Of course, determining the extent of the defect via ultrasound was virtually impossible.

Yes, I've neglected to get into sharing the sex of the baby. Obviously, boy or girl after January 25th became irrelevant. The naming of our baby had evolved into the second biggest insignificant discussion before the cleft news struck. It too, felt like a monumental obstacle to overcome as well. I mean, what do you name a baby with a defect? Certainly, what we as a couple had hoped a long time ago would be some of the sweetest and most pleasant nine months of memories began to feel bitter and unfulfilling. Our feelings were in disarray and our heartache grew at just how bad it might be or how bad it might look.

My wife's frequent bursts of high blood pressure gave her issues throughout the month of May. Thankfully, this was a time when she was able to take some time away from work to care for herself and that growing baby of ours. While the due date of June 13th was looming, we both knew getting through May was unlikely.

The strife of more than eight months of worry, fatigue, sickness, exhaustion, and stress evaporated forever on the evening of May 23, 2012 when my wife delivered a beautiful, and I mean beautiful, baby girl with a cleft lip. That's right, my baby girl!

The cleft was a minor one, a unilateral notch out of the left side of the upper lip with no indication of palate involvement. Despite that circumstance, her smile was absolutely beautiful and the defect became virtually unnoticeable to us as parents. Our friends and family were a blessing throughout the nearly four-month long period of waiting for the next step: a cleft lip repair at Riley Children's Hospital.

As I mentioned at the beginning of our story, time flies. Our beautiful girl is now more than nine-months-old. Her lip was repaired with precision on September 18, 2012 by some of the best craniofacial experts in the field. The so-called 'defect' has now healed. Plastic surgery has restored her to what the world sees as normal. Looking back, special beats normal hands-down.

All the wrenching guilt, the needless worry and the dreaded word 'defect' seems like a distant memory. So, too does my mindless, selfish preoccupation of boy or girl and what to name our newborn. For the record, we finally settled the "What do we name her?" dilemma. Our girl is Brynleigh Shae and this is her story.

I Wish I'd Known... how all the worries would fade away as soon as I saw her face!

Nico

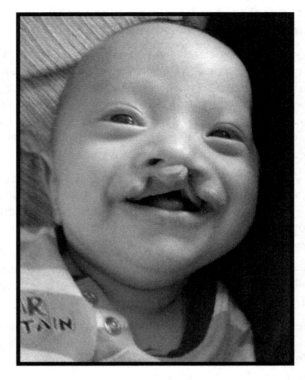

Country: United States of America
Type of Cleft: Bilateral Cleft Lip and Cleft Palate
Birthdate: August 10, 2012
Cleft Team: Inova Fairfax Hospital
Found Out About Cleft: 20-Week Ultrasound
Cleft Device: NAM
Surgery Date: December 3, 2012 (Lip repair), March 14, 2013
Family History of Clefts: No

I got a call on a Friday afternoon from my doctor that my maternal alpha-fetal protein was elevated, which could be a sign of Spina Bifida. She recommended that I do a Level II ultrasound and an amniocentesis to know with certainty. I was a nervous wreck all weekend, particularly after doing research online on Spina Bifida.

During the ultrasound, the technician was very friendly, revealing my son's gender as we'd asked, patiently going over his vital organs, especially his spine which is what we were concerned about, and carefully taking the usual measurements. But, the tech got quieter and quieter as she studied his face. We had one funny moment when we caught him sticking his tongue out at us. Looking back on it now, I had a strange feeling that something was wrong when she wasn't able to get a really good shot of his head facing us.

When she left the room, we excitedly discussed the names we'd picked out now that we knew the gender. When the doctor came in, it was all business. She immediately gave us the good news that she did not see any indications of Spina Bifida, although she also recommended an amniocentesis to confirm. She told us that she saw signs of a "craniofacial abnormality." When I asked, "What do you mean, like a cleft lip?" She responded affirmatively. My heart just dropped into the pit of my stomach. Strangely enough, just weeks before my mom and I had been discussing autism and how no one really knows the causes. I remember saying, "It's like babies born with cleft lips; doctors just have no idea how it happens." Here it was, coming true for my son. I was a mess all night. I was sad and scared for my son and what he would look like as I sat on the couch doing research on cleft lips and palates.

We went in the next day to see the maternal-fetal medicine specialists and I was completely nauseated the whole time. The ultrasound tech was very serious. The tension in the room was palpable. Not being the most patient person in the world, I just wanted to get it over with and just know what was going on. After the ultrasound, we waited for a bit to meet with the genetic counselor and then it really got bad. She confirmed a bilateral cleft lip and cleft palate.

In addition, she thought that my son might have a chromosomal abnormality like Trisomy 13 or 18 or Downs syndrome because we don't have a history of clefts in our families. His head was in the one percentile and I still had an unexplained elevated maternal AFP. She explained that if my son had Trisomy 13 or 18, his chances of making it to term were minimal. She told us about the amniocentesis and other genetic tests they could perform, but at that point I couldn't really understand a word she was saying. I could barely hear her through my own crying. I was totally devastated. In four days I had gone from thinking that my son might not be able to walk, to thinking he might have a cleft lip, to thinking he might not make it at all. It was without a doubt the absolute worst day of my life and, as I think back on it now, I still can't really even come up with the words to describe what I went through.

I got through the amniocentesis and I ended up staying home from work with my fiancé the rest of the week because all I could do was cry and wait for test results. The next three weeks, life became a new level of normalcy. I went back to work and constantly did research on Trisomy and cleft issues. I also found a cleft group on BabyCenter.com that told me everything I ever needed to know about clefts, so that I could feel more informed and thus, more comfortable telling family, friends, and co-workers.

I also went in for another ultrasound, and it turned out that the tech had incorrectly measured his head and that it was actually a totally normal size. I found out much later that ultrasound measurements are notoriously imprecise and that ultrasounds are more of an art than a science. When the results finally came in, I was informed that my son didn't have any chromosomal abnormalities. Frankly, I was relieved that it was "just" a bilateral cleft lip and palate because, by then, I felt somewhat better prepared. I was still sad and scared for him that he would have to go through surgeries and molding and possible speech therapy. But, the more time I spent online in the cleft group on BabyCenter, the better and less alone I felt.

When Nico was born, as everyone will tell you, I fell in love with him at first sight and the cleft didn't make any difference whatsoever. Overall, I think that dealing with his cleft related

issues has been manageable. There have been some hard moments, like being told by his pediatrician that he needed to be admitted to the hospital to be put on a feeding tube because he'd lost too much weight after birth, or having to tape up his adorable face to put in a NAM every day and the surgeries, of course. But, I know that we can get through anything that comes our way and that all scars, physical and emotional, will heal with time.

I Wish I'd Known... that despite his clefts, my son is just like any other baby

Dear Pregnant Mom,

Your cleft baby will be strong and you will be a stronger person for having him or her. Everything you feel (shock, anger, grief, sadness, embarrassment, or fear) is all normal and it's all okay. You are not a bad person or a bad mother for feeling those things. Let yourself feel them so you can move forward. Cry when you need to cry.

People will tell you, "Oh that's easy to fix." Comments like this may make you angry. That's okay too. Just keep in mind that they are trying, in their own way, to make you feel better. Most don't know what to say.

In my experience, telling others about the cleft (we found out via ultrasound) made me stronger. It pushed me to learn more and allowed me to educate my family and friends.

There are much worse birth defects and diseases that your baby could have, but it's still hard to think about what your child (and you) will have to go through. The first year, they say, is the hardest, but I can tell you it hasn't been as bad as I imagined.

This journey would not have been this calm without the guidance, support, love, and friendship of so many wonderful people in our lives and in the cleft community. I suggest connecting with other parents either online or even asking your doctor for the name and contact info of someone local that can talk with you and has already been down the same road. It will help you understand the daily routine of raising a cleft affected child, because most doctors can't speak first hand to this. Most of all, just remember that you are not alone. You have all of us.

Linked together by a cleft.

Support

"The one thing I need to say about this journey is that it helps to have support... Without these people, it would have been so much harder."

Brayland

Country: United States of America
Type of Cleft: Incomplete Unilateral Cleft Lip
Birthdate: November 17, 2010
Cleft Team: Plastic Surgeon and ENT through the Bureau for Children with Medical Handicaps
Found Out About Cleft: At Birth
Surgery Date: May 2, 2011
Family History of Clefts: Yes

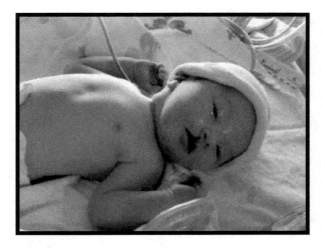

I didn't know my son was going to be born with a cleft lip. I had several ultrasounds done during pregnancy due to the fact I was told my son was going to be a big baby, yet, not once did they catch it. I remember going to the hospital to be induced. I was nervous, as any first time mother would be. After13 hours of labor, I gave birth. They told me he had a cleft lip, but it was minor. I was worried at first. I was not expecting news like that. However, when they put him in my arms, he was the most beautiful baby I had ever laid my eyes on. My fears melted away for the time being.

My family didn't even seem to notice his cleft. They just saw a beautiful baby boy. We hardly even talked about the cleft; it didn't seem to matter. I knew nothing about clefts at this point in time. I did, however, learn that it ran on my dad's side of the family.

At first, I had to hold my son's lip together to feed him so he got less air. Eventually, I was able to feed him normally. I think my first big shock about having a baby with a cleft is how people reacted. I hated how some people would just stare as though my child was less than human. It didn't bother me when some children stared at him or asked their parents what was wrong with my son; they didn't understand.

When my son was around one-week-old, we took him to his very first appointment with the plastic surgeon. He told us that my son would probably only need one or two surgeries. The first one would be to repair the cleft and a possible second surgery to remove the extra skin from the lip. He also told us that Brayland might not get his teeth in the cleft lip area, even though he didn't have a cleft palate. I am happy to report that my son did get all of his teeth.

We had first scheduled his surgery for April, but we had to cancel because Brayland was sick. He had Bronchitis and an ear infection. So, we rescheduled for May. We were nervous about the surgery. We didn't know much about what was going to happen. The doctor told us about the surgery, but not much about the recovery. He had explained it somewhat, but not like someone who had a child go through this could. So, we got in contact with my cousin who had a cleft child. She was very helpful in explaining to us how the surgery and recovery would go. She really put us at ease.

The wait for surgery felt like forever. Even though he didn't eat much, he was still very good up until about the last hour before the surgery. After that he started getting cranky. Then came the toughest part for us as parents; they took him away for surgery. He didn't understand what was going on. He was reaching for us and crying. We were in tears, too. The surgery didn't take as long as we thought it would. It lasted around two hours. When we finally got to see him, he had tape over where his cleft was. He was very out of it and had splints on his arms.

The next step was finding the best way to feed him. We tried an open cup, which he hated. We tried using this little tube over a syringe, but that was hard and he hated it. Finally, we just used the syringe itself and that worked. We had to do this for two weeks because he wasn't allowed a bottle.

Brayland was the best baby. Even after the surgery, he didn't cry much. He was and is such a tough little guy. The next two weeks proved to be difficult because we couldn't let him bump his lip. He wasn't able to roll over or really play so, he got bored easily. After a week, he had his stitches taken out. His first real smile since his surgery was after the stitches came out. He tried to smile before, but it was hard.

I remember shortly after this we were sitting in my sister's shop and a guy asked us what happened to him. I told him about the surgery. He told us he wasn't talking about the lip. He figured he had fallen because of the splints. We then explained the splints were to keep him from touching his lip. This really made my day. No one even noticed. I was never ashamed of my son. To me he was always beautiful. It was just nice to know that he probably wouldn't be made fun of as he got older.

After two weeks, we happily took off his splints and gave him back his bottle. He had been cranky the last few days. It turned out he had another ear infection. He averaged an ear infection a month until he was about one-year-old and had another surgery to put tubes in his ears. Since then, he hasn't had any. He has been back to see his plastic surgeon, who says his lip looks good. We also saw a speech therapist. We were told he was advanced in speech.

The one thing I need to say about this journey is that it helps to have support. I had my boyfriend, my parents, my siblings, and had someone to talk to who had been through this. Without these people, it would have been so much harder. It also helps to have someone with you at the time of the surgery.

My son is now two-years-old and has the most beautiful smile. You can barely tell he ever had a cleft. I just want to say no matter what anyone tells you; cleft babies are beautiful!

I Wish I'd Known...
about the cleft ahead of time.

Anthony

Country: United States of America
Type of Cleft: Left Unilateral Cleft Lip and Palate
Birthdate: June 26, 2012
Cleft Team: Kosair Children's Hospital
Found Out About Cleft: At Birth
Surgery Date: October 9, 2012 (Lip and nose repair)
Family History of Clefts: No

Anthony's journey began on November 15, 2011; the day I found out I was pregnant. This pregnancy was smooth until the last three months. We made many trips back and forth from the hospital because I was going into preterm labor. Three times they were able to stop it so our baby could 'bake' a little longer. With contractions on a daily basis I was counting the seconds until he arrived.

On the twelfth visit to the hospital for contractions, the doctor finally told me I was progressing and that little Anthony would finally be allowed to make his appearance into this world. I was at 37 weeks and three days. I was already four centimeters dilated and had lost my mucous plug months ago, so this delivery went very fast. It only took two pushes and I heard a scream. At 9:47 a.m. he was born and weighed in at five pounds, 15.5 ounces, and 19 inches long. Something was different.

The doctor did not put him on my belly right away. The doctor and all the nurses fell silent. The doctor stopped and said (words which I still hear every day), "Now, before I show you your son, there is something that I have to tell you so you will not be shocked." A million things went running through my head. I had no idea what to expect and I never expected a cleft lip and palate. All I had really heard or seen about them were the commercials on TV, which in those, they always seem to use the worst pictures that they can find. She then put him on my belly and I didn't even look at his mouth, I just looked at his eyes.

I really felt alone through this because I did not know anyone personally that had walked in my shoes. Everyone in my family and my husband's family came to the hospital, but I didn't really talk a lot to them. I did not want to talk to anyone. On the second day, I finally looked at Anthony's cleft and I didn't see what all the fuss was about. It looked nothing like I had imagined.

A lot of people came to talk to my husband and me including counselors and social workers. One even asked if I wanted to put him up for adoption. I looked at her and said, "Are you freaking kidding me?" How can someone ask something like that?

So far, we have been through two surgeries; the lip/nose surgery and the palate surgery. Both were difficult, especially handing over your baby to people that are practically strangers. The lip surgery was the most difficult, I think, because it was the first one he had. That day was very hard on me, as I knew it would be. They brought Anthony back into the room after he woke up. He looked so different to me. Before he went into surgery the doctor gave me a marker, told me to put a dot somewhere on him, and then left the room. I honestly had to look for that dot because he looked nothing like that little man I gave to him at the beginning. Normally when Anthony cries, I always put him on my shoulder, but I couldn't because he was not allowed to be on his belly until his lip healed. That was my break down point. I asked everyone to leave the room because I could not hold it together anymore. I had been holding it in since the beginning and it all just exploded at that point. After a few minutes, I pulled myself back together and let everyone come back in. Through all of the emotions, we made it through and were sent home that evening. He recovered quickly from the surgery.

Anthony did very well when he had his palate surgery and just had to stay one night. Everything went exactly as it should have with no complications. When we were finally called to see him and given our room number, I could NOT get to the fourth floor quick enough! He looked the same, a little swollen, but other than that I couldn't tell he even had surgery until I heard him cry. He sounded so different. They told me of the gauze that would be stitched to his palate for a day and would make him sound very muffled. We tried to get him to eat right away but all he wanted to do after he received his pain medicine was sleep. He slept until almost 4:30 p.m. and finally ate two ounces of formula. That was all he ate for the first day. The nurses kept his pain medicine coming and he slept for the most part and would wake up right as the next dose was due. We stayed overnight and slept through most of the night. He only woke up for his pain medicine.

This will be a long road to recovery, but I can tell he is glad to be home and be back with his big brother and to also be where he belongs. He has also healed very well from that surgery and it was a lot less stressful. We knew better what to expect and were better prepared for the emotions. We have found out that he will need a lip revision sometime within this next year as his lip has not healed as well as they hoped, but this is one more hurdle we are ready for. Anthony is now up to par with his age for milestones and is currently crawling a mile a minute and enjoys chasing his brother all over.

I hope my story will help others going through this so they will not feel alone like I did at first. I want people to see where we came from, to where we will be one day. My little man is strong and he IS beautiful, no matter what.

I Wish I'd Known...
the daily struggles.

Paxton

Country: United States of America
Type of Cleft: Bilateral Cleft Lip and Palate
Birthdate: April 7, 2011
Cleft Team: Children's National Medical Center
Found Out About Cleft: 5 Months Gestation
Cleft Device: Latham device
Surgery Dates: At 3 months, 5 months and 9 months
Family History of Clefts: Unknown

During the fifth month of my pregnancy, we found out that my son was going to be born with a cleft lip. I will always remember that day and how I reacted to the news. I had seen children born with cleft lips and heard of it, but didn't think it could or would have happened to my child. My husband had never even heard of a cleft lip. After hearing the news, he seemed to be in shock. I called my mother soon after and poured out the news to her. I remember doing a lot of crying and I felt guilty. I had also decided to tell my close friends and family the news. They were all very understanding and helpful.

After a few weeks, I decided there wasn't any way to change what had occurred and went into research mode. I couldn't seem to stop looking at the computer and found tons of information. I was even able to make our first appointment with the children's hospital and visit with our plastic surgeon, who was and is amazing!

Once Paxton arrived, he had to spend a few weeks at the NICU. We found out that Paxton not only had a cleft lip, but a cleft palate as well. I spent quite a lot of visits in the NICU with Paxton, learning how to feed him with a special type of bottle, which I found very difficult to use. I even spent a night there just trying to figure out how to use the bottle. I had to have it at a certain angle for Paxton to get any liquid out of it.

Once we brought him home, things got a little bit easier. After a few months of being home, we had our first visit with Paxton at the Children's National Medical Center. It went really well! Paxton was fitted for the Latham device, which would be surgically placed in his mouth to help the palate come a little closer together for a few months before his lip repair. We met with seven different doctors that day, which made up his cleft team. I couldn't even begin to tell you how amazing each of them were!

At about five months, Paxton went in for his lip surgery. I can't even begin to explain how hard this was. To know he was going to be put under for several hours broke my heart. During those hours, I was blessed to have my family there for support. My brother and parents took time off just to come in for a few days and help me take care of Paxton or step in if I needed a few minutes to myself.

Once we were told we could take Paxton home, I felt pretty nervous. The first few days were pretty nerve wracking. The arm restraints helped keep Paxton from ripping off his tape or stitches from his lip and nose. They were annoying little things, but did a good job. After a few weeks, Paxton's lip healed quite nicely. His surgeon was quite impressed. We also noticed that he was able to produce a few more sounds, which was incredibly amazing.

When Paxton turned 11-months-old, he went in for his palate repair. Again, this was very difficult for me. My family was there again to help and provide support. His surgery lasted eight hours! When his surgeon called me back to tell me that he was done, I literally cried. I gave him a huge hug, told him he was a blessing and thanked him. Once we took Paxton home, the healing process was quite rough. Paxton didn't care one bit about feeding from the syringe. I literally had to force feed him and had to think of several types of ways just so he could eat and drink. It probably was one of the most difficult things I have had to do.

Since then, Paxton has healed and looks fantastic! His speech is still coming along, but he is now saying quite a few words. Car seems to be his favorite word so far. The journey has been rough, but we made it through and I wouldn't change a thing about it!

I Wish I'd Known… honestly, nothing.
I'm blessed to have had this journey!

Fuhe

Country: Canada
Type of Cleft: Right Unilateral Cleft Lip and Palate
Birthdate: September 23, 2001
Cleft Team: Winnipeg Children's Hospital; Dr. Ross, MD
Found Out About Cleft: At Adoption Referral
Surgery Dates: In 2004, 2005, 2008, 2009, 2010, 2011 and 2012
Family History of Clefts: Yes

Fuhe was six years old the day he walked into our lives. After three years of waiting, our adoption journey had taken us to China. At two days of age, our son had been placed outside a police station. His birth certificate stated: place of birth unknown, birth parents unknown. We were told the Cantonese pronunciation for Fuhe sounds like "food" without the 'd.'

He was small for his age, below the zero percentile on a Canadian growth chart. His referral stated, "repaired cleft lip with two failed right cleft palate repair surgeries." No further surgeries would be done in China. My mother also had a right cleft lip and palate. Therefore, Fuhe's little face reminded me of her love for family.

The second day in China, we legally adopted Fuhe. It was on the third day that I asked my husband, "Do you think he can talk?" My husband replied, "Obviously not, so get over it and never cry in front of our son again!" He was right. Our son did not need any sympathy. With renewed spirit, I started learning Fuhe's basic sign language and teaching him to print. It was day four when our teenage daughters told me that Fuhe couldn't hear really well. I responded, "We will fix that too."

Coming home, Fuhe quickly learned how to live in a family. Coming from an orphanage with 55 kids, he loved his six new siblings. He found great joy in flushing the toilet, taking every electronic device apart, and hoarding food in his closet.

Our first visit to the Cleft Palate Clinic was overwhelming. However, there were three words that gave me reassurance, "team" and "over time." Over the next few visits, we were given a list of specialists including a dietician, speech therapist, plastic surgeon, an ear, nose and throat surgeon, an audiologist, dentist, an orthodontist, oral surgeon, and a pediatrician. We realized how fortunate we were to be Canadian with universal health care.

With two failed surgeries, scar tissue was a major concern. Since coming home, Fuhe has had six surgeries in four years including facial artery myomucosal flaps, bone grafting, and orthodontic work. The cleft palate team has supported our family through all the diagnostic workup and the pre and post-operative care. After the first set of T-tubes were placed in his ears Fuhe woke up, pointed to the window and excitedly started waving his fingers up and down. I hugged him, "Yes, you can hear the rain!"

The latest surgery was a cosmetic revision of his nose and lip; a surgery my mother never had. Our son is a typical 11-year-old who is outgoing, cute, bright, competitive, funny, and chattering nonstop. He devours every meal and has soared up the growth chart. Tonight, I retold him his life story of how his birth mother loved him very much. However, because of the cleft palate, she could not feed him and, therefore, chose a safe spot to leave him. She hoped for a miracle that someone, somewhere, somehow could help her son. Then, we pray and thank Fuhe's birth parents, the orphange staff, and all our friends at the Cleft Palate Clinic. With a goodnight kiss, I tell him our love is like a circle, with no beginning and no end. Life has given us Fuhe; we could not ask for more.

I Wish I'd Known... how wonderful the entire cleft team was.

Cody

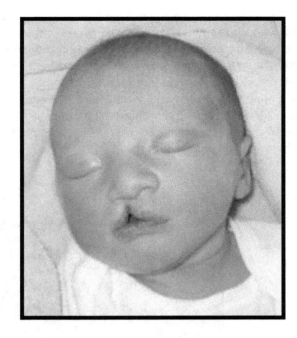

Country: United States of America
Type of Cleft: Right Unilateral Cleft Lip and Palate
Birthdate: October 10, 2006
Cleft Team: Presbyterian Hospital; Dr. Luis Cuadros, MD
Found Out About Cleft: 20-Week Ultrasound
Surgery Dates: March 2007, August 2007, 2008 and 2010
Family History of Clefts: No

New Mexico has one of the highest incidences of clefts in the country. I am a pediatric nurse of 14 years, a wife of ten years, and most honorably, a mom of two healthy kids. My son, Cody, was born with a cleft lip and palate. I'd like to share our journey in having a child born with an abnormality. Well, that's at least the term used when Cody's cleft was detected at our 20-week ultrasound.

I will never forget that day. It started as a day full of excitement and joy. Whether the baby would be boy or a girl was really all I was thinking about. Then came the bombshell. The ultrasound tech turned to my husband and me, and informed us that our child had a cleft lip and a probable cleft palate. Tears immediately formed and streamed down my face. The nurse in me, not only visualized the faces of every severe cleft child I had cared for in the past, but also the syndromes that are often associated with cleft lips and/or cleft palates. My husband, on the other hand, took the news very well and was overjoyed to know that his first child was a boy who had a healthy heart, vital organs, and that as he grew older he had the ability to grow a mustache.

My expectations were to have perfection and at that moment, I felt that I was being handed less than perfect. It is now hard to hear myself say that or even to know that I had those thoughts. All I can say is that unless you have been told something less than what you expected, you go through a mourning process. Through talking with other moms faced with the unexpected news of their precious infant having a cleft, they too experienced those similar feelings. Feelings like doubt, anger, frustration, fear, and even devastation. I now look back and feel like I was able to mourn, grow, and move forward in those early stages of grief after finding out that Cody was going to be born with a cleft.

It is through that experience during my pregnancy that completely transformed my perspective on the meaning of true perfection. I know now that my eyes were opened to a new found ideal of true perfection when I held Cody for the first time. All those feelings of uncertainty disappeared and now I was able to focus on being a mom and providing Cody with the care he needed to grow and start the journey ahead of us; a journey that consisted of coping, adapting, delicate feedings, preparing for surgeries, and Doctor visits to follow his hearing, speech, and dental concerns.

Cody had his first surgery at five-months-old which consisted of repairing his lip. A short seven days later, he went back into the operating room to have his sutures removed. He had his third procedure at ten-months-old which consisted of repairing his palate and placing ear tubes. This was the most invasive and painful of his operations. To make matters worse, he could not put anything in his mouth for seven days to ensure that the palate would heal. This included his bottle, pacifier, hands, and toys. He had to wear elbow restraints and was fed with a device called a Zip-n-Squeeze or through a syringe.

Cody was 18-months-old when he had his first lip revision, then a second lip revision at three years of age. Through all of this, Cody was such a trooper and is now a very normal, active, and energetic six-year-old. He is full of love, kindness, and laughter. At an early age, he was able to accomplish more than most adults can. He was able to look past an imperfection and see beauty at first glance. He is not defined by his cleft, but has grown to know that it is a part of who he is.

As a result of my journey and as a mom of a child born with a cleft, I saw a need in New Mexico. It was a need for an organization whose primary purpose was to provide these children and their families with the support and companionship needed to help them cope with feeding difficulties, surgeries, self-esteem issues, and to help them build lifelong friendships with other children who have faced similar challenges. It is important to me that each of these children and their families know that they are special and that their smile has a story to tell.

Out of this vision, an organization called SmileFest was created. SmileFest is a non-profit organization that provides an annual event for children born with a cleft and their families. SmileFest is fully supported by donations that are generated through bake sales, fundraising events such as cleaning the Pit and football stadium, silent auctions, and donations from individuals throughout the community. There are numerous opportunities for individuals, companies, and organizations to get involved with SmileFest and help support kids and families in New Mexico going through the cleft journey.

As you can see, six years and five cleft surgeries later, my family's journey is one marked by much love, unexpected joy, unforeseen obstacles, and victory in everyday challenges. I can only hope that Cody's smile and our family's journey has inspired you with not only the desire to support SmileFest, but to also live each day to its fullest. May you plant seeds of love, joy, hope, and smiles wherever your road travels!

I Wish I'd Known... how much my family members had gone through in having a child born with a cleft, prior to me having to experience it myself. It would have changed me as a nurse and the care I gave.

Dear Pregnant Mom,

Just take it one day at a time. You are going to cry. It's okay. Always know that your feelings are completely normal and valid (anger, fear, sadness, worry, etc.). Don't let anyone downplay those feelings. Take the time you need to process the news and emotions. We are all different and handle things differently. Now, you need to be strong and love on that baby. It is too hard to worry about the future before it happens.

Fear is normal. Do as much research as you can and stay away from the web pictures! There is so much good and bad information on the Internet. Get your cleft information from valid cleft organizations and your cleft team.

It's a rocky journey at first. I was lucky in that my son's cleft lip was fairly minor, but it was hard watching people stare at him oddly as though he were less than human. Once the lip is fixed, people tend to back off because it's not as noticeable.

Do not think you are alone. There are more parents than you would think going through the same thing. Take advantage of them and their journeys. Find healthy support groups and stay away from anyone negative!

You can do this!

Don't Google

" *Google is scary as hell when you are trying to find* "

medical information.

Ivy

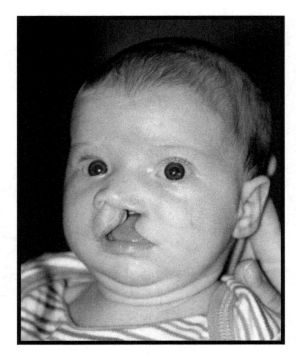

Country: Australia
Type of Cleft: Complete Unilateral Cleft Lip and Palate
Birthdate: December 20, 2010
Cleft Team: Mater Children's Hospital
Found Out About Cleft: 19-Week Ultrasound
Surgery Dates: April 20, 2011 (Lip repair), November 9 2011 (Palate repair)
Family History of Clefts: No

It was a Wednesday. I was at my 19-week scan and when I saw the look on the technician's face, I could tell something was wrong. I was ecstatic to be told we were expecting a little girl, but the excitement soon waned as I saw the guarded look on the technician's face. "We think we've detected an anomaly on your baby's face, maybe a cleft lip. Do you mind if we call in a senior for a second opinion?"

After many frowns and whispers amongst the ultrasound technicians, it was decided that our baby girl most likely had a unilateral cleft lip and possible palate involvement. Most of that ultrasound appointment is a blur, but I clearly remember two things the technicians said: "Oh, they can do so much for that these days," (something I would get used to hearing) and "Whatever you do, don't Google 'cleft lip' when you get home, or it will just scare you." I remember thinking, what a stupid thing to say. Of course, I was going to do exactly that. This is my child; I am her protector and biggest advocate. Why wouldn't I gather as much information as I could?

When I got home, I surfed the net for the next three to four hours. It was difficult. I was saddened, but inspired by what I read and saw. Then, I got angry. Why us? Why our child? Was it something I did? After that, I cried for three days and grieved for the trouble-free life our daughter would not have.

After my initial heartbreak, I just got on with it. I researched clefts and prepared for the arrival of our princess. I was torn between excitement and trepidation for what was to come. I just knew she would be beautiful. I knew we would love her. But knowing she would be born with a difficult road ahead made everything bittersweet.

We decided to call her Ivy. Christmas is our favourite time of year and I wanted her to have a festive name. We also knew that Ivy, the evergreen, is a tough and resilient plant. No matter what you throw at it, it always flourishes. It is binding, and she was the final piece of our puzzle. Our little family was complete.

Soon after her birth, it was confirmed she had a unilateral cleft lip and palate. The cleft in her lip was at least one to two centimeters and her cleft extended all the way back to her soft palate. We spent some time in neonatal intensive care just to monitor her feeds.

After four days of monitoring, we were free to leave the hospital on Christmas Eve, just in time to celebrate her first Christmas with her older brothers. They were (and still are) enamoured by her, and curious about her 'broken lip'.

Before we knew it, we had our first appointment with the plastic surgeon and orthodontic team. We were shown how to tape her lip in preparation for surgery. We were unwavering and made sure she wore the tape 95% of the time. I'm so glad we did, because it really helped. On the day of her lip repair, the cleft had closed to only half a centimeter apart.

At four-months-old to the day, she was admitted for her cleft lip repair. She was also having bilateral grommets inserted in her ears. I was a mess. I remember thinking "Why am I handing over our perfectly healthy baby, to endure a scalpel and general anesthetic?" Of course, I was also relieved that this part would soon be over. A box ticked, so to speak.

After a three-hour surgery and an anxious wait in the parent's room, she was awake and I could go see her. I cannot explain exactly how I felt when I first saw her. I was ecstatic, relieved, shocked, and felt guilty. I just held her and stared in awe. Despite some initial bruising and swelling, she looked so beautiful. Amazing!

At ten-months-old, she was ready for her cleft palate repair. She also had another set of grommets inserted because she had outgrown the others. Waiting out the surgery was a little easier the second time, but the recovery was harder and the hospital stay was longer. She was not impressed with being confined to a cot and IV drip for four long days. The surgery was a success and thankfully she didn't have any issues with infection or fistulas.

Ivy is now almost two-years-old and we can't believe how fast the time has gone.

Sometimes I even miss her cleft and her big wide smile. After everything she's been through, I think she's definitely come out stronger. Her journey isn't over and she has a long road ahead. Something that I learned and accepted is that the cleft condition is something we will manage through to adulthood. It is not just a case of having a repair and then it's fixed. Unfortunately, she will be challenged, but hopefully continue to rise to the occasion.

Although Ivy was born with a cleft, she is not defined by it. She is a gorgeous, funny, feisty little girl. We can't wait to see the kind of girl and woman she grows into. We are incredibly proud of her and thrilled to be able to say that Ivy is our daughter.

I Wish I'd Known... how strong she would be.

Joshua

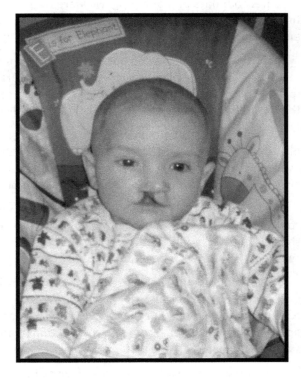

Country: United States of America
Type of Cleft: Unilateral Cleft Lip and Palate
Birthdate: September 29, 2011
Cleft Team: The Craniofacial Center; Dr. Jeffrey Fearon, MD
Found Out About Cleft: 20-Week Ultrasounds
Surgery Dates: January 2012 (Lip and nose repair), August 2012 (Palate repair)
Family History of Clefts: No

My husband and I happily went to our ultrasound still deciding if we thought it was a girl or a boy. The only news we expected to hear was the sex of the baby. Our ultrasound technologist didn't give anything away. She was friendly as ever, laughing with us, and was pleased to tell us right away that it was a boy.

We waited to see the doctor for my regular appointment, all excited about our son. Our doctor told us right away that the baby had a cleft. The room seemed to close in on me. She was talking, I was listening and responding, but I was going numb and don't recall most of the conversation. At one point, I broke down into tears. My husband was frozen in his seat, staring at the floor in complete shock. He seemed to just shut down with the news.

Our OB showed us the scan they got of the face; it was obvious. She set us up with a specialist, recommended a doctor, and did what she could to help us. I remember being glad I took off that afternoon because I didn't want to face anyone at work. My co-workers were anxiously waiting to find out the sex of the baby.

Our mothers had gone to the ultrasound with us, but not to the doctor appointment. So, they were in the waiting area when we came out. We'd been through a lot to get pregnant. We had fertility issues. This seemed like another kick in the gut. We were finally pregnant and now our baby had problems. I made it out of the office and then started bawling in my mom's arms as I told her the news.

The next few days were a blur. Google is scary as hell when you are trying to find medical information. By good fortune, I soon found a group on BabyCenter.com, just for cleft lip and cleft palates. I thank God every day that I found them. I stayed up late reading posts about surgeries, issues, and looking at pictures. Finally, I was brave enough to join and share my story. What a warm and welcoming bunch of people. I had support from my family and now I had it from moms and dads that had already been through this same journey.

After a few days of grieving for the loss of my 'perfect' child, I felt better. Prayer, time, and new information made things easier. But, those first few days were hard. I'm embarrassed to admit that many of my first thoughts were things like, "What will people think of my son?" "Should I bother with announcements?" "What if someone makes fun of my baby's looks?" All very superficial and all very trivial, but all things I was thinking. Those thoughts eventually all went away. I started telling people at work right away and no one batted an eye. Everyone was supportive and still couldn't wait to meet my son.

Once we found a surgeon we felt we would like to use, had contact with him, and had a plan, I was back to normal. I just wanted to meet my son.

I had to have a C-section because Joshua was breech. This was another thing we never planned on, but by this time it didn't faze us. After Joshua was born, I didn't get to see him for a few minutes. They were checking him out and determined he was breathing too fast. They brought him to the nursery to put him on oxygen. The nurse stopped by with him so I could at least see him before they whisked him away.

Not long after I was in recovery, the nurse told me our baby was fine. He was only on oxygen for a few minutes and they brought him back to me. He was absolutely beautiful. I never knew I could fall in love so fast.

Three weeks after he was born, we took him to Dallas to meet our cleft team. The first step was a feeding evaluation. They had us stop using the Haberman and move to regular bottles using a red preemie nipple. It's softer than regular nipples and they showed us how to make the holes bigger. Our meeting with our surgeon went very well. He explained the basics, answered our questions, and we were on our way.

The next few months were a blur of regular newborn stuff (i.e. little sleep and lots of diaper changes). People were wonderful when we were out with our son. His big smile seemed to win everyone over and he smiled at everyone. We had opportunities to educate a lot of people.

Nerves kicked in as surgery day approached. That day was one of the hardest of my life. Handing over my sweet, happy, little boy for surgery made me cry. His surgery went extremely well and we were given regular updates throughout the two hours it took. In recovery, we quickly discovered that Joshua and anesthesia don't go well together. He was making this dreadful moaning sound. I don't know if he was in pain; he was just slow coming out of the anesthesia.

He looked completely different. I was instantly glad we'd had photos taken the week before surgery to capture that big beautiful smile he had. It took a while, but Joshua finally woke up a bit more and calmed down. That's when I started crying. The stress of it all finally got to me.

We had so many friends and family anxiously waiting for news and picture, so we texted updates to everyone all day. We were all exhausted. A few hours after surgery, Joshua took his entire bottle! I was so thrilled! We were released eight hours after his surgery was over. Our surgeon was pleased with his recovery.

Recovery wasn't what I expected. Joshua seemed to physically recover very well and quickly. He was smiling at us the morning after surgery. A strange new smile with a little swollen face, but it was so good to see. Our biggest recovery issue was sleep. Joshua didn't return to his pre-op sleeping patterns until a month after surgery. His new smile is gorgeous, the lip healed well, and the scar faded over the months

I wasn't nervous for his palate surgery until the week before. Handing him over was a little easier and I managed not to cry. The surgery took the same amount of time and once again was a big success. We stayed one night in the hospital. Once again, Joshua was amazing with eating. A few hours after surgery, he had milk and applesauce. He loves to eat! Again, our biggest recovery issue was sleep. He was fussy and cranky for ten to 14 days after surgery, but he didn't return to sleeping through the night until eight weeks after surgery. That was a rough, rough time for me. I was used to sleeping all night again.

Now, the surgeries are behind us and the next one isn't for a few years. It was a busy first year, full of extra anxiety, worry, and doctor appointments. But it's all behind us now. If I could go back in time to the day we found out about the cleft, I would tell myself that it's not as bad or as hard as it seems.

My son is an extremely active, happy, smart, silly, and independent toddler. The cleft issues did not slow him down one bit. He held his head up the day after he was born, he walked at nine months, he says a few words, and can use a little sign language. Most people don't even notice his scar anymore. He is slightly delayed in his speech, but not by much. I wouldn't have asked for a child with a cleft, but I wouldn't change a thing now. The experience made us grow as parents. It made our son even more special. I am in awe of his strength. I've met many wonderful people, in person and online, because of a little cleft. The experience has been a good one; scary at times, but good.

I Wish I'd Known... I would barely notice your cleft when I first saw you.

Lainey

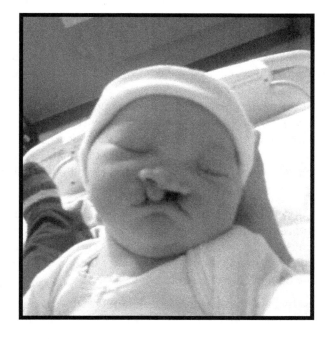

Country: United States of America
Type of Cleft: Bilateral Cleft Lip and Palate
Birthdate: August 28, 2012
Cleft Team: Seattle Children's Hospital; Dr. Tse, MD
Found Out About Cleft: 25 Weeks Gestation
Cleft Device: NAM
Surgery Date: December 7, 2012
Family History of Clefts: No

As a little girl, I never dreamt of a big wedding or becoming a princess. Instead, I dreamt of becoming a mom. Most of all, I wanted a baby girl. On Christmas Eve, we found out that we were expecting and could not have been happier! I prayed and prayed for a little girl.

April rolled around, and in fact it was a girl! During the ultrasound, I asked questions like, "How's the brain?" "Does she have ten fingers and ten toes?" "How is her spine and her heart?" You know, the "normal" stuff. All seemed well. My doctor later said that they needed to do another ultrasound because my little girl kept her hands on her face through the ultrasound. My thought was, "Sweet! I get to see her again!" The ultrasound technologist stated that she still didn't get great pictures, but that they would work and printed off a few for me. When I was looking over them, I thought that the profile of her face didn't look right. I decided that the doctors would tell me if something was wrong and I decided to let it go.

During my 25-week visit, I asked my doctor for the follow-up results. She mentioned that everything looked good, but that it was detected our baby had a bilateral cleft lip and most likely palate. At that point, I felt like everything was crumbling down around me. I had never suspected that I could have a child born with a cleft. I was absolutely devastated and most definitely in shock. I cried for about seven days.

I let myself be sad, but decided that being sad was going to make for a long last three months of pregnancy and it wasn't fair for my young son or anyone around me. Instead, I informed myself. I began doing lots of research. I started with Google, which was a big mistake. Then, I stumbled upon a cleft lip and cleft palate group on Babycenter.com and began to read about all of these everyday moms having cleft babies too. I began to feel at ease and realized that it was going to be okay. I learned so much in a short amount of time. I started to contact insurance companies, doctors, support groups, supply stores, etc. I wanted to be prepared for when my little girl arrived.

On August 28th, Lainey graced us with her presence. And boy, did she come fast! When I met her, it was love at first sight! She was absolutely beautiful. They examined her and told us that she was healthy and began trying to get her to eat right away. It took about 12 hours and two different types of bottles before she started eating like a champion! We were able to leave just two days after she was born.

Three days into her short life we started making trips to the Children's hospital where they did a full exam on her and determined that she would be a great candidate for the NAM and explained all of the pros and cons of choosing this route. We decided that it was the best route for Lainey and our family. This meant weekly trips in the car, three hours each way for a 30 minute appointment. Initially, seeing her with tape on her face broke my heart. There were times when I would look at her and just wish that we could take it all away and have a "normal" life. The NAM had its good days and its bad days. But, I told myself if I'm going to tape her face, then I need to dedicate myself to it 100% so that we could be done with it as quickly as possible. She cried when I put it in and took it out. While it was in though, she truly didn't mind it. It was like a built in binky that never fell out!

They moved her surgery up seven weeks and surprised us with her having her first surgery at just three-months and nine-days-old. I had read that I would miss her wide smile and that people didn't want to make their babies go through surgery. I didn't really understand this until we had reached that point. I struggled with handing her over for them to "fix" something that, in my opinion, didn't need to be fixed.

When we first saw her, I was amazed at the surgeon's work. He did a fabulous job and I instantly fell in love with her "new look." We weren't even admitted 24 hours before being allowed to go home. As I write, she is a week post-op and doing absolutely amazing.

I want parents to know that it is how you look at the situation that will make or break your experience. A cleft baby will smile brighter than any other child I've seen. Lainey has taught me more about life in the last three months, than I have learned in the last 20 years. I have had to take risks and cross paths that make me uncomfortable, but feel that it's made me a much better person. I've come to realize a lot about myself and about others. She has introduced me to many wonderful, caring, kind, and giving people on this Earth. She's brought me closer to God and an understanding to what matters most in my life. Our family has grown stronger and our bonds are tighter. When I look at Lainey, I can see her soul; it's beautiful, pure, and peaceful.

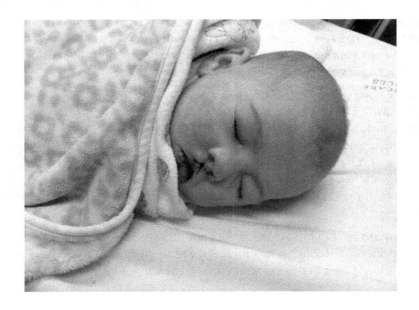

I Wish I'd Known... that everything would be better than I had anticipated.

Callan

Country: Australia
Type of Cleft: Unilateral Cleft Lip
Birthdate: June 8, 2012
Cleft Team: Westmead Children's Hospital
Found Out About Cleft: 19-Week Ultrasound
Surgery Date: October 9, 2012
Family History of Clefts: No

Going in for my 19-week ultrasound, I remember how excited my husband and I were to find out the sex of our baby. I was very happy and excited when the lady said, "It's a boy!" Our excitement soon turned to concern and disbelief when the technician paused, looked at us, and said, "I think your baby may have a little cleft lip." She continued on, saying that it looked like the left part of our baby's lip had not formed and that she was going to have to get the doctor to have a closer look. I was in complete shock and fear. As she left the room, I remember praying to God to please let her be wrong.

The doctor had a look, and then pointing to the ultrasound screen she said, "If you have a look here, you can see your baby has a little bit of its lip that has not formed." I felt my heart sink. She asked us if we knew what a cleft lip was. We had no idea. The doctor then began to explain to us that our baby would need surgery to close up the lip and that we would hardly even notice he had it. She finished by telling us not to go on the computer and Google it. I had so many unanswered questions. I had no idea what they had just told us. The car ride home was long and quiet as I fought back the tears. My excitement of having a little baby was shattered. I wasn't even sure I wanted it anymore.

All my family and friends were waiting to hear the sex of the baby. I just couldn't talk to anyone and I didn't want to talk about the baby. My husband contacted our family and close friends, explained to them what was going on and told them that I didn't want to talk to anyone. I searched Google and read some horrible things, saw some pictures that scared me, and read that the baby wouldn't be able to have surgery until he was at least four-months-old. I then went straight to bed and cried. I cried all night long. My eyes were so swollen and I didn't want to talk to anyone. I couldn't eat. I couldn't sleep. All I did was cry.

The next day, I woke up after the tiniest bit of sleep and began to cry again. I was completely devastated. Days went on and I just knew I had to get myself together for my family and this baby. My husband would tell me that this baby is going to need us to love him, "He needs you." So, I met with a close friend and counsellor who helped me through my emotions, prayed for me, and offered much support. I held onto my faith and trusted that God was in control and had a plan for this baby.

Each scan from then on, I would always get them to check if the cleft lip was still there and if they could tell if the palate was involved. At one scan we got some hope, as the lady said that the baby's tummy looked really full, meaning that he was getting plenty of fluid through his mouth, which was good sign that he may not have a cleft palate. I held onto that hope.

At birth, I was really scared and hoped Bub was going to come out normal but, unfortunately, Callan was born with the cleft lip on his left side and his left nostril was flat. But, when they looked in his mouth, his palate was fine. This was fantastic news.

I found it hard to bond with Callan. I had so many mixed emotions. During a little time alone with Callan, I was telling him how much I loved him, how we were going to make him all better and that he was perfect just the way he was. I began to sing to him and kiss him as I held him close.

As time went on, our bond grew so strong. Everything I had feared about what other people would think or say about him didn't matter. He was mine and he was perfect just the way he was. Things were hard when people on Facebook started to ask for a photo of Callan. I was scared, as I had not told everyone about Callan's lip. So, I would always put up pictures of him with a dummy in or hiding his mouth. I just wanted to protect him. I already felt like I was on an emotional roller coaster and telling everyone just seemed too hard. It was tough, but I eventually put up a picture and explained to everyone about Callan. They were all so loving and encouraging and made me feel so much better. It was a huge weight off my shoulders that there was no more hiding.

The first few weeks were very hard with adjusting to the feeding challenges, but once we figured out how to feed him with his pigeon bottle, it got easier. It took about a week or so to get the hang of it. I found squeezing the bottle hard and often got sore aching hands. I even had to go see a physiotherapist a few times and take medication for my sore muscles. We had regular visits from a local area health nurse (put in place for special needs babies) and Callan was doing well. He was putting on lots of weight and doing everything a normal baby should. She made our first few weeks so much better, as she helped us with any problems we had and kept a close eye on Callan's health.

We did have many little challenges in the first few weeks, but we worked together as a family and got through it together. I won't lie, at times it was really tough and we were exhausted emotionally and physically.

When it was time for surgery, Callan was four-months-old. Surgery was another big hurdle for us. It was very tough and my heart broke for Callan. I felt every pain, probably even more than he did. I hated seeing him all swollen, with blood on his face. I will never forget that image. Handing him over to the surgeons was too hard for me, so my husband offered to. As we walked away, it only took a few steps up the hallway before I burst into tears. I just wanted to hold Callan. I didn't want him to have to go through this. I didn't want him to wake up scared. I just wish I could have gone through it for him. But, I knew it had to be done.

The two and a half hour wait felt like forever. As soon as our buzzer went off, I couldn't get to recovery fast enough. I was pretty much running. When I first saw him, I burst into tears again. I could hardly recognise him. He was so swollen, had blood on his face, and had a horrible cry; a sound I'll never forget. That night in the hospital was long and tiring. We needed to keep his nose clear because it was bleeding into his open nostril, blocking it, and waking him as he couldn't breathe. I spent all night holding his hand, making sure he knew I was with him. It was a challenge to feed him due to the pain and he lost a little bit of weight. With some pain medication taken just before a bottle, it was easier for him to feed well. After regular medication, feeding, and lots of wakeful nights, Callan began to heal. Within three days, he was smiling again.

I couldn't believe how well and how quickly he was recovering. I was so happy that we were through the worst. Within two weeks of surgery, he was back to his normal, thriving self. It was all over and I could not have been happier. We could move on. I could take him out and not have people stare, wondering what was wrong with him.

It all went by so fast and I never thought I'd say this, but part of me even missed his cleft smile. Callan is now eight-months-old and when I tell people who don't know Callan's story, they can't believe it. They say they had no idea and didn't even notice his scar until I mentioned it. Callan may still need a couple surgeries in the future, but whatever happens, we will get though it together as a family and give Callan all the love and support he needs. Callan's cleft journey has been extremely difficult and emotional, but it has made us stronger as a family and as individuals. Callan is such a cute baby. He is incredibly adorable, has a very happy personality, and loves to play with his best friend and big brother, Zeke.

I Wish I'd Known... that when I would hold him in my arms, nothing else would matter. He was precious and perfect just the way he was.

Adley

Country: United States of America
Type of Cleft: Bilateral Cleft Lip and Palate
Birthdate: September 17, 2012
Cleft Team: University of Texas Health Science Center; Dr. Teichgraeber, MD
Found Out About Cleft: 24-Week Ultrasound
Cleft device: NAM
Surgery Date: January 18, 2013
Family History of Clefts: No

Jason and I had been trying to have a baby for almost a year. When I finally started my first round of Clomid, we immediately fell pregnant on our first round! At around 11 weeks pregnant, we got the results of the blood test to find out the sex of the baby and we were having a girl. Her name would be Adley!

At our 20-week scan, we never got to see her face because she had her hands in the way. When we left, the doctor said she wanted to do another ultrasound at the next appointment because she would not move her hands.

Four weeks later, we headed to the doctor again. My grandmother was with me this time. It was the first appointment my husband had missed because he had a meeting at work that day. As I lay on the table, I was so excited to see my sweet little angel again. I love ultrasounds. The doctor was taking her time looking. Finally, she looked at me and explained that she is about 90% sure that Adley would have a cleft lip.

I do not think it really registered with me until I sat up. When I sat up on the table I lost it. I remember thinking, "How am I ever going to walk out of this room and keep it all together until I get to the truck. How am I going to tell my husband? What do I tell him? How do I tell my family? What if she was wrong and that 10% was going to be us? What does this mean? Is she going to be made fun of?" Thoughts and questions were running through my mind at 100 mph. I had planned to spend the rest of the day with my grandmother and soon realized I would not be able to do anything else for the rest of the day. I was overcome with emotion.

When I got in the car, I called to tell my husband what the doctor had said. He didn't take the news well either. One million thoughts went running through his head as well and I didn't have all the answers to them. His brave soul immediately turned to Google. Do not do this! It was terrible. The things people say and the things you see will make you crazy.

When we met with the maternal fetal medicine doctor, she did the 3-D scan and confirmed our sweet girl did have a bilateral cleft lip. She was 90% sure it would involve the palate as well.

My water broke on September 16th, three days before my due date. I was officially ready to have our baby. At the hospital, they started me on some Pitocin and we waited for Adley. She didn't arrive until the next morning around 11 a.m. All of the fears, questions, and worries I had didn't matter anymore because she was here and she was the most beautiful little girl I had ever seen. She immediately stole my heart. She was perfect. The moment they put her on my chest, I felt love that I had never felt before. She was the best gift from God anyone could ask for.

Within the first week, we met with the craniofacial doctor and started using the NAM. The NAM gave us amazing results. As I look back and ask myself the question "Would I do it again if I had to?" Well, I am going to say yes! It wasn't that terrible. With that being said, I am going to say there were days I called my dad and said, "I broke the NAM! I need super glue and by the time you get here it may not be able to be fixed." There were also days that I called saying, "Jason is working late and your granddaughter will not let me tape her. I suggest you get over here fast."

My grandmother stayed with us in the beginning to help me with everything. There were plenty of times that I would have to walk off after taping in the beginning because Adley was screaming and I felt so bad. I would go lock myself in my room while my grandma rocked her. I

would just wait for her to calm down because I felt terrible for making her scream like that. Then, it became a game. I would play with her as I taped her and she would laugh. I would put a piece on and say, "I got you!" She learned to love the NAM. She was always smacking on it and loved to pull it out just to make mommy crazy.

I pray to God that if and when we decide to have more children, we don't have to do it again. But, in the spectrum of things, it didn't kill me. Adley had surgery on January 18th. It was a tough day but things turned out beautifully. We plan to have surgery on her palate in July 2013.

I wish I'd known that she would steal my heart from day one and that I would fall in love with her wide smile and her new smile. I wish I'd known that the cleft made no difference in how we loved her or how we allowed other people to view her. The cleft was just a small bump in the road that, in the end, seems so minor.

I Wish I'd Known... that I would come to love this smile so much and that I would be sad when the cleft was gone.

Dear Pregnant Mom,

It's okay to be sad. It's okay to be scared of all the things your little monkey will have to go through in the short term and over the course of his or her life. It's okay to be angry. Allow yourself the time to heal and grow strong for each other and your little one.

Don't forget to be grateful for the understanding and support of family, friends, and medical staff, for the kindness of strangers, and for the silent embrace from other parents like us who are on this roller coaster ride right along beside you.

That perfect, tiny spirit, that little miracle you're holding chose YOU as parents. You have everything your little muffin will ever need to get through this; all the love in your heart at this very moment, plus a whole lot more you never knew you could fit in there.

Everything is going to be okay.

I Love My Cleft Team

"*Our opinion mattered and we were part of one of the best teams in the world.*"

Sean

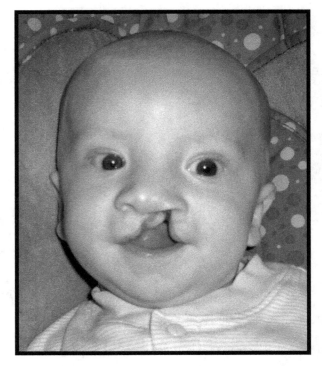

Country: United States of America
Type of Cleft: Unilateral Cleft Lip and Palate
Birthdate: September 12, 2006
Cleft Team: Shriners Hospital for Children
Found Out About Cleft: 20-Week Ultrasound
Cleft Device: NAM
Surgery Dates: January 2007 (Lip repair), June 2007 (Lip revision and ear tubes placed), June 2009 (Ear tubes replaced), March 2011 (Pharyngeal flap surgery), June 2012 (Lip revision)
Family History of Clefts: No

Our cleft journey began during a typical 20-week ultrasound. This is when we found out that Sean would be born with a possible cleft lip. We ended up having a 3-D ultrasound that same day to confirm he did have the cleft lip with a possible cleft palate. The first thing that came to my mind was what I had done. From that moment forward, after all the emotions ran through us, we began researching how we would care for him and feed him.

I was 36 weeks and Sean decided to come early. We were both scared and had no idea what to do. We had no insurance and no family close by to lean on, but knew this baby needed us as much as we needed him. The same day he was born, the two doctors from the local cleft team came to the hospital to meet Sean and help us figure out what our next step would be.

After coming home with Sean, both my mother-in-law and mom suggested we look online for information about Shriners Hospitals. To me, personally, it seemed way out of reach. I mean why would they want to help us? We had nothing to offer in return. We talked and decided to fill out an application and submit it. In less than three months' time, we were on our way to the Shriners Hospital. Since that time, Sean has had a total of five surgeries.

We are scheduled to return to Cincinnati Shriners Hospital in June to start planning for his next surgery. We do not know how many more he may have. All I can tell you is we are ready and know he is always in the best hands, starting with his favorite drivers, Wayne & Wally. He is my little hero and I'm so proud of him.

Sean is a wonderful, six-year-old boy. He enjoys karate, basketball, baseball, and helping others in the area notice he has no scar because he was born perfect (in his words). He is a straight-A student, on the honor roll in first grade, and enjoys sharing his journey with all his friends and teachers. He was featured by our local Al Chymia Shrine Temple as honorary ringmaster for the 2013 circus. When he grows up, he plans to be a Chef on the Moon at Ihop because he loves to cook and, well, astronauts will still need to eat. Like my other kids, I tell him he can do anything he sets his mind to. He is one amazing little boy to me as he won't let anything hold him back. He has no fear in anything he is faced with. We are so proud of him.

He loves to educate others about his cleft journey. If you ask him about his scar, he will tell you that he has no scar, only extra love. He has had five surgeries so far and will have many more to come. His first surgery was done at three months of age. We are facing a bone graft operation soon. Personally, I am scared to death of things to come, but he is not. He is simply amazing to me just the way he is.

I'm so thankful for the Nobles and Ladies at Al Chymia Shrine Temple for welcoming us into their family with open arms. We feel truly blessed to be part of such a great organization and be able to give back in our son's honor. I'm proud of my husband for making the decision to become a Mason and Shriner. They all are our extended family and we look forward to our two youngest growing up there. Thank you to Shriners International and Shriners hospitals for the philanthropy and care in which Sean has received, thus far. Also, a special thanks to Dr. Billmire and the staff at Cincinnati Shriners Hospital for Children and Dr. William Parris, orthodontist, and Dr. Betsy Barcroft, DDS.

I Wish I'd Known... exactly how many surgeries he would need.

Christopher

Country: Canada
Type of Cleft: Unilateral Cleft Lip and Palate
Birthdate: November 3, 1970
Cleft Surgeon: Dr. Hazelwood, MD
Found Out About Cleft: At Birth
Surgery Dates: At three months, 18 months, 12 years and 20 years
Family History of Clefts: No

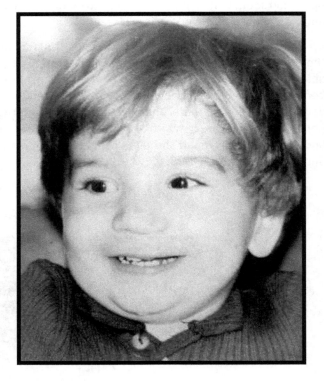

November 3, 1970, I gave birth to my first child. I was a recently married 17-year-old girl, who had little to no knowledge of healthy "normal" babies, let alone a child born with a cleft lip and palate. This would be both a blessing and a curse.

Christopher was born three weeks past his due date. I had a normal pregnancy except for one very bad cold where I had been prescribed a cough syrup and an antibiotic. There was little to no information available to me about pregnancy and motherhood; no "What to Expect When You're Expecting" books, no Internet, or computers.

Christopher was born in the days when fathers were not allowed in the delivery room or even the hospital room when the babies were being fed by the mothers. I was told that my baby was a boy, that he had a cleft lip and that I would probably never be able to feed him. My son was then taken to an intensive care nursery where he would be isolated for three weeks. I never got to hold him during my entire five day stay at the hospital. I would stand outside the window of the nursery, gaze at my baby boy and wonder how I could possibly love anyone as much as I loved him. I was determined to look after him and care for him as best I could.

I remember standing outside the hospital room of my then family doctor's wife. She had just delivered a daughter. When he was visiting his family, I asked him if I could hold my new son. I was told, "No." They didn't want to risk infection. They were feeding him through a gavage. After I was discharged from the hospital (without baby Chris), I was allowed to go back and learn how to feed him. We did this until he was three-weeks-old and we were finally allowed to take him home.

The attitude in those days was that these children were different. They believed that every effort should be made to make them look as normal as possible and then everything would be fine. In fact, I was once told by a plastic surgeon whom I was interviewing, that he believed these children should never be able to reproduce. Needless to say, I didn't have a second visit with that doctor.

At three months, Chris had his first lip repair. He was in the hospital for three weeks. Isolated again, we were denied access to him to comfort or care for him. We were told that this was because of danger of infection. Up until that point, we were feeding him with a nipple with the end cut off. We thickened the formula with Pablum (I had been told that I couldn't breast feed) to slow the flow of the liquid. I can recommend this mixture to anyone who needs a cement-like substance that will never give way. Because we knew nothing of babies, this was not any more difficult than it would have been for us to adjust to feeding a baby without a cleft. We had the gift of youth and ingenuity and managed just fine with our beautiful boy.

At 18 months, Chris had his first palate repair surgery and again we were not allowed to be in his hospital room. He had splints on his arms so that he would not touch his face. We peeked at him through a little window so he would not see us and cry for us. Can you imagine how barbaric this was for us? One time, he did see us and I will never forget his cries for his mommy and daddy. During this time, I was learning about cleft children, their treatment, and searching for a better, more progressive alternative.

After his second surgery, I found Sick Children's Hospital in Toronto, Canada. We were introduced to a newer, progressive way to cleft treatment; a way where the parents are part of the caregiving team. There was a whole group of therapists, surgeons, and E.N.T specialists who were caring for our boy. Our opinion mattered and we were part of one of the best teams in the world. We learned so much. Although Chris had to have several other surgeries to repair and fine tune his growth, our experiences were hopeful and happy.

Christopher has always been my greatest teacher and although those early times were some of the worst of my life, I learned, became stronger, and am forever grateful for the gift of his existence. He is now a successful 42-year-old, network engineer with a beautiful wife and daughter who is the love of his life. The journey was long but worth every step.

I Wish I'd Known...
that I could have held my
child when he was born and
that he was in no more risk
to infection than any other
baby.

Patrick

Country: United States of America
Type of Cleft: Unilateral
Incomplete Cleft Lip with Cleft
Gum line
Birthdate: March 16, 2011
Cleft Team: NYU Medical Center -
Institute of Reconstructive Plastic
Surgery
Found Out About Cleft: 24-Week
Sonogram
Cleft Device: NAM and Post-
Operative Nasal Stents
Surgery Date: July 11, 2011
Family History of Clefts: No

I found out that I was
pregnant with our second son in
July 2010. We were thrilled to
have a sibling for my son, Liam. My pregnancy was smooth sailing until my 20-week sonogram.
The doctor informed us that our baby's kidneys were measuring on the higher side of normal. It
was terrifying to hear that something was abnormal with our baby, but our doctor said that it
was common in many pregnancies. They started to monitor the baby's kidneys every two weeks
to make sure that they were not getting worse.

At my 24-week sonogram, we found out that our baby had a cleft lip with a possible palate.
My husband and I went through a crazy few weeks of tears, doctors' appointments, and
research to find out what exactly this meant for all of us. It was determined that our baby was
cleft affected in some way, but we would not know the severity of the cleft until birth.

The time before his birth was very difficult. We decided to only share our news with close
family and friends. I knew nothing about clefts and was so anxious and worried that it was hard
to get through each day. However, we still had my older son Liam to brighten the tough days.
My husband and I stayed together as a team and we had wonderful support from family and
friends.

We also found out that our baby was a boy and we decided to name him Patrick Daniel. In
January, we met with the Cleft Team at NYU who would be helping us with Patrick's journey.
The team is made up of a speech therapist, nurse, pediatric orthodontist, social worker, and
surgeon who led us through his surgeries and care. We felt comfortable with the idea of a team
and everyone was so warm and supportive.

The cleft team said it best when they told us that we were expecting a baby on March 17th,
not just a cleft. We were very lucky when Patrick came into the world an hour before St.
Patrick's Day. Patrick was born with a unilateral incomplete cleft lip on the left side. His palate
was formed, but he did have a notch in his gum line. We have been so in love with him from the
minute he was born.

At eight weeks, Patrick had a NAM inserted to help mold his nose and pull his cleft closer
together. This was very labor intensive for us and uncomfortable for him. However, Patrick was

such a trooper throughout the whole experience. We had to go to NYU for weekly adjustments and the taping was tough on his skin. The strength of Patrick kept us positive and moving forward in his journey. On our toughest day, Patrick would be smiling and happy which made everything so much easier for all of us.

His surgery was on July 11, 2011. There is no way to sugar coat it; it was heartbreaking to see our baby boy in so much pain during recovery. It was the most difficult part of his journey and I am still in awe of Patrick's strength to this day. Patrick wore nasal stents for three months after surgery to help with scar tissue. He got used to wearing them, but it was difficult because they frequently fell out and required tape on his face.

As I write, Patrick is nearly two-years-old. I can't believe all that he has been through and we have all learned so much from his journey. My close friend told me that Patrick has the most amazing, sparkling eyes. His smiling, Irish eyes have lived a lot of life in such a short amount of time. He continues to inspire me with his sweet disposition and strength. I believe children born with clefts have a remarkable spirit that enables them to face the challenges they face in life. I am so proud to be part of the cleft community and I feel our lives have changed for the better going through Patrick's journey as a family.

I Wish I'd Known… how completely in love I would be with our son's original smile and how much we would miss it.

Nathan

Country: United Kingdom
Type of Cleft: Cleft of the Soft Palate
Birthdate: May 19, 2005
Cleft Team: Spires Cleft Centre
Found Out About Cleft: Two Hours After Birth
Surgery Date: October 2005
Family History of Clefts: No

Nathan is our first child. He was born in May 2005, after a relatively trouble free and lovely pregnancy. Shortly after he was born, our midwife broke the news to us that she had discovered a cleft of the soft palate. My husband and I were shocked.

The cleft nurse visited us in hospital and showed us how to feed Nathan with squeeze bottles. He fed really well, and as soon as we felt able, we were allowed to take Nathan home.

Over the next few months, there were frequent visits from the wonderful cleft nurses and trips to Oxford for appointments. Early in October that same year, we took Nathan in for his palate repair. The surgery went very well and over the following years, he has had few problems.

I Wish I'd Known... that everything was going to be okay.

Evie-Beau

Country: England
Type of Cleft: Incomplete Unilateral Cleft Lip
Birthdate: June 3, 2012
Cleft Team: Birmingham Children's hospital
Found Out About Cleft: 20-week ultrasound
Surgery Date: October 4, 2012
Family History of Clefts: No

At my 20-week scan, the midwife thought she could see that there was something wrong with Evie's lip, but couldn't tell as she had her hand to her face. I was called back two weeks later to check again. This time, the midwife suggested that Evie simply had a prominent Cupid's bow and that there was nothing medically wrong.

June 3, 2012, Evie-Beau entered the world with an incomplete unilateral cleft lip. It came as quite a shock as I had not known about it during my pregnancy. After a few days of it sinking in, the cleft nurses from Birmingham Children's Hospital came to visit us at home and ran through the whole process with us. Trying to rule out why it had happened was tiring.

A few weeks later, Evie had her operation. As the day slowly approached, I was filled with emotions. Evie went down to theatre at 1:30 p.m. and retuned at 5 p.m. The hours dragged on and every negative thought raced through my head. Then the ward doors opened and here she was, mouth as perfect as ever!

We stayed in hospital that night. Evie had Paracetamol, Ibuprofen, antibiotics, and Codeine to kill any pain. Four days later, she was put to sleep again to have the stitches out. And that was it; it was all over!

It was a lengthy process and I wish I had known more about it. But, it's all over now and Evie is more perfect than ever! Thank you to the team at Birmingham children's hospital and Miss Slator, Evie's surgeon, for giving my daughter the opportunity to look as every other child does. She will be very thankful when she is older.

I Wish I'd Known... other people's journey stories. I felt like I knew nothing and my child was the only one with a cleft.

Kaydence

Country: Canada
Type of Cleft: Unilateral Cleft Lip
Birthdate: November 26, 2010
Cleft Team: Stollery Children's Hospital
Found Out About Cleft: 20-Week Ultrasound
Surgery Date: March 15, 2011
Family History of Clefts: Yes

After my 20-week ultrasound, I received a phone call from my family doctor. He told me that our baby was growing well, all the organs looked like they were functioning well, but the baby had a cleft lip and they were unable to confirm whether there was cleft palate involvement. Being a respiratory therapist, I knew what clefts were. When I heard the news, it was like someone popped my perfect pregnancy bubble.

I felt disappointed that I wasn't having a perfect baby like all my other family and friends. I was worried that I wouldn't think she was beautiful and that I wouldn't love her as much. I was scared for what her life would be like. I felt blame. We are nearly two years post-surgery and recalling these feelings are painful. It's painful to think that I blamed myself for something that might not have been my fault or might not have even been preventable.

After finding out about the cleft, I followed up with my doctor who referred us to the Cleft Lip and Palate clinic at the Stollery Children's Hospital. I was surprised that they met families even before the baby was born. My husband and I went to the appointment, not knowing what to expect. We brought with us lots of questions and Sharon, the speech language pathologist, had all the answers and then some. We felt much more prepared after leaving the clinic.

Kaydence was born via C-section on November 26, 2010. She weighed in at seven pounds, 14 ounces and 19 inches in length. I think I asked the nurse if she had a cleft palate about three times. She told me, "No, just a cleft lip and she's beautiful." It's one thing for a parent to think they have a beautiful baby, but when someone else confirms it, it means so much more. When I first saw her, I instantly fell in love with her and her beautiful smile.

At about two-weeks-old, Kaydence had a follow-up appointment with the Cleft Lip Clinic. Sharon checked to make sure she was feeding okay and answered a few more questions. At about two-months-old, Kaydence had her first Audiology appointment with the Cleft Lip Clinic. The audiologist put little sensors in Kaydence's ears and then we waited for her to fall asleep. Once again, Kaydence surprised me with great results on her first test.

By the time March rolled around, it was time for surgery. A big challenge was when Kaydence had to fast starting the night before surgery. The poor baby was hungry and I felt helpless as a parent not being able to feed her. It was a good thing that her surgery was scheduled early in the morning. The most difficult part of Kaydence's surgery was giving her to the surgeon and watching her being taken away to the operating room.

It was such a relief to see her after surgery. She had a weird, weak cry from the anesthetics. She looked like a totally different baby. I found that her smile almost looked weird and incomplete without her cleft. She took antibiotics to prevent infection. We gave her Tylenol with codeine for pain and kept the stitches moist with Vaseline regularly. She had to wear cute little arm braces so that she wouldn't pick at her face or suck her thumb. Kaydence was a little Houdini and we really had to get creative for them to stay on once she went to bed. She was a very smart little baby.

We did regular follow-ups with the Cleft Lip Clinic including Audiology, Speech Language Pathology, Social Work, ENT, and appointments with the Surgeon. When Kaydence started getting her teeth, they were all growing in fine. There was a space where her cleft used to be. I was concerned that no tooth would grow there. After all her other teeth grew in, a really weird-looking tooth finally dropped where the cleft was. The only way I can describe it is that it looks like the end of a Phillips screwdriver. I brought her to the dentist because it looked really painful. They did a small x-ray and it turned out to be simply a harmless and weird-looking tooth. The dentist also commented that the adult tooth looks normal.

I think one of the biggest struggles of having a child with a cleft was getting over my own insecurities and realizing that not everything is about appearances. Most people are accepting to other people's differences. Not everyone is perfect.

Kaydence has such a beaming smile and big bright eyes that we would get stopped in the mall, the grocery store or anywhere and strangers would comment on how beautiful she is.

At present, Kaydence is a normal two-year-old, running around, walking, talking (with a huge vocabulary), and testing her limits. I can't stress how much of an awesome experience we had with our Cleft Lip Clinic. It was fantastic having a support system to ask questions and get a reliable answer. I really do wish I'd known how beautiful, smart, and perfect Kaydence was going to be.

I Wish I'd Known...
how beautiful, perfect,
and smart she would be.

Nathan

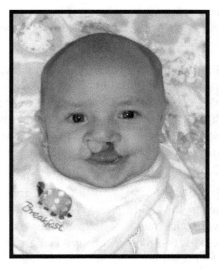

Country: Canada
Type of Cleft: Complete Bilateral Cleft Lip and Palate
Birthdate: February 19, 2005
Cleft Team: Winnipeg Children's Hospital; Dr. Ross, MD
Found Out About Cleft: At Birth
Surgery Dates: June 2005, January 2006, November 2013
Family History of Clefts: No

After a perfect pregnancy, Nathan decided to arrive eight days early. After he was delivered, the room fell silent and my baby was taken over to a table. A nurse called, "Get NICU." I could hear him crying and I asked, "What is it?" No one would answer me. I then started yelling, "What's wrong?" After what felt like forever, I was told I had a baby boy and there was a problem. "He has a small hole in his lip," I was told. They made my husband go and sit down before they would show our baby to him. I remember the sound of my husband sobbing before the nurses took Nathan away. I remember looking into Nathans eyes; they were amazing, big, blue, and full of wonder.

Our first experience with the pediatrician on call was awful. He would not look us in the eye when talking about Nathan. He made it sound like we were handed a life sentence. He explained that Nathan would be in the hospital a long, long time. We were delighted when Nathan was released after only six days.

Nathan's first surgery was done at three and a half months. That was when we met our amazing cleft team. Our surgeon, Dr. Ross, is nothing short of a miracle worker. He used to joke that Nathan reminded him of Bam-Bam from The Flintstone's. The support provided by Cindy, the nurse clinician, cannot be put into words.

The night before surgery, Nathan slept in my arms. I watched him sleep knowing I would never see his smile again. I still miss his wide smile; the way his entire face smiled. Surgery day was awful. It was horrible handing our baby over to a "stranger." But, with the support of our parents that day, we got through it. In a way, we were waiting for our baby to be born all over again. The result was truly amazing! We knew it was going to be okay when later that day, Nathan showed us his very first new smile.

Nathan is amazing. He is a better person because he was born with a cleft. He has a compassion about him that I am shocked a child can have. He is caring and reaches out to others because he was reached out to. He has developed friendships with doctors and nurses and wins the hearts of everyone who meets him.

I Wish I'd Known... what a blessing the cleft would be.

Susanna May

Country: United States of America
Type of Cleft: Bilateral Cleft Lip and Palate
Birthdate: November 19, 2010
Cleft Team: Johns Hopkins Children's Center; Dr. Redett, MD
Found Out About Cleft: 22 Weeks Gestation
Surgery Date: February 15, 2011 (Lip repair and ear tubes placed), May 21, 2011 (Lip revision), August 31, 2011 (Palate repair), April 2012 (Ear tubes replaced)
Family History of Clefts: No

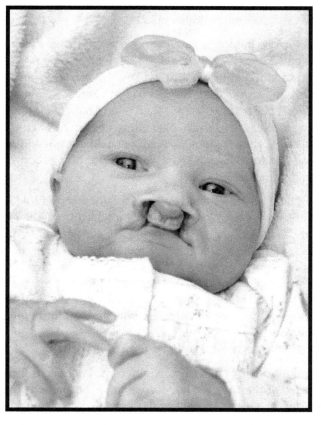

Our story began in March of 2010, when we found out we would be expecting our fifth child! The pregnancy was going just as expected with symptoms of extreme exhaustion and headaches. In July 2010, my routine AFP test came back positive for Down Syndrome. I was not too worried, as we had been through this before with our second pregnancy.

At my next ultrasound, we found out our new edition had a bilateral cleft lip and palate. I completely lost it when the doctor and tech revealed what was found during the scan. Our hearts sank. We were overwhelmed at that moment – fear and sadness completely overcame us.

As soon as we arrived home, we called to make an appointment at the Johns Hopkins clinic. I spoke with a sweet lady over the phone who told me everything was going to be okay. She scheduled an appointment for us to meet with her and the doctor a few days later. We met with Dr. Redett and right away we felt very comfortable with him. We had a book of questions. He answered all of them and helped with all of our concerns. I left feeling great about the team we would be working with. We were a little more educated about the condition and what to expect after birth. I was still sad and I felt like I was mourning the loss of my "perfect" baby for weeks to come.

I spent the next four months being monitored twice a week for high amniotic fluid and constant contractions. I was so nervous to give birth. As this being our fifth child, it was not the labor that scared me, it was the unknown as to what was going to happen with our baby afterward.

On November 19, 2010 our beautiful daughter, Susanna May, was born. After a normal delivery and no medical intervention needed, she was placed into my arms. My heart melted.

She was absolutely perfect. All of our fears just blew away. Her gorgeous little face just shimmered at us with pure love.

Everything was the same with Susie as far as having a newborn, except for the way she ate. She sometimes seemed to get fluid stuck in the back of her throat, so we kept her propped up in car seat, swing, or Boppy pillow.

The day before Susanna's surgery, I was a nervous mess. I kept telling myself everything was going to be okay. We did not sleep a wink the night before. Susie slept peacefully while daddy and mommy had anxiety! Luckily, she was calm and happy during our two-hour wait. I was good up until the anesthesiologist came in and started to go over the possible side effects. This was our first experience with one of our children needing surgery and it was a little scarier because she was so small. Tears began to flow from my eyes uncontrollably. I held it in for so long but I couldn't stop. My husband held us tight and reassured me she would be fine. We chose dad to go back with her into the operating room until she went to sleep because I knew I wouldn't be able to.

About an hour later, Dr. Ishman came out and told us her tubes were in and there was no permanent hearing loss. We were thrilled with the news. We continued to wait, and two hours later the nurse called for us come back and see her in the recovery room. I was a nervous wreck. I had been dreading this moment. The nurse showed us over to her bed and my heart dropped. Her little body was so swollen and her face a little bloody. I again began to cry. My husband stood strong by her bed and held me tight. Susie then began to thrash around a little and I couldn't stand to watch her in pain. I walked out and went back into the waiting room to get myself together and process what I saw. Dad stayed and held her. I went back in a few minutes later and felt more in control. She lay quietly in our arms, at times, whining from pain but nothing as terrible as I had tried to prepare for.

We could not believe how different she looked! Right away we missed her cleft, but were amazed at the work Dr. Redett had done. Susanna did not wake until that evening, but when she did she was amazing. She woke, smiled at us, did some baby talk, and then took her bottle. We were amazed! It was as if she never had surgery a few hours ago. The night went by with no concerns. She was eating and going to the bathroom, so we were sent home the following afternoon. The past few months of panic and concern were over and it was not as bad as I had imagined. Susanna came home her happy self and right back into her routine. To be over this first hurdle was such a big deal to us; we made it. It was over!

May 21, 2011 was her second lip revision and we were a lot more calm. We knew what to expect first hand and it helped tremendously. Again, she came through like a trooper and sprung back immediately. Susanna had stents in her nose as well as stitches between her nose and top lip, but it didn't seem to bother her. The stitches were taken out a week after surgery and the nose stents, six weeks after.

In June, we received a letter saying her next surgery would be August 23, 2011. August came and we headed back to Hopkins for her third surgery. This was the most difficult time we had with her being hungry. Poor thing kept saying, "Eat," and of course, we couldn't feed her. Palate surgery took about four hours. We were warned this time she would be swollen and have a bloody mouth. Susie was restless in her bed and was on stronger pain meds for this surgery. She had blood coming out of her mouth and they kept her on her side to let it drain out. To add to all our stress, an earthquake hit after we were placed in our room. We swayed in a tall building as we tried to focus on Susie's post-op care.

We attempted to give her a bottle after she woke up a little more, which she rejected right away. We waited a bit and tried a syringe and that worked. Dr.Redett stopped by our room and was very pleased she was eating. The night went by with no troubles and by morning, Susie was attempting to eat from her bottle and eating Italian ice. We were sent home that afternoon and continued her pain meds every few hours. She was a bit fussier than usual, but nothing we couldn't handle. She kept sticking her tongue out of her mouth, I guess, in order not to touch her palate. This lasted well over a month!

Before we knew it, our baby was turning one. In November 2011, we had a lovely party for her and celebrated her first year of life. I think all the different stages and surgeries made her first year fly by. We made a wonderful slide show that showed from sonogram, birth, every surgery, and first birthday pictures. It was a great walk through of her first year.

Susanna is now two and is absolutely amazing, spunky, smart, gorgeous, and brave. You can barely see her scars and many people do not notice them. We now see Dr. Redett and his team yearly. Her next surgery will be around the age of five and that will be a nose revision. We have been unbelievably blessed to have her in our family and the journey we have experienced with her has been hard, yet educational. Our entire family has grown so much and have become better people from everything we have been through with Susie. We have an amazing family and we wouldn't change a thing about the path we've been given. Every day we thank God for our children and give a little extra prayer for our amazing Susanna May!

I Wish I'd Known...
that everything
would be okay. Our
journey would not be
as bad as we thought
it would be.

Dear Pregnant Mom,

Stay strong – even when close family members are scared. My mom and husband seemed to hurt so much for our daughter that she had to go through this. It wasn't always easy being the strong one, but my daughter needed me to hold it together. Surely, I could keep mixing concentrated formula, taping her cheeks till they bled, feeding her with an open cup that spilled all the time, pump every two hours, and all while entertaining our three-year-old.

I did what she needed, I prayed, and talked to friends who were positive. I reflected on the fact that our little girl would soon get through this and she was counting on us. I found some Bible verses that I read daily for support. I spoke to a mom who had already been through this.

I also tried to take my little sweetheart out and about and showed her off to the world. She always had a flower in her hair and a smile on her face. We carried on with life because she deserved that. I showed our beautiful daughter off to the world!

Love, your empathetic fellow cleft mom.

Beauty of the Cleft

" *I wish I'd known how amazing his smile would look;*

best baby smile ever! "

Kestrel

Country: United States of America
Type of Cleft: Incomplete Unilateral Cleft Lip
Birthdate: July 27, 2011
Cleft Team: University of Rochester Medical Center; Dr. Girotto, MD
Found Out About Cleft: 20-Week Ultrasound
Surgery Date: December 7, 2011
Family History of Clefts: No

At our 20-week ultrasound, my wife and I discovered that our daughter had a cleft lip. At the time, we thought it would be a complete cleft. We felt sad and overwhelmed. Despite the lack of other concerning symptoms, the doctor threw around terms like Trisomy 18, a fatal birth defect. I had an amniocentesis and, two weeks later, we discovered that the cleft was an isolated birth defect.

We told our family and friends, we worked through our own difficult emotions, received support, and we found out everything we could about caring for a child with a cleft lip. We got over being afraid and began to celebrate the impending arrival of our little girl.

At 33 weeks, I was diagnosed with Intrahepatic Cholestasis of Pregnancy (ICP). ICP is a rare liver disorder that can occur during pregnancy. It is unrelated to the cleft. However, it is much more dangerous. Suddenly, the cleft was the least of our worries. It faded into the background of what was now, a much more difficult pregnancy. We faced the reality that our baby could be born much earlier than expected and that I would need an induction.

From then on, I began having weekly ultrasounds and twice weekly non-stress tests. The baby did wonderfully with all these tests. Our doctor scheduled an induction for 39 weeks, which was later than the recommended induction with ICP. I wanted an un-medicated delivery. Breastfeeding was very important to me and I wanted us to have the best possible start. At 38 weeks and five days, I had acupuncture to help induce labor naturally. It worked and 36 hours later, Kestrel Marjorie was born, weighing eight pounds and five ounces.

We barely noticed her cleft at first. When we did, we realized it was incomplete. I tried nursing her, but she couldn't latch very well. A few hours later, she was admitted to the Special Care Nursery with a pneumothorax (collapsed lung), which was related to the ICP. Kestrel spent five days in the Special Care Nursery. The first day, she was under an oxygen hood and was unable to eat by mouth. I was heartbroken that these early days of bonding would take place in the midst of wires and machines.

She did amazingly well and was very strong. The first several weeks were some of the most difficult of my life. She seemed constantly hungry and distressed. She couldn't latch well and I was in a lot of pain. At nearly two months, after visits with a lactation consultant and trying numerous interventions, Kestrel had not regained her birth weight. We began supplementing with donated breast milk and formula. Our nursing journey had been further complicated by a hemorrhage during birth and again twelve days postpartum that resulted in a D&C for a retained placenta. It would be months before I felt normal again and only after an increase in antidepressants.

Once Kestrel began getting enough to eat she was a much happier baby! We began bonding and enjoying our lives together. We found her wide smile so charming. It was hard to imagine her looking any different. We grieved the idea of surgery and changing her face.

On December 7, 2011, Kestrel had her cleft lip repair at Strong Memorial Hospital. The surgery was uneventful, successful, and we were blessed with the presence of friends. I went to Kestrel as soon as she was in recovery and tried to nurse her. I had hoped that nursing would be comforting to her, but she refused. It was too difficult and painful for her. It surprised us how much she looked like herself and yet totally different.

The next month was very difficult. Kestrel developed an oral aversion and getting her to take any formula was a struggle. After a couple weeks of this, we took her to a chiropractor at the advice of our family doctor. We were stunned by how much that helped. She soon began taking bottles eagerly and began to gain weight slowly.

Kestrel is now 15-months-old and we have just received a referral to Speech Therapy. She is tiny for her age, weighing only 18 pounds and one ounce. Named after the smallest of the hawk family, she is just as feisty and as fierce. While the spoken word eludes her, American Sign Language helps her communicate. We've all had a lot of fun learning a new language with our hands. I wish I'd known that everything was going to be okay.

I Wish I'd Known... how beautiful her smile would always be.

Garner

Country: United States of America
Type of Cleft: Incomplete Bilateral Cleft Lip and Cleft of the Soft Palate
Birthdate: September 13, 2012
Cleft Team: UNC Chapel Hill; Dr. Golden, MD
Found Out About Cleft: 24 Weeks Pregnant
Surgery Date: March 14th, 2013 (Lip repair)
Family History of Clefts: Yes

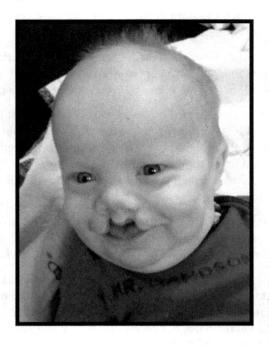

Our cleft journey started when I was 24 weeks pregnant. I went in for a routine fluid measurement. I had always had a large amount of fluid, but they weren't really sure why. They explained that it could be many things: diabetes, a birth defect, or just a lot of fluid. Well, we ruled out diabetes and by the end of this appointment, we found out the reason why.

It started out as normal. They checked the fluid, and then decided to get a good look at the babies. Yep, that's right, I said "babies." My son has a twin sister. During the ultrasound though, the tech kept focusing on his face. I started to pay closer attention to the ultrasound to see why she was spending so much time on him. She switched to the 3-D ultrasound and that's when I saw it. She took a few more photos and said she was going to go talk to the doctor. My husband had no clue. He noticed the focusing on his face, but really didn't know why she was. I told him it was because he had a cleft lip.

The doctor confirmed it that day and gave us some information on it. I didn't know everything about clefts, but I was aware of them and knew they could be fixed. That was good enough for me. I never really got upset over it. He was my son and I was going love him no matter what. I admit, though, I did cry after reading stories of others' interactions with some people. I didn't want my son judged or treated differently. I was afraid I wouldn't be able to protect him from other peoples' looks and whispers.

After we found out, we scheduled an appointment with the cleft team. Before we were able to go to the appointment, my twins decided to come early. I was 28 weeks and three days, and labor was very fast; so fast that they couldn't stop it. My biggest worry, the cleft, became the last worry on my mind. Out of both of them, he was my little troublemaker. He had a long, hard road. He was intubated a couple times for not being able to breathe and the doctors were not sure why he couldn't. This had his surgeons concerned, so we were sent three hours away to a bigger hospital.

Once we had all of our appointments set for the new hospital, it all went pretty quickly. We met with the doctor one week, and in two weeks we had his surgery. Again, they were concerned about his breathing, so when they put him under, the ENT doctor scoped him to check his airway. Then, they did the lip surgery and also put tubes in his ears. I think it was one of the longest days of my life. They decided to use glue for his sutures. We were told this would be better for scarring. When he came out, though, he had tape over it. You could tell he looked different, but you couldn't get the full effect.

I fell in love all over again. He stayed in the PICU so they could monitor him closely. My husband stayed with him that night because I had his sister with us too. That night he told me all he did was cry and they had to give him morphine for pain. The next day he seemed a little better but all he wanted was to be held. They kept him one more night just to make sure he was doing okay, and then we were released to come home. It took him about one week before he didn't seem to be in pain or uncomfortable.

I had really hoped to get his tape removed at the follow-up appointment, but the doctor wanted to wait till it fell off. Sure enough, later that day, we got home and it came off. As I write, it's still a little red and we were told it could look worse before it looks better, but I am amazed on how it looks. I think our surgeon did a wonderful job and I am very hopeful for Garner's future.

I Wish I'd Known... how amazing his smile would look;
best baby smile EVER!!

Lucas

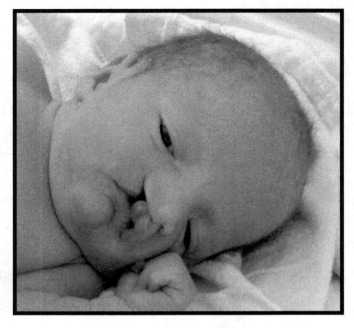

Country: Canada
Type of Cleft: Complete Unilateral Cleft Lip and Palate
Birthdate: April 18, 2012
Cleft Team: John McGivney Children's Centre
Found Out About Cleft: 21 Weeks Gestation
Cleft Device: NAM
Surgery Date: November 6, 2012 (Lip repair), April 9, 2013 (Palate repair)
Family History of Clefts: No

We had it all planned out. My 19-week ultrasound was scheduled for early December and I was going to ask the tech to put the sex of the baby in a Christmas card and seal it. This would be our Christmas Surprise. We placed the card in the tree and awaited our big surprise. We opened it on Christmas morning to learn that our baby was a boy. We were excited! Our son Noah (who was three at the time), was going to have a brother. However, an even bigger surprise came a few days after Christmas at an OB appointment.

While reading the ultrasound report for the first time, she read, "Possible cleft lip." She continued, "Oh, okay. Well, it looks like the baby may have a cleft lip. We will do a 3-D ultrasound to confirm." My mind raced and my heart was pounding. I didn't really even know what a cleft lip was. She explained a little and then wrote the two little words on a piece of paper, 'cleft lip.' "I know you will want to look this up when you get home," she replied. No other information was given, that was it. I cried as my husband held me, and at that moment I prayed to God to let my baby be okay. I would have done anything to know that he would be okay.

I spent the rest of my pregnancy worried and afraid. Each morning, I would try to convince myself that everything was going to be okay. But, my worries grew as I researched and educated myself about clefts. I already loved him so much and didn't want him to experience any pain. I got in touch with our cleft team which was a blessing to us. We started to feel like we weren't alone.

In the morning of April 18, 2012, Lucas Maximus made his entrance. He was born with a complete unilateral cleft lip and palate. The cleft was more severe than they had expected. I cried because, at first, his cleft looked painful and raw. Within hours, I didn't see the cleft. All I could see was my beautiful baby, whom I adored. He did well right from the beginning; no NICU, no breathing difficulties, and he fed pretty well with the Haberman bottle. My love for my special baby was like no love I had ever experienced before. I felt like we had been given this special job to protect and love him even more. He was going to be okay.

On day two in the hospital, the nurse reported a sacral dimple. Immediately, I became worried of Spina Bifida. My mind was racing again. An ultrasound cannot confirm its closure, but he was functioning okay. They wanted us to go home and return in two days for an MRI. Yes, he needed an MRI at five-days-old. This news put the cleft into perspective for me really fast. I thought, "A cleft I can handle, we can fix that. But, Spina Bifida may mean he wouldn't walk, talk, or live a full life!" I cried for the two days leading up to the MRI. The MRI was quick and the nurse reported that they found what they needed quite quickly. Our doctor called a few days later to report that there indeed was a closure and Spina Bifida was no longer a worry of ours.

When he was eight-weeks-old, we started the NAM journey. We drove two hours away for his NAM appointments once a week. We were first advised to do the LATHAM. I knew it required more surgery as it is surgically implanted, so I inquired about the NAM. They said that the NAM could lead to the same results; it would just be more work for us. They were right. The NAM was a lot of work. The NAM had to be cleaned and replaced a couple times a day. It never seemed to stay in properly. We used tape and Polygrip, but it was a constant battle. Lucas hated that retainer or his "NAMmy whammy," as I liked to call it. He would cry out in pain as I placed it in his mouth and held it there so that it would stick. I think a little piece of me died as I tortured my little angel for six long months. Our NAM journey was long and painful. I often wonder if the Latham would have been a better choice.

Surgery finally came on November 6, 2012. Lucas was almost seven-months-old and we were all excited to be done with the NAM. I was a little sad to be saying goodbye to his wide smile that I had grown to love so much. Surgery went well. When they took him that morning, I felt like my heart stopped beating until I saw him again two and a half hours later. The transformation was incredible and, yes, I cried. The first day, he mostly slept off the drugs. On the second day, the swelling began and his discomfort was apparent. It took three to four days before he felt well again.

We kept the No-no's on for a week. He didn't seem to mind them at all, but the nasal stents were another story all together. He hated those and so did I. We kept them in for four and a half weeks. The surgeon would have liked us to keep them in longer, but I couldn't take it anymore.

We are currently preparing for his palate surgery which will happen sometime around his first birthday. He is ten-months-old now and he is coming along with solid foods. He doesn't seem to be interested in crawling or rolling to his tummy. I worry that it is because during our NAM days we were so careful, trying to avoid him hitting his face that we didn't do much tummy time. Our cleft team is going to have him seen by an occupational therapist and physiotherapist just in case. I worried and prayed that my baby would be okay and he is. The past year has been a challenge for us as a family, but we have survived it. We love our little 'clefty' to bits and we pray that he will forget the pain and suffering and remember the love we have for him.

I Wish I'd Known...that a tiny scar would make me love you that much more!

Benjamin

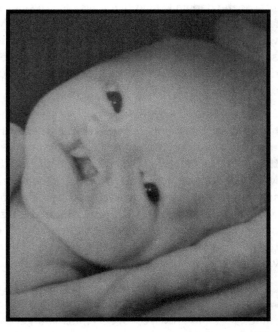

Country: United States of America
Type of Cleft: Complete Unilateral Cleft Lip
Birthdate: February 26, 2012
Cleft Team: Children's Hospital of New Orleans
Found Out About Cleft: 20-Week Ultrasound
Cleft Device: DynaCleft tape
Surgery Date: August 10, 2012 (Lip repair)
Family History of Clefts: No

After ten long years of trying for a child, we were blessed with our little angel. We went for our initial appointment and had our very first ultrasound at 12 weeks gestation, something I had initially accepted I would never have. For the next three months, we would gaze at this tiny little face in the black fuzzy photo. Not until later, would I know why I always looked at that photo and wondered why my angel's lip looked as if it was raised in the corner. Of course, I had just assumed it was nothing and it was just me reacting like a mother. Now, we know it was my motherly instincts telling me that something just was not right.

At 20 weeks gestation, we went for our anatomy ultrasound. The whole day felt surreal. We couldn't contain our excitement, especially when we were told we were having a boy! Dad instantly knew that there was something wrong. He had two children from a previous relationship, so this was not his first ultrasound. The tech did her examination and printed photos for the doctor. She just so happened not to have printed us a photo of our baby boy and kindly started the scan again. She began to focus on getting us that perfect shot of our baby's face to take home with us. That was the moment she discovered that there might be something wrong with our baby. I was elated and in my own little world and still was not aware of the concern on her face or dad's face.

Our doctor called about an hour after we left the office while we were celebrating our wonderful news. Sadly, we were told that it looked as if our baby had something called a cleft lip. I was devastated and scared for us and our baby boy. We knew he needed to have a strong name because he was going to have to be a strong little boy. So, we decided on the name Benjamin. Dad was so supportive and positive after we had received the phone call, and our obstetrician was our cheerleader. We looked forward to seeing her every month for her positive and lovely words of encouragement throughout the process.

A week later, we went to the specialist and had another ultrasound done to confirm the cleft lip. We proceeded with an amniocentesis to rule out Edwards's syndrome and Down's syndrome. The waiting for these results were gruelling. The results came back that Benjamin just had a cleft lip and these syndromes were not detected.

We were sent to the Children's Hospital to meet the wonderful cleft team. As we were sitting in the waiting room anxiously waiting and unaware of what to expect, we were graciously introduced to our surgeon. He is a wonderful surgeon, does such beautiful work for babies with cleft lips, and he eased our worries and anxieties. At this time, I was 36 weeks gestation and after looking over the ultrasound photos, Benjamin's surgeon confirmed a diagnosis of a unilateral cleft lip and possible cleft palate.

We had spent these last 20 weeks educating ourselves about cleft lip and palate. Many hours were spent on the Internet, just soaking up all the information we possibly could. The big day had finally arrived. We were overwhelmed with joy. Our miracle baby boy was here. He had ten fingers, ten toes, he was crying, and he had the most adorable top lip we had ever seen. Dad and I were instantly in love but most of all, instantly in love with his lip. I can honestly say that when we first laid eyes on our baby boy we were a bit saddened that his lip would have to be fixed. We loved it that much, that fast. Benjamin's cleft lip was a part of him; a special baby for a special family.

Benjamin was able to eat from a cross cut nipple right away. He did very well at first, but as the night drew on, he started to get tired from having to work so hard to eat that he stopped eating. One amazing nurse with experience in cleft care got him to eat like a champ with the Haberman Feeder. Benjamin was doing so well with his eating that we were sent home the very next day.

All we did for days was stare at our beautiful baby boy. We were overcome with the emotion of loving his lip so much and having to someday soon say goodbye to it. Surprisingly, we had nothing but adoring smiles and comments for our son's cleft lip. During our pregnancy, we anticipated getting his lip fixed as soon as possible. It never crossed our minds that we would be so reluctant to proceed with the surgery due to our love and everybody else's love for his beautiful lip.

Benjamin used the Haberman Feeder for three months and started to develop a sore on the roof of his mouth due to the reflux he was developing. At this time, his pediatrician had suggested that we try the cross cut nipple once again. Benjamin would stick his thumb in his mouth at feeding time in order to help control the speed of his formula from coming out too fast and to help him swallow. We also added two teaspoons of oatmeal to help thicken the formula and reduce the choking.

At two-weeks-old, Benjamin was fitted for his DynaCleft tape in order to help pull his lip together non-surgically. He wore the DynaCleft tape for five and a half months in the anticipation of his first surgery to repair his cleft lip. All the while, we were showing that lip off proudly.

The day of Benjamin's first surgery finally arrived. We were ready, or at least we thought we were ready for our baby and ourselves to begin this long journey. His surgery took a gruelling two and a half hours. Dad and I were led into recovery to hold our baby in our arms and comfort him. The cleft was gone. It was no longer there. His lip was repaired. This had hit Dad like a ton of bricks. He was not prepared for the emotions that were running through him due to this loss. The thought of his cleft lip honesty terrified us in the beginning of this journey. But, having to wrap our hearts around the loss of it, we think was the biggest struggle of this journey for us so far. Benjamin's older brother and sister, and his little cousins would ask and say, "Why do we have to fix it? We love it so much!"

The next two weeks following surgery were difficult due to the pain, arm restraints, and the nasal conformer. We just wanted to take it all away for our baby. After those long two weeks, he was back to his normal self – this time, with a new lip that everybody had to adjust to him having.

Benjamin is now one-year-old and continues to put his thumb in his mouth to help him swallow certain foods. The scar is very minimal and everywhere we go we are told he is so cute and what an adorable baby we have. We are now in the process of preparing for his palate surgery. He will need tubes for his ears as he has been fighting off ear infections. Benjamin has been receiving speech therapy from a local therapist whom he loves very much and she is wonderful. She has been a very supportive and positive influence throughout Benjamin's journey. I don't know what we would have done without her or the doctors, family, and friends.

I Wish I'd Known... How much we were going to love your lip!

Philippa

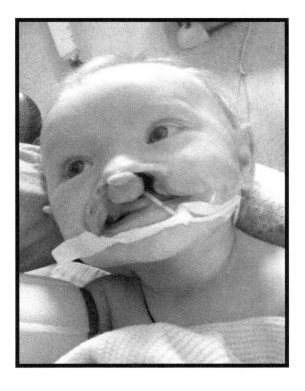

Country: United States of America
Type of Cleft: Complete Bilateral Cleft Lip and Palate
Birthdate: May 5, 2012
Cleft Team: International Craniofacial Institute; Dr. David Genecov, MD and Dr. Elizabeth Sperry, MD
Cleft Surgery Dates: November 20, 2012 (Partial lip repair), February 6, 2013 (Second lip repair).
Family History of Clefts: Yes

I got the call on a cold December day right after Christmas. We had only just discovered that, unsurprisingly, our baby would be a little girl (daddy's fourth!). I was busy unpacking boxes after having spent our first night in our new home. I was brooding in my own melancholy, as daddy and I were in the midst of our first great lover's quarrel.

The phone rang without forewarning; on the other end was a not cruel, but certainly distant nurse. "We think there is something wrong with the baby." All the depths of the universe of madness and grief swelled within me and I felt the cold and pain wash through my body, ripping out my made-frigid heart and discarding it upon the floor. I was desperate to end the call; to go back to only a few moments before, when life was normal, when my greatest worry was being mad at daddy, how to reconcile it with the karma he deserved, and then how best to make up. I wanted to return to the normalcy I had just had stripped from me, but she continued. In my angst, soft tears began to pour down my cheeks. "Are you crying?" the woman asked, surprised at my reaction.

It would be a solid month before we could pursue a certain answer, as the indicators on the original sonogram may have only been shadows. While those around me pretended it away, certain that it wouldn't be the case, I did my research. Even with all the hopefuls around me, I just knew that not only would she have a cleft, but it would be the boldest of them all.

I fell into varying shades of anger, disgrace, and despair. The world suddenly became so cruel and so corrupt, and everybody from strangers in the super market, to my own friends and family became an "enemy." The guardian instinct came out within me with a maddened growl. I was ferocious and poised to strike. I was so desperate to protect my new baby from a cold, calculating world. But, was I protecting, shamefully, the world from her?

Something miraculous took place on an early May Monday afternoon in 2012. After a splendidly simple labor, they thrust our newborn upon my breast. I saw the cleft, but I didn't. I heard the different, airy texture of her uniquely newborn cry. But as she cried, I saw the dimples on her cheeks and I wept with shameless joy at the sight of her, my precious, Philippa. I fell madly, deeply, and passionately in love with her that day. A love that was born out of those long months of aching speculation, and a love that would be tested in the coming weeks and months as new challenges began to unfold.

After initially doing fairly well with a modified preemie nipple, she shut down. Her weight decreased dramatically and, after being home for only nine days, Philippa was admitted to the NICU for failure to thrive. It was two and a half months by the time she came come home again.

The hospital became utterly befuddled by her "case." After all attempts at oral feeding failed, they implanted a G-tube, which went even more horribly and dramatically awry. Four days after her surgery, and after much subtle and timid prodding on my part, they removed Philippa's wound bandages only to discover that a huge portion of skin had disintegrated. The wound was gaping, and I could see into her tiny belly. Philippa writhed in pain as the wound care nurses marveled and the nurse struggled, vainly, to convince me that it wasn't that bad. "We see much worse than this all the time," she told me. After the surgeon came a couple hours later to inspect the wound, he assured the nurse that it was, indeed, as bad as it appeared; if not far worse.

Instead of admitting their weaknesses and uncertainty, they continued to facilitate their god-complex. In my naivety, I permitted it. What happened to that angry, ferocious mommy-dog I had been all throughout the last half of my pregnancy?

After weeks of further healing, they implanted a J-tube that would feed Philippa through her upper small intestine and, after several more weeks, she was able to come home. Two nights later, her untreated reflux reared its ugly head, and she aspirated in my arms during the witching hours of the morning. As I sat there holding my baby, watching her writhe and contort, desperate for air and fighting for breath, I had the sick and horrifying feeling that she was about to die in my arms and there was nothing I could do to stop it.

She eventually adapted, caught her breath, and fell into the ironically sweetest slumber I had ever witnessed. When the paramedics and fire fighters finally arrived and pronounced her vitals stable, I placed my head wearily upon hers and wept openly, unabashedly, with all the fear and utter devastation that comes when someone gazes into the face of Death itself.

We settled into some sort of attempted normality. In September, Philippa underwent another operation to replace her J-tube because it was irredeemably clogged. After that, without any request of follow-up by any of the medical providers responsible for Philippa's care, and coupled with the atrocious memories of her NICU stay, we severed ties, unapologetically, with that hospital. We have yet to look back over our shoulders.

It has been a struggle, to say the very least, to maintain her weight. In January 2013, when Philippa was eight months, she weighed in at 11 pounds and three ounces. We had not seen an increase in her weight since the beginning of November. She was, once again, admitted to the hospital. Fortunately, the week we spent there, though long and challenging, was altogether life-changing for us all. They removed her J-tube, performed tests the other hospital had never even entertained, put in a G-tube, and began Philippa on a specialty formula. The change was instantaneous. Within a matter of hours, her skin took on a healthier, pink glow. She began to smile and play and even sleep more peacefully. Within a day, she began gaining weight. Less than a week later, Philippa had gained two entire pounds! She went from a human-like creature, clinging to survival, to a full-fledged baby girl. She went from scarce mechanical acts to holding up her head and finally attempting to sit upright. I fell in love with her all over again.

Philippa is now almost ten-months-old and less than a month away from the second stage of her lip repair. Mommy and Daddy are busy planning our April wedding and, not long thereafter, her palate repair, first birthday, hospitalization for G.I. studies, and one last surgery.

If all goes as planned, after the last surgery, we should have a few years of greatly appreciated reprieve; from craniofacial surgery, at least.

I wish someone had told me, that all my insecurities were perfectly normal and "okay." My hope is that parents do not make the mistakes I did regarding our baby's care. A parent's intuition is such a phenomenon. When I look back on this long and incredible journey we have had, the only times I regret are the times I did not trust my instinct. You are your baby's best, and sadly, sometimes only, advocate.

When we got the news she would have a cleft, though I didn't remotely fathom the struggle we would have throughout her first year of life, I knew that regardless of the specific details, it would be tough. But, with the difficulty I anticipated and steeled myself for, I wish I had known how beautiful my little girl would be; how captivating her eyes and how intoxicating her smile! I wish I had known how greatly I would change as a human being, how having this special child would open up my eyes to a far greater world than I could have fathomed; the compassion, caring, and empathy for others it would come to instill in me.

When I was told I would miss her smile, I scoffed. But, I ache to see that wide grin again. It is certainly beautiful to watch her navigating through her new smile, but there is nothing like that first one you fall in love with. I wish I had known all this and so much more, but true knowing is "having-done." I know this because I have lived it.

I Wish I'd Known... how beautiful my little girl would be.

Corbin

Country: United States of America

Type of Cleft: Unilateral Cleft Lip

Birthdate: April 30, 2010

Cleft Team: Sanford Hospital; Dr. R. Hussein, MD

Found Out About Cleft: 20-Week Ultrasound

Surgery Date: June 22, 2010

Family History of Clefts: No

At our 20-week ultrasound, we were delighted to find out that we will be having another boy. Unfortunately, the ultrasound revealed some abnormalities. We found out that our son had a cleft lip and palate, which is sometimes a marker for chromosomal abnormalities; most notably Trisomy 13 or Trisomy 18. It could, however, have nothing to do with those disorders. We did opt to have amniocentesis done under the advice of the perinatologist.

We prayed fervently for the best case scenario, because if he did have Trisomy 13 or 18, the outcome would likely be fatal. My husband and I were understandably very upset, but tried to remain positive. It was a very scary time for us, full of the unknown. Yet, we had every faith in the world that we would pull through this. The range of emotions we went through felt like a roller coaster ride, but at the end of the day, we were extremely thankful for all of our blessings including our new baby. While we waited for the amniocentesis results, we hoped, we prayed, and we waited.

The results were in and our son did not have any chromosomal abnormalities. We felt so much relief, but the worrying didn't end there. The fact that my son would have a cleft consumed every part of me. What would he look like? Would he be treated harshly? Would I love him the same as a "normal" child? How would others treat him? Would his cleft negatively impair his health?

Our little man entered the world at the end of April 2010. It was a planned C-section not because of his condition, but because of my failure to progress with my first child. We had planned and prepared for so many possible scenarios and we were ready, or so we thought. The C-section went perfectly and when he came out, my first question was, "Is he okay?" My husband assured me that he was. The team, of course, had to check him out before we could see him. It is crazy to think of all the emotions that can cross your mind in such a short period of time. I was anxious to meet my little man, but sad because we thought he would be spending his first few days in the neonatal intensive care unit. To our surprise, they handed him to us and left. What? This was not the plan. He surprised us all when he came out with a palate that was intact. He surprised us yet again when he breastfed like a champ and hasn't stopped surprising us in his two and a half years!

He has only had one surgery to repair his unilateral cleft lip on the left side. We were very lucky to have a very skilled surgeon. Those days seem like a distant memory now. There were so many things I wish I would have known back then. I wish I would have known that love would pour out for our little man. I wish I would have known how perfect he was going to be; even before his repair and that people would love him regardless of how he would look. I wish I would have known how strong this would make me as a mother and as a person.

Before Corbin was born, I was afraid of other's reaction to him. After he was born, I felt sorry for people who judged him based on his lip, because there was so much more to him than that. I read somewhere that scars tell a story; that scars build character! I wish I would have known what a beautiful story my Corbin's first scar would tell.

I Wish I'd Known... that scars give character.

Dear Pregnant Mom,

It is okay to be terrified. We love our kids more than life itself, so we *should* be terrified when they are struggling with something. Ask for help from others and don't be afraid to share your feelings with others. Talk to other families who have had children with clefts. They can offer comfort because they truly understand what you and your child are going through.

Remember: We can't change many things about our situation, but we do have total and complete control over our own attitude and actions. Finally, remember that your child loves you and try to enjoy him or her. He or she will be all grown up in a blink of an eye!

Sending you hugs and peace.

Medical Concerns

"*The doctor leaned over me and said with kindness, "I believe your baby has a serious heart defect, I'm sorry.*"

Declan

Country: United States of America
Type of Cleft: Bilateral Cleft Lip and Palate
Birthdate: September 13, 2012
Cleft Team: Kids First Clinic
Found Out About Cleft: 24 Weeks Gestation
Surgery Dates: November 13, 2012 (Lip repair), November 23, 2012 (G-tube placement)
Cleft Device: Paper clip and Rubber band, and DynaCleft tape.
Family History of Clefts: Yes

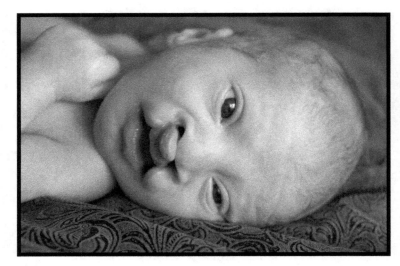

Declan Ray, my sweet boy! I found out at 24 weeks gestation that I was having a little boy and that is also when I found out about his bilateral cleft lip and palate. I was so sad, "Where had I gone wrong?" It took me a few days to realize that being sad wasn't going to change anything. My little boy needed his mommy to love him and be strong for him. So my research began. I already knew a little from my brother, who also had a cleft palate and Pierre Robin Sequence. Yet, I needed to know more. Over the few months before he made his arrival, I learned a little bit more of my baby boy's condition.

Then on a warm September afternoon, it started. I didn't think it was time yet, I still had two more weeks until my due date. After dinner I decided to go for a walk because the contractions weren't regular, but that short walk did the trick. I had a horrible contraction that stopped me in my tracks and I knew it was time to go. I was in labor and delivery for 45 minutes when they admitted me. I was dilated to four centimeters and was having contractions every three to four minutes. Not even four hours later, I met the most gorgeous little boy my eyes had ever seen. When I first saw him, I looked at his lip to see how severe it was and then I saw him. He was absolutely perfect; all five pounds, nine ounces, and 19 3/4 inches of him.

We attempted to breastfeed the first time, but I was worried, so we bottle-fed as well. He did very well. He had an echo done his second day of life. The echo showed two heart defects, neither were really a big deal at the time.

We went home on day three. On day five, we went in for his palate impression to get his obtruator. We ended up staying five days because he started to desat and had to be placed on oxygen. That is when we learned that my son, just like my brother, had Pierre Robin Sequence. We came home with an apnea monitor to make sure he was breathing alright. Everything seemed to be going great, except Declan wasn't really gaining weight. At three-weeks-old, he was five pounds, 11 ounces. So, we increased his calories to 24 kilocalories and it worked for a while.

On November 13th, the day he turned two months, he had his lip repair. Let me tell you, that was the longest two hours of my life. When we got to his room in the pediatric intensive care unit (PICU) and I saw him for the first time, I fell in love all over again. He looked incredible! He started eating right away and was released the next day.

A week later, we went in for a swallow study because he was breathing over 100 respirations a minute. We then received a pulse oximeter. He failed and it was horrible. He was admitted immediately. On the 23rd of November he had surgery to place a G-tube. It seemed to be working great. He was in and out of the hospital for the next little while.

We went in on December 14th because he threw up mucus and started to desat again. After two days of being there and the doctors saying, "We'll have to wait and see what happens," I decided to transfer him to Riley Children's Hospital in Indianapolis. We rode in the ambulance there and even got to go lights-and-sirens for the last bit because the ambulance was breaking down! Once we got there he was admitted to the PICU. The first doctor we saw was told he had a bilateral cleft lip and palate and without seeing him, asked me if he had Pierre robin Sequence. I knew at that point I made the right call to send him there.

On December 19th, Declan went under the knife again for a jaw distraction. When I saw him, I lost it. He was intubated and had metal coming out of his jaw. It was a hard thing to see, but he started to do well once they started turning the pins. I even had to turn them a few times.

Two days before we were supposed to go home, he started to throw up and then began struggling to breathe. A PICU doctor came to check him out and sent him down to the OR right away to be intubated again. Something still wasn't right. They ended up doing a scope of his airway and found that he also has laryngomalacia, which is just an extra flap on the voice box. So, they had to do another surgery, supraglottoplasty. He came back on only one liter of oxygen. It was amazing. He started to thrive and was finally gaining weight.

They have decided to let him grow out of the rest of his breathing problems. His pins will be removed soon. For now, we are home on half a liter of oxygen, a pulse oximeter, an apnea monitor, and an infinity feeding pump 29 millilitres per hour and 27 kilocalories. He is ten and a half pounds at five-months-old. It sounds tiny to most, but he is a big boy to me. I can't wait to see where else this journey takes us. He's the strongest person I know and nothing will ever hold my determined little man back.

I Wish I'd Known...
how rewarding, but
difficult this journey
would be.

Kalob

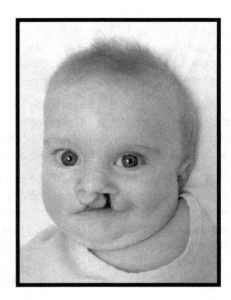

Country: United States of America
Type of Cleft: Complete Bilateral Cleft Lip and Palate
Birthdate: May 9, 2012
Cleft Team: Children's Memorial Hermann Hospital; Dr. Teichgraeber, MD
Duration of Hospital Stay: 29 Days After Birth
Found Out About Cleft: 32 Weeks Gestation
Cleft Device: NAM
Surgery Date: November 27, 2012
Family History of Clefts: Yes

Kalob was born May 9, 2012 at 8:20 p.m. I was not able to hold my son after birth until the next day. It was very hard listening to all the babies cry in the rooms next to me. The nurses took him to the NICU immediately because of other health issues he was born with. He has some very rare medical issues and has a medical record the size of a text book. The doctors were anticipating heart surgery not long after his birth. He made it until four months before he needed his vascular ring repaired. He is a tough boy.

There were many things we didn't find out until after he was born, which made things a little harder. He was much more fragile than we had expected. He stayed in the NICU for 29 days. Feeding and breathing issues were his main health concerns.

I was with him every day that he was in the NICU. I fought for what I felt was right for him and am glad I did. The doctors wanted to place a peg tube since he struggled with his feedings. I managed to convince them to allow us to take him home with an NG tube. It wasn't until he was six-months-old that we were able to wean him off the NG tube.

He has had three surgeries to date; one emergent abdominal surgery, heart surgery, and lip surgery. Kalob may need a little help with gross motor skills, but he sure is a fighter and is extremely determined. He is developmentally delayed, but is stronger-willed than any healthy child I know. He may have low muscle tone, but he has a beautiful heart that makes him stronger. There is nothing more beautiful than seeing him accomplish a milestone that he has been working so hard on.

Having a child with special needs makes you realize what is really important in life. My husband and I celebrate the little things in life because they are a big deal to us. I will do ANYTHING for my son. He is my life and the anchor that keeps me grounded. He has opened my eyes and showed me what pure love is all about.

I Wish I'd Known... how long the hospital stay was going to be.

Ivy

Country: New Zealand
Type of Cleft: Bilateral Cleft Lip and Palate
Birthdate: March 11, 2011
Cleft Team: Middlemore Hospital
Found Out About Cleft: 18 Weeks Gestation
Surgery Dates: November 14, 2011 (Lip repair), March 30, 2012 (Palate repair), November 24, 2012 (Gastrostomy to place Mic-Key button feeding tube)
Family History of Clefts: No

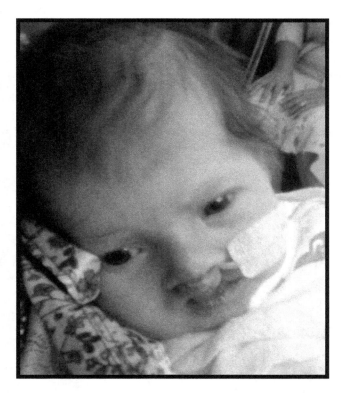

When I was 18 weeks pregnant, I went for my routine scan. This was when I was first handed the news that Ivy would be born with a cleft. At the time, all they knew was that she had a cleft, but not the extent of it.

Two weeks later, I went to Auckland Hospital and was told that Ivy had a bilateral cleft lip and palate. It was also at this same appointment that I was offered an abortion. This was not based on any other unknown health issues, but just because she would be born with a cleft. Let me tell you now, a cleft will send you on a journey that you may not feel prepared for, it may scare you, terrify you, bring you grief, or any wide range of emotions. I knew that I loved my unborn child with all my heart even though I knew there would be surgeries, feeding issues, hearing and speech problems, and possibly more. I also knew that for my baby, I would overcome any doubts and be strong for her.

The first time I saw my daughter, cleft and all, I thought that she was 100% perfect. I'd read the good and a little of the bad, so I knew there was the chance that things wouldn't go textbook. Which, for us they didn't. Ivy spent almost three weeks in the Special Care Baby Unit (SCBU). She was mainly fed by a Nasogastric (NG) feeding tube while we were there. After a talk with the charge nurse, Ivy was sent home with both her Haberman bottle and NG tube.

Ivy was fully fed by NG tube by the time she was five-months-old. Due to various issues with trying to tape down her cleft, her feeding, and weight gain, Ivy was seven-months-old by the time she had her first surgery. One thing I remember reading from other mums, but not really understanding until I was in that position, was the overwhelming feelings at the change with not only her face, but her smile. It was two days after her lip repair when the drugs were wearing off and her personality was shining through again, that I felt like she was my little girl again.

Ivy's second surgery was just after she turned one. Like her first, there were some problems after surgery, but she handled it well and was home after only three days in hospital. She still has a hole in her palate and we don't yet know when anything will be done to it.

Ivy is nearly two-years-old, and she now has a gastrostomy tube. Ivy has issues that aren't directly related to her cleft having to do with her tummy, bowels, feeding, swallowing, and weight. She also has some hearing and speech issues. At nearly two-years-old, she only has a vocabulary of seven words and is currently waiting for her ear canals to grow enough so that she can get grommets.

Finding out about the cleft that Ivy would be born with has sent us on one heck of a ride. One in which we are still on today. It hasn't been easy at times, but she has surprised us with how she takes everything in stride. She is nothing short of amazing.

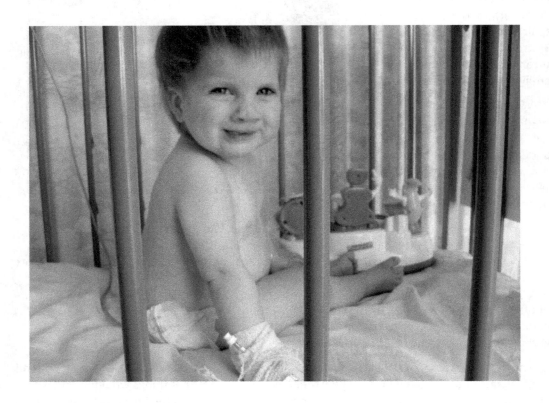

I Wish I'd Known... how ignorant people can be.

Aiden

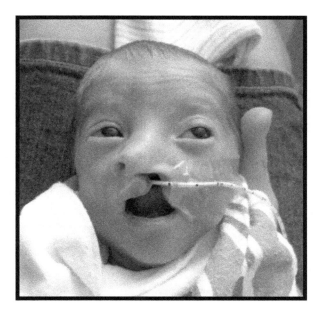

Country: United States of America
Type of Cleft: Complete Unilateral Cleft Lip and Palate
Birthdate: June 9, 2010
Cleft Team: Louisville Surgery Center Outpatient Facility; Dr. O'Daniel, MD
Found Out About Cleft: 28 Weeks Gestation
Surgery Dates: November 17, 2010 (Partial lip repair), May 3, 2011 (Complete lip repair), September 21, 2011 (Palate repair)
Family History of Clefts: No

Aiden was born 12 weeks premature, with a complete unilateral cleft lip and palate. We were blessed to find an amazing plastic surgeon, Dr. O'Daniel, who works miracles for beautiful babies like Aiden.

Aiden has had two surgeries to correct his cleft lip; in November 2010 and May 2011. Both were very eye-opening experiences. Even after his two-month NICU stay, countless tubes, wires, tests, and procedures, nothing quite prepares you to send your precious baby off to surgery. We did this for a third time in September 2011. He had his palate repaired and did wonderfully.

We pray the Lord continues to bless our little boy with strength and healing. We know he is in the best hands with Dr. O'Daniel leading the way. We still have a long road ahead of us, including speech therapy and more surgeries, but we know that Aiden will continue to do just fine. He is a true miracle and the toughest little boy I know. He was born with a beautiful wide smile and now has an even more beautiful smile that I am so lucky to see every day.

I Wish I'd Known...
it truly isn't the end of the world! It will all be OKAY!

Taylor

Country: United States of America
Type of Cleft: Complete Unilateral Cleft Lip and Palate
Birthdate: November 1, 2006
Cleft Team: Wake Forest University Medical Center
Found Out About Cleft: At Birth
Surgery Dates: March 2, 2007 (Lip repair), May 22, 2007 (Soft palate repair), September 18, 2007 (Hard palate repair), March 14, 2008 (Fistula repair & ear tubes), February 2, 2010 (Fistula repair), October 11, 2011 (Nostril revision & fistula repair)
Family History of Clefts: Yes

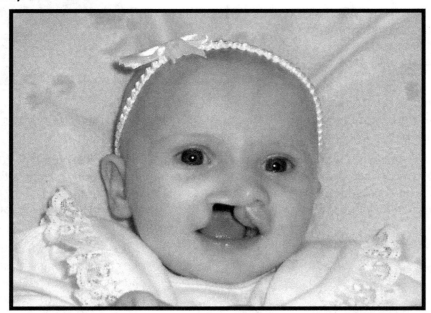

Our granddaughter, Taylor, is our son's child. He and his girlfriend became pregnant while they were engaged. Taylor's maternal grandmother lived far away, so her mom asked me to be with her in the delivery room. 20 minutes after midnight of Halloween, our little one was born. As soon as I saw her face, I recognized that she had a cleft lip. When her mom asked me if she was okay I replied, "She's the most beautiful baby in the world."

When Taylor was six-hours-old, they airlifted her to a children's hospital two hours away. The parents, my husband, and I followed in our car. We spent a week with Taylor in the NICU learning how to feed her, learning first aid, and CPR. It soon became evident that Taylor's parents were incapable of dealing with a child that was high maintenance and with such medical needs.

Taylor had her first surgery at four months of age. It was the most difficult thing to have to watch her go through. When Taylor was six-months-old she needed her second surgery and due to a series of circumstances, her parents signed voluntary custody of her over to us. We were pleased to take her.

Since that time, we have watched our baby go through a total of seven surgeries. In addition to them, she has been diagnosed with sensory processing disorder, post-traumatic stress disorder, separation disorder, and insecure attachment.

It has been a long road, but one filled with so many blessings along the way. Taylor is six-years-old now, excelling in kindergarten. She is a happy, verbal and beautiful girl, with many gifts and talents. She brings joy and happiness to our home each moment of the day. She will face many more surgeries. A lot of orthodontic work is in her future as well, but no matter what her future holds, we hope that we will always share that future with her.

I Wish I'd Known... she would have been born with the cleft.
Knowing would have eased the shock.

Riley

Country: United States of America
Type of Cleft: Left Unilateral Cleft Lip and Palate
Birthdate: October 27, 2010
Cleft Team: Shriners Hospital Cincinnati
Found Out About Cleft: At a Routine Ultrasound
Cleft Device: NAM
Surgery Dates: March 2011 (Lip repair), September 2011 (Palate repair)
Family History of Clefts: Yes

At a routine ultrasound we were told that it appeared our son had a cleft lip and they were unsure of any palate involvement. They could not see all of his heart and they also noticed a two-vessel cord. We were sent to a High Risk Obstetrician and one month later our fears were confirmed, only much worse. Our baby's grandmother was born with a cleft lip and palate and we prayed and hoped that maybe they were wrong.

Our High Risk OB confirmed the cleft as well as a serious heart defect known as Tetralogy of Fallot. Our son's cleft quickly took a backseat to his heart. We were unsure of any genetic issues and declined any tests offered. We were given appointments weekly with the obstetrician until a delivery date was set. Riley was born blue, quickly stabilized, and was then transferred to Riley Hospital for Children. Ironically, we had his name years before he was even born. Expecting surgery within a few days of birth for his heart, we were surprised that he was doing quite well and they had a new plan in place for heart surgery at eight-months-old.

With his heart stable, our efforts returned to his cleft and feeding. He could not breastfeed and the team at Riley tried for several days to find the "right" bottle, which turned out to be the pigeon bottle. We went home after one week with the instructions to put as much weight on him as possible. Born at 37 weeks at five pounds, 12 ounces, fighting a heart defect, and a cleft lip and palate, we had a challenge ahead of us.

Riley's mother pumped for 12 months to give Riley the best chance she could. His cardiologist said it made a difference. Once home, we were contacted by the Shriners who wanted to assist Riley with his cleft. A heart catheterization was scheduled for January as a diagnostic procedure only to confirm his heart was strong enough for lip closure surgery. With the go ahead from Cardiology, Riley had his lip closed in Cincinnati at the Shriners hospital in March.

It was a successful surgery and we were home only a few days later. Riley was five-months-old at this time and had not yet mastered breathing out of his mouth while sleeping. We took turns sleeping in a chair, holding his mouth open so he could sleep. He couldn't breathe out of his nose due to the swelling caused by surgery.

In June of 2011, we brought our son to Indianapolis for his heart surgery. His open-heart surgery lasted eight hours and he had complications that kept him in the hospital for 24 nights. Finally, bringing home a happy and healthy boy in July, we could concentrate our efforts on his cleft palate.

We were home only a week when we had to go back for an outpatient surgery to remove a problematic suture from his sternum. After two short months without any surgery, we travelled to Cincinnati for palate surgery. Again, with the go ahead from Cardiology, Dr. Billmire operated on Riley. It took about an hour and a half to close his palate and Riley stayed in the hospital for an additional five nights.

Riley is a happy two-year-old who had a busy first year. He still has several more surgeries ahead, including another open-heart surgery, but everything is looking great for our son. We thank God and the many wonderful doctors who have brought him to where he is today.

I Wish I'd Known... that everything would be okay.

Olivia

Country: Australia
Type of Cleft: Unilateral Cleft Lip and Palate
Birthdate: November 18, 2011
Cleft Team: John Hunter Hospital
Found Out About Cleft: 19-Week Ultrasound
Surgery Dates: June 12, 2012 (Lip, nose and soft palate repair and ear tubes), May 14, 2013
Family History of Clefts: No

Olivia Jaide was born November 18, 2011 via C-section and weighing five pounds, 13 ounces. She was born with a unilateral cleft lip and palate, which was discovered on our 19-week scan. From the minute I saw Olivia, I thought she was a perfect little angel.

Olivia was tube fed for three days and then went onto a pigeon bottle. She struggled with gaining weight. We had appointments every two weeks to check her weight and get tips on how to help her gain more.

Olivia had her first surgery in June 2012, which included repair of the lip, nose, soft palate, and ear tubes put in. Handing her over to the surgeon was one of the hardest things

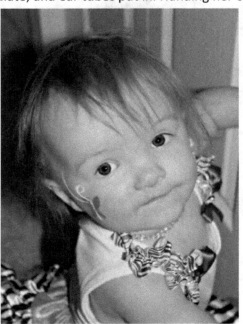

I have had to do. Nearly four hours later, we saw our beautiful girl with a new little face. I couldn't stop staring at her. It was like she was just born again; she looked so different. The next morning, my heart melted when she showed me her new smile. She struggled a bit after her surgery. She wouldn't take any liquids and was in a fair bit of pain. It took about nine days till she was her normal self again.

Since then, Olivia has grown and developed her own personality. She is our gorgeous, cheeky, brave little girl.

I Wish I'd Known...
about weight issues and I wish I had researched a little better.

Caleb

Country: Canada
Type of Cleft: Left Incomplete Unilateral Cleft Lip and Palate
Birthdate: October 31, 2012
Cleft Team: Children's Hospital of Eastern Ontario (CHEO)
Found Out About Cleft: At a Routine Ultrasound
Surgery Date: April 2013
Family History of Clefts: No

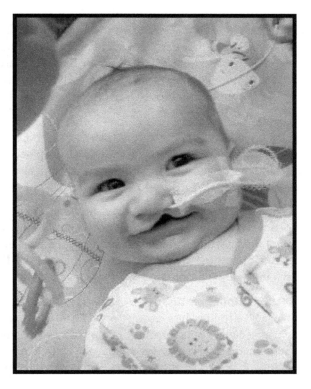

Nine and a half years after my first son, Justin, I had a baby daughter, Caitlin. We were overjoyed and told I was very lucky to have even conceived my daughter and would probably not be able to ever conceive again. We accepted that fact, but were very surprised to learn when my daughter was only two-months-old that I was pregnant again! After all the effort to conceive our daughter, we spontaneously got pregnant with Caleb.

I was very happy and didn't mind the fact that my babies would only be 11 months apart. Caitlin was healthy and I fully expected the little one on the way to be as well. Every time we went for an ultrasound, it was always the same story; the baby was moving around well, growing well, heartbeat was good, and everything appeared perfectly normal.

In August, a couple months before I was due, I had an ultrasound booked. My husband couldn't get off of work, so I went by myself for the first time. I expected the usual, to hear the technician say that all was well, and I would be on my way. The next thing I knew, the tech told me, "I need the doctor to look at the ultrasound right away." All of a sudden, there were five people in the room instead of one, finely going over the ultrasound and saying all kinds of medical terms I couldn't understand. My heart was racing and I knew something was very wrong. I was so distraught that this had to happen when my husband couldn't be there. I felt helpless, lying there on the exam room table. The doctor leaned over me and said with kindness, "I believe your baby has a serious heart defect, I'm sorry." I felt the world around me begin to crumble.

In a very short amount of time, baby Caleb was diagnosed with Tetralogy of Fallot and would need open-heart surgery just days after birth. Two ultrasounds later, we were told he most likely had a cleft lip and cleft palate as well. We were not expecting more bad news and I began to feel hopeless and in despair. The next ultrasound showed our baby was missing his right kidney. At this point, I didn't want to hear that anything else that was wrong. It was heart-wrenching. We were told that he may have a syndrome of some type and to fully expect it at birth. We were confused as to how all this was happening. There was no cleft lip, cleft palate, or syndromes of any type on either side of our families. We were saddened, but knew we would love our child, regardless.

By late in the evening on October 29th, 2012, I had been induced and things were not going well. Caleb's heart would start to slow and then barely beat. He was fading. The doctor stopped the induction and his heart beat corrected itself. The baby and I were given 24 hours to rest. Then, on October 31st at 3:25 p.m., baby Caleb Zachary was born via C-section. After Caleb was born, I saw him right away. He did have a cleft, but my heart swelled with pride and love at the sight of him. He was whisked away for a quick cleaning and assessment, and then taken over to the NICU at a different hospital.

He stayed in the NICU for the first 39 days of his life and came home for the first time just in time for Christmas. His first heart surgery took place when he was only six-days-old. He received tube feedings due to the cleft lip and palate and also due to the fact his little heart just didn't have the energy to bottle feed for a long period of time.

The genetic tests came back and we finally received some good news. Caleb had no syndrome of any type and all chromosomes were present. He will function normal mentally and after all the heart, lip, and palate surgeries, he will live a fairly normal life. After the April 2013 surgery, Caleb's first repair of his lip will happen late May or in early June 2013; then, the palate to follow a couple months later. I do believe we will miss that little cleft smile.

Now, at four months, Caleb is a happy, good-natured little baby and always has a smile for us. I just love to hold him close to my heart. He is so precious in every way. We all love him so much, especially his big brother, Justin, and baby sister, Caitlin. I wish I'd known how much a unique, devoted, and ever-loving journey I would embark with him. He gives me strength and has shown me how strong I can really be. He has brought us incredible joy. He truly is a gift.

I Wish I'd Known... how much strength he would give to me.

Abigail

Country: United States of America
Type of Cleft: Complete U Shaped Cleft Palate
Birthdate: June 22, 2011
Cleft Surgeon: Dr. Robert Glade, MD
Found Out About Cleft: At Birth
Surgery Dates: September 16, 2011 (Supraglottoplasty and ear tubes placed), June 25, 2012 (Cleft palate repair and ear tubes replaced)
Family History of Clefts: No

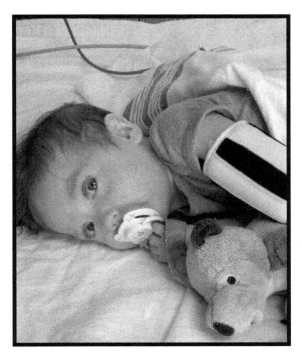

Abigail was born on June 22, 2011 at 33 weeks and four days gestation. I had fallen on father's day and went to the hospital to make sure everything was okay. Abi was fine and we were sent home. By the next morning, I was back at the hospital; I was dilated and ready to have my baby girl. They tried to slow it down as long as possible. 46 hours of labor later, I welcomed my angel face at 3:34 a.m. She was six pounds, six ounces, and 18 1/2 inches long. She had a full head of hair and was incredibly precious. Honestly, the first few times I saw her I didn't notice that her jaw was not developed. She just looked beautiful.

They took her away about 15 minutes after she was born. Once her apgar scores came up from their initial low numbers, they let me hold her for a second. I kissed her face and told her how much I loved her. It ripped my heart out when they took her to the NICU. They told my husband, he could go see her after an hour and a half. By this time, my daddy showed up. My husband and my father went to see her as soon as they were allowed. They came back downstairs after 30 minutes with pictures to show me. My husband looked at me and said something that stopped my heart for a moment. He told me that they were evaluating her when they got there. He told me that they do a routine check for a cleft palate on all babies and as the nurse was explaining what she was doing, she looked at him and said, "Yes, she has one."

I think my heart literally stopped. I couldn't breathe. I was so scared. We didn't know anything about cleft palates. I had heard of it in passing. That was all. We had no answers. The doctors decided that they would not try to feed Abi for the first 24 hours, so they could do some testing and make sure she would be able to take my milk.

Finally on day two in the NICU, they put in a feeding tube and gave my angel two milliliters of my milk. She was only able to digest about half of that. Abi developed jaundice and was treated with bili light therapy. She was hooked up to oxygen on a continuous positive airway pressure machine (CPAP) to help a little. She had IVs in her because she was not able to take much of my milk at all.

They only let us try the bottle once a day in the first two days. She was to be in the NICU until she could drink 45 millilitres at a time out of a bottle in a 24 hour period. But, they weren't letting us give her the bottle very much. Therefore, I pushed it and they brought it to twice a day. That was still not enough. I pushed even more and the doctor finally said that if we were there, we could give her the bottle every feeding. After two days of this, Abi was ready to go home.

Abi was a tiny, six pound, little baby doll. She was tested for everything under the sun, including diabetes. Everything came back negative. Abi was gaining approximately one to two ounces a week. When we came home, we had doctor appointments with her pediatrician weekly to monitor her weight. Plus, she had appointments every two to three weeks with her ORL doctor.

At five weeks, they did a sleep study on Abi because I kept noticing that she would stop breathing if on her back. The results were back in a few days. Abi had severe obstructive sleep apnea. The doctor ordered oxygen at night when she was asleep and a pulse oximetry monitor when she was lying down. Needless to say, he wanted to do surgery as soon as possible.

We had three options. Option one was to do a tracheostomy. Second, they could sew her tongue to her bottom lip for a few months or they could break her jaw and pull it forward. I prayed and prayed, "Dear Lord, no!" All of these options scared me to death. I couldn't do this to her. Dr. Glade took us to meet with his partner because we had decided on the tongue and lip adhesion. Dr. Dugoy took one look at Abi and suggested a supraglottoplasty. He explained that they would go in and shave off a micromillimeter of her airway. This sounded a lot better. Her surgery went well and she was home after three days.

On October 3rd 2011, Abigail went with daddy and me to the airport. She sat with her daddy for two and a half hours. Then Daddy kissed her face, kissed me, handed Abigail to me, and turned to walk away onto the plane waiting to take him to Korea for the next year. I was terrified. I was hurting. I was sad. I had a baby that needed so much.

As time went on, Abi gained weight but had constant ear infections. In early December, my angel weighed in at 13 pounds and five ounces. Over the holidays that year, Abi and I took time to get over our bronchitis, pneumonia (Abi), upper Respiratory infection (Abi), and double ear infections (Abi). At a routine appointment in February, I had noticed that she was the same size as at Christmas. At eight months, she was still in newborn clothes and her chest looked caved in. You could feel every rib and bone in her body. She weighed in that day at 13 pounds and five ounces.

We discussed what to do. They decided to do a check of her airway and place a feeding tube. So, on the only snowy evening in Oklahoma in 2012, we drove out for her examination. The next morning, we went to Children's Hospital where, instead of doing the test, they admitted Abi due to a 102 fever. They ran test after test to see why she wasn't gaining weight and to rule out cystic fibrosis. I missed my husband every day. It was a lot to do alone.

While in the hospital, she started to eat eight ounces of food instead of four. After a week, they hadn't placed a feeding tube because she was finally eating on her own. Once we came home, Abi started gaining weight. At ten-months-old she weighed 16 pounds and six and a half ounces. She still has sleep apnea but it's moderate now, instead of 'severe obstructive.'

On Abigail's first birthday, her daddy flew home from Korea to surprise her! Three days later, on her daddy's birthday, she underwent palate repair. Surgery was five hours total and she did great. Daddy was able to be home for a month and Abi was always in her daddy's arms. She finally started growing and at one-year-old, she was wearing six-month clothes. She was my happy girl again.

Daddy left again in July and Abi continued to learn to eat and changed day by day. Daddy came home for good in October of 2012 and Abi saved her walking for daddy.

At 19 months, Abi currently weighs 22 pounds and is 32 inches long. She is going to be tested for stickler syndrome. We still have feeding issues and are working on those. She is a very picky eater and possibly has a food aversion.

God has been my strength through this whole thing. He has held my hand and carried us through these hard times. I am proud of Abigail. She shows me every day how strong she is. She doesn't let anything keep her down.

I Wish I'd Known... about her cleft before birth so we could have been prepared.

Dear Pregnant Mom,

Finding out about the cleft has sent us on one heck of a ride; one in which we are still on today. Nothing has gone as we expected. We have encountered a whole new world that we were near oblivious to. That is, until we joined the ranks of other parents like us; parents who learn so much that you feel like a nurse yourself at times.

Life may not be easy at times. Perfection brings on a whole new meaning. You get to celebrate and enjoy things that everyone else takes for granted. There will be tears, but lots of smiles too. Remember, mum and dad really do know best. If your gut is telling you something is up, go with it, stomp your feet on the ground, and throw a tantrum to rival any three-year-old if need be. You are their voice, so make them heard. As for your gorgeous boy or girl, they're going to surprise you with how well they just take it all in stride. These kids of ours are nothing short of amazing!

From one proud mum to another.

Breastfed Babes

"*The six-week delay in the diagnosis of my son's cleft palate was actually the blessing in disguise that enabled him to nurse.*"

James

Country: United States of America
Type of Cleft: Cleft of the Soft Palate
Birthdate: May 2, 2012
Cleft Team: Boston Children's Hospital; Dr. Meara, MD
Found Out About Cleft: 6 Weeks After Birth
Surgery Date: March 6, 2013
Family History of Clefts: No

My son James' cleft palate was not diagnosed until he was six-weeks-old, which made for a confusing first month and a half for my husband and me. We knew something was not quite right almost immediately. We enjoyed the benefits of breastfeeding with our first child. Nursing, for me, became an integral part to my experience as a mother, cultivating a sense of intimacy. There was no question of trying to offer the same benefits to James. However, James was not able to stay latched on to my breast for long. He would slide off as if it was too slippery and he made a distinctive clicking sound as he swallowed. Nurses and lactation consultants streamed in and out of our hospital room at our requests; adjusting the baby's head, my hands, and pillows that propped up the two of us. They inserted gloved pinkies and scrutinized his flared lower lip as we repeatedly fit him over my nipple together. They acquiesced to my request for a nipple shield to get us going, tried refitting nipple shields of other sizes, all the while offering optimism. "It's just an immature suck. He'll outgrow it." "Boys can be a little lazier." "He's still just 24 hours old, give him some time to learn."

The attending pediatrician listened to our concerns about the clicking, chalked it up to a nursing issue, and discharged us. Breastfeeding James in my bedroom proved even more difficult in the ensuing days. My husband would catch my eye and we would both softly chuckle about what seemed to be James' enthusiastic medley of slurping and clicking, and we would joke about how loud our son was in the dead of night. We were so delighted to be reacquainted with the noises of a newborn, and yet so much of this felt unfamiliar. Milk would stream out of James' downhill lip corner. I'd adjust more pillows and change both of our milk-soaked clothing. Frustration surged through me. James would fall asleep, visibly exhausted by all of his sucking. The searing electric shock whipped through my body at each latch on as my nipples became more abraded. I'd press Soothies on between feedings and reassure myself that every nursing mother of a newborn has sore nipples, and that our situation was normal. Milk would drip out of James' nose. I knew that had never happened with his sister.

The first few weeks at home, I had the sensation that I was never quite making enough milk. I convinced myself it was a supply issue on my part and began a regimen of fenugreek tea and pills, oatmeal, beets, and intense hydration consisting mostly of juice cocktails with ginger ale. At a friend's suggestion, I would pump even without extracting milk to help generate production; creating the demand artificially that James' weak suck could not do naturally. I quit the nipple shield, fearing it was holding my body back from naturally creating a larger quantity of milk. I immediately came down with mastitis, as painful dried milk became infected in the ducts. The best cure was constant nursing and pumping, but I couldn't count on my baby's suction to keep my milk ducts freely flowing and I didn't know why.

The first visit to the South Shore Hospital's Lactation Consultants reassured me that I was not imagining our nursing difficulties that first week. At the time of the visit, I was fairly positive the problem was with James' latch and after all the adjusting that first week, and agony for my nipples, I doubted I had the stamina to see us through a rigorous re-training of how to latch. The idea of switching to formula and bottles seemed, for the first time, appealing and preferable. I bumbled into the nursing room, bleary from lack of sleep from consecutive nights of sitting up, breastfeeding nearly constantly, and frustration. Linda, a wonderful lactation consultant with a long white lab coat and kind eyes, listened to my complaints that James could not create a vacuum. She tried the same adjustment routine we saw in the hospital and saw no discernible reason for James' clicking, and adamantly said that with a normal nursing baby, there should be no clicking. There had to be "something" there. She told me how to get a prescription for the fabulous pharmaceutical compound APNO to help my nipples heal. Then she peered down James' throat with a flashlight and concluded that yes, there was "something" there. She informed our pediatrician, whom we were due to see for the scheduled five day checkup the next day anyway.

Our much-loved pediatrician seemed doubtful that there was "something" since James was gaining weight so well. "I could not ask for a better weight gain for a breastfed baby in the first week," was her summation. When James gave a wide-mouthed wail while lying down, she had a straight-shot view down his throat, looked up startled, and said that yes, there was "something." We were then referred to an Otolaryngologist, who gave us an appointment over a month away. At a subsequent weight check a few weeks later with our pediatrician, I first heard the word "cleft" to describe the "something" in James' mouth. "Cleft palate" felt too strong of a phrase for what James had. I felt stunned and hopeful that the Otolaryngologist would diagnose weak muscles as the reason for the weak suck.

We had the chance to try out the phrase again when James was five-weeks-old and hospitalized through the ER with a dangerously high fever, which turned out to be part of a virus. Three days in the hospital gave us ample opportunities for nursing, pumping, and explaining about the clicking. The feeding team came to have a look. The physician and medical interns making the rounds heard me float our pediatrician's theory that James had a cleft palate. She turned to me, her expression not scornful exactly, but a mix of incredulity and amusement. "Your pediatrician thinks he has a WHAT?" Given his size (always in the 80+ percentile) and ability to nurse with a nipple shield, it seemed an absurd diagnosis. Embarrassed, I trailed off in that conversation and stopped mentioning the situation, even when milk drenched our clothing and dribbled out of his nose. The feeding team recommended trying one feeding a day without the nipple shield, to strengthen his suck muscles. When I later remarked on that conversation with our pediatrician, half expecting that I was letting her know gently of her own error in using the word "cleft," she brightly responded with a charitable explanation; "They didn't see it? Well, it is awfully far back."

Soon we were in the chair at the Otolaryngology office, and our "little mayor", as the doctor called our inquisitive and regal-looking son, was officially diagnosed with a cleft palate of the soft palate. I felt an immense sense of relief. Not only did Dr. Nuss reassure me that it is a fluke of nature and never the mother's fault, but his diagnosis validated my six weeks of confusion. I was not imagining problems. I had not done anything wrong. It explained everything and I felt justified in spending so much time nursing. James and I really were in the rare position of successfully nursing a baby with a cleft palate. I see it everywhere on the Internet: "Cleft palate babies cannot nurse." The six-week delay in the diagnosis of my son's cleft palate was actually the blessing in disguise that enabled him to nurse. If we had been told in the hospital that he was physically unable to breastfeed, I would have listened, understood, and used formula with a Haberman nipple.

Free reign at the breast, on demand, through sleepy nights in our bed, my healthy roly-poly buddy had gained a remarkable amount of weight. He was healthy and thriving. After the first few months, his muscles compensated in just the right ways to nurse normally. I hold no illusion; it was not due to his hard work, although he worked incredibly hard. It was not due to my diligence. It was due to the fact that he was lucky that there was just enough palate adhered together to facilitate a swallow. Most cleft palate babies physiologically cannot generate any suction. James had some, but the suck-swallow sequence also got remarkably easier over time.

My advice to any mother of a baby with a cleft palate who is interested in nursing is to try what you can. If it doesn't work at first, try it for the relationship, know that it will get

easier over time, and maybe even develop into true breastfeeding as the baby grows. I am now grateful that I did not know that James had a cleft palate when he was born. The delayed diagnosis gave me the freedom to try and to succeed at cultivating our nursing relationship. Had the pediatrician in the hospital noticed James' cleft, I would likely have been deterred from breastfeeding. The birth hospital doctor's failure to notice the cleft palate was absolutely my blessing in disguise.

As I write now, James will have surgery a week from today to repair his cleft palate. I am nervous, especially about restrictions in nursing post-surgery, as it is his main form of comfort and way to relax to fall asleep.

I Wish I'd Known...
that a missed diagnosis can be a blessing in disguise.

Eleanor

Country: United States of America
Type of Cleft: Unilateral Complete Lip and Gum Notch
Birthdate: October 17, 2012
Cleft Team: Children's Hospital Colorado
Found Out About Cleft: At Birth
Surgery Date: January 15, 2013
Family History of Clefts: No

On October 17th 2012, Eleanor was born. She was immediately placed on my chest, which was a bittersweet moment because that is when I saw she had a cleft lip. How could so much happiness be combined with shock and concern? I immediately started looking for other possible issues as the midwives worked with me to deliver the placenta. Eleanor was cleaned on my chest as the midwives continued to examine me and Eleanor. She remained on my chest for the next two hours as the midwives said that both of us needed to be transferred to the hospital. I required a repair, there was some concern about her breathing and it was standard procedure with a baby with a cleft lip.

We had to be transferred in separate ambulances due to space constraints and procedures. I went to have my repair and Eleanor was examined in the NICU. My husband followed us there, met with the doctors and stayed with Eleanor.

Just four hours after birth, I was reunited with my daughter. I was able to attempt to nurse her, which is difficult for babies with a cleft. I could not stay in her room because I needed to be examined as well. My husband and I visited her every three or so hours to nurse. The next day, both of us were discharged as healthy and were home just 24 hours after leaving the birthing center.

Eleanor has successfully breastfed since day five. We are so proud of her. We decided to have her lip repaired at three months through Children's Hospital of Colorado. We had a great team and they did a great job. It is amazing how different she looks. Recovery was difficult for all of us, but we are happy to have it behind us.

I Wish I'd Known... about the cleft before birth.

Peyton

Country: United States of America
Type of Cleft: Incomplete Unilateral Cleft Lip and Alveolar Ridge
Birthdate: October 30, 2011
Cleft Team: NYU Craniofacial Center; Dr. Court Cutting, MD and Dr. Barry Greyson, MD
Found Out About Cleft: 20-Week Ultrasound
Cleft Device: Pre and Post-Surgical Nasal Stents and Lip Taping
Surgery Date: February 13, 2012 (Lip and alveolar ridge repair)
Family History of Clefts: No

After a long road of fertility challenges, we were ecstatic when we found out we were pregnant with our little miracle baby. The first four to five months was a pretty normal pregnancy and we were starting to make plans for the arrival of our little one. We went to our 20-week ultrasound ready to see our munchkin on the big screen and count fingers and toes. I honestly didn't even know the extent of screening that was involved in a 20-week ultrasound or that cleft lip could be detected by ultrasound.

The nurse was quiet during the scan and took lots of pictures. At the end, she gave us pictures of the hands and feet before leaving the room. She came back in with the doctor, who started asking questions about our quad screen and family history. When she found that everything was negative, she then told us that the ultrasound indicated that the baby had what they believed was an isolated cleft lip. My stomach dropped. I immediately started crying and asked what I had done wrong. I was terrified of what it all meant and couldn't calm down. They soon called in our OB, who gave me a big hug, told me that there was nothing I had done wrong, and encouraged us to have additional testing.

We did choose to have a higher resolution ultrasound that afternoon and even decided to do an amniocentesis to test for chromosomal abnormalities which, in some cases, can cause cleft lip and palate. We even decided to find out the sex of the baby that day. We wanted to know as much as possible about our little munchkin so that we could prepare for his arrival. Yes, we were having a boy!

Although he wouldn't give us any guarantees, the doctor who performed the ultrasound indicated that Peyton would be born with an incomplete unilateral cleft lip and cleft of the alveolar ridge with an intact palate. He was spot on.

The next few weeks were challenging, to say the least. We first told our parents and siblings. They were extremely supportive, and reassured us that our baby would be okay. I admit, I was afraid how people would react to hearing the news and meeting him. In retrospect, I spent too much energy worrying about people's reactions and comments.

Peyton was fortunate to be born into a family with so much love and affection. His cleft was never an issue. When family was around, we barely got the chance to hold him at all!

Before Peyton was born, we spent a lot of time researching doctors and craniofacial centers. We live in the NY metro area, so we focused on NYC hospitals. We chose to go to the NYU Craniofacial center as they have a wealth of experience with cleft lip and palate. We chose Dr. Court Cutting, who dedicated his career to perfecting cleft lip and palate surgeries. We have become quite close with a few of the staff members at the center. They truly became a part of our family and we are grateful for their dedication to the patients at the center.

When Peyton was born, we were ecstatic to see a healthy (screaming) baby, ready to be loved. Because his palate was intact, he was able to breastfeed. Yet, we did hit several bumps in the road with breastfeeding and had some challenges with latching in the beginning. I spent a lot of time pumping to get my milk to come in and we didn't get the hang of breastfeeding until he was about four-weeks-old. It was worth the wait, though. We had a wonderful breastfeeding relationship that continued until he was 15-months-old.

When Peyton was a few weeks old, we had his first visit to Dr. Court Cutting and Dr. Greyson, the surgeon and pediatric orthodontist at NYU. We began lip taping at that time. When he was about six-weeks-old, we began using a nasal stent for pre-surgical molding. We had the option to use a NAM, but chose to use the less invasive nasal stents. Had Peyton been born with a cleft palate, the NAM would have been required to help close the gap prior to surgery. The nasal stents did substantially improve Peyton's nostril prior to surgery and gave Dr. Cutting a great starting point for surgery. The stents and lip taping were quite a bit of work and caused some irritation to our little guy's cheeks. We did give him some time off from taping for special occasions and to allow his cheeks to heal.

Peyton started daycare at 11-weeks-old. We were fortunate to find a daycare that was very willing to go the extra mile for him. We taught one of his teachers how to fix his nasal stents when he pulled them out. We even left extra tape with her for emergencies. They became quite familiar with the process, as Peyton wore nasal stents for three months after surgery to prevent collapse of the nostril due to scar tissue formation.

Peyton's cleft lip repair was scheduled for about four months after his birth. I was with him when they put him under. I couldn't hold back the tears. The surgery took several hours. We were so relieved when Dr. Cutting came out to say that his surgery was a success and he was in recovery. We couldn't wait to see him and his new smile. He took quite a while to come out of the anesthesia and his oxygen levels were low. Because of this, he was put in a step-down unit to be monitored overnight. I slept in a chair next to him and my husband slept in the lounge down the hall. He didn't want to nurse or take fluids during that first night. He certainly disliked the squeeze bottle we were told to use to feed him. The next day we were discharged.

As soon as we got him home, Peyton was ready to nurse. I was so relieved that he had his appetite back and that he could still nurse. He also tried to smile that first day home, even though we could see that it hurt to do so. The first few days home proved challenging with regular peroxide cleaning of the incision site and constant wearing of arm restraints. We also swaddled him at night to prevent him from wriggling out of the arm restraints. I stayed home with him for two weeks and exclusively nursed him. He quickly bounced back to his old playful self and wanted to get back to the business of being a baby. A week after surgery, the stitches were removed and we were amazed at how well the surgery had gone.

We will always miss his first wide smile, but we love the new one too!

Peyton may need additional surgeries as he grows up. His alveolar ridge was repaired in the initial surgery, but we won't know if it was successful until he is eight or nine-years-old. If the bone did not fuse, he will need a bone graft at that time. He may also need a lip and nose revision as a teenager. He did have significant scar shortening a few months after surgery and a noticeable hypertrophic scar, which has improved considerably over the past year. We have been told that it will continue to improve over time and he can be evaluated at the age of four to five to see if any revisions are required.

Peyton is 16-months-old now and is doing great! He is walking everywhere and talks up a storm. We rarely think about his cleft now and any challenges we face are the "normal" kid challenges of constipation or temper tantrums. His teeth are slow to come in and it is already clear that he will need orthodontics (but so did I).

We feel so blessed to have Peyton in our lives. He is an imaginative, happy, and slightly stubborn kid who likes to climb and get into trouble. We can't wait to see what the future holds for him. Being born with a cleft has given him an added challenge in life, but we know he will learn to take it in stride and make the most out of every opportunity he has in life.

I Wish I'd Known... that once Peyton was born, the joy would outweigh the fear and anxiety we felt after finding out about his cleft.

Dear Pregnant Mom,

Take everything one day at a time. There are going to be good and bad days, just like anything else. Things will slow down and feel normal again before you know. I know it may be hard and frustrating in the beginning when you find out, but you will be rewarded by this beautiful baby that is unique in their own way. Everything gets better and all that is left is happiness.

Don't forget to live life while moving through the cleft journey. First and foremost, your child is a child and you are a family. Make sure you remember that! It's difficult, but don't sweat the little stuff. Don't get frustrated. Try to do the same things parents of non-clefted children do. Sleep when they sleep, feed them when they're hungry and smile when they smile.

Worry less, love more.

Soft Palate Princesses

"What did this mean? The short version – it meant a very different first year than we had ever anticipated."

Maggie

Country: United States of America
Type of Cleft: Cleft of the Soft Palate
Birthdate: January 31, 2012
Cleft Surgeon: Dr. Ruben Bueno Jr., MD
Found Out About Cleft: After Birth
Surgery Date: February 1, 2013
Family History of Clefts: No

We were blessed to have our third child, Maggie, on January 31st 2012. She was born mid-morning and when she was, our OB-GYN said to check her palate. The nurse came back and said it is there, just high. Everything was going fine until about an hour later. I had a post-partum hemorrhage. My husband had gone home, just a few blocks away, to be with our other children and help with lunch and nap time. I sent him a text to come back to the hospital right away. The nurses and doctors were excellent. By the time my husband got back I was already in the OR having a D&C performed. He came back to an empty room.

Then our pediatrician came in; he had just checked on Maggie. He informed my husband that she had a soft cleft palate. This was quite a shock to us. We had no prior knowledge of this. When I came back into the room I was pretty out of it for the rest of the day. I had to receive four units of blood, two units of plasma, and two units of platelets.

When we got home from the hospital, my husband and other two children were staying at my parent's house because they were all sick. We could not chance Maggie getting sick. It was about four days before we were all together again.

We had an appointment to see the plastic surgeon, Dr. Bueno, and our feeding specialist, Laura Walbert. In a week, Maggie had lost around one pound due to her not being able to eat very well. Once we met with Laura, she explained to us how to feed Maggie better and gave us a Mead Johnson bottle to use. She had us hold Maggie upright and on her hip, so that the formula went in her cheek instead of straight back in the mouth. She told us that anything over 30 minutes of eating is just wasted calories because eating is such an aerobic exercise for babies.

We finally felt like we were getting a handle on things, but by June she still was struggling with the amount she was drinking. Therefore, Laura recommended that we try a new bottle. We went to her office and tried the pigeon nipple. Maggie took one suck on it and that was it. She did not care for it at all. Next, we tried the Haberman feeder and it worked like a charm.

We finally set a date for surgery for February 1st 2013. Once we had the date set, everything became real to us. It was a year of planning, talking, and preparing for surgery. By Christmastime, she was completely off the bottle and doing great with a cup. Then, we had to prepare ourselves for the surgery part of it.

We celebrated Maggie's birthday with family and friends the weekend before her first birthday. Maggie's surgery turned out to be the day after she turned one. After we celebrated her birthday, we prepared to go to the hospital. She was also having ear tubes put in at the same time as her cleft repair. She had six ear infections since June and always had fluid in her ear. For me this was not a big deal, a minor surgery to go with her major surgery.

We arrived at the hospital at 5:45 in the morning and waited in the surgery prep area. Our church pastor had come to pray with us for the doctors, nurses, and for Maggie. It was a great comfort to have that done. The nurses were great. They gave Maggie a blanket, teddy bear, and surgical hat. They were also blowing bubbles at her, which she loved. It was a little bit of wait in the prep area. When they were ready for her, I carried her as they rolled the bed to the surgical ward. We said our "goodbyes" and "I love you's," and they took her into the surgical ward.

The first half hour went by fast. Dr. Woodson came out and told us that the ear tubes were in and she had lots of thick fluid in her ear but the tubes should help that. Finally, the volunteer told us that Dr. Bueno would like to talk to us. We went into a family conference room and waited for him to come. After what felt like forever, he came into the room and told us that everything went very well. Hallelujah! It went just as they expected.

They called us back in recovery and we were so excited to see our little girl again. They had us put on gowns and hats, and then took us to see her. She was crying when we got in the room, but stopped once I held her. There was a lot of blood drainage coming from her mouth. She had to stay in recovery for an hour. But, we were there longer, waiting for a room to be ready. I was able to sit down with her and rock her. That first day was filled with lots of cuddles and rocking. She slept most of the day, just waking up to peek around and whimper a little bit.

Maggie and I were just relaxing throughout the night. She was receiving Motrin every six hours around the clock. At seven or eight o'clock at night, her IV became kinked at the site of where it was put in. They had to remove it. I knew from seeing four pricks in her hand and a couple in her feet after surgery that it was going to be difficult to get it back in. I had no idea how difficult. It happened right before a shift change, so we saw a couple different nurses during this time. One came in and put some numbing cream on her wrists, elbows, and feet where they were going to stick her. Then about an hour later two nurses came in, one to help hold her still and one to put in the IV. She tried several times and then gave Maggie a break while they called in another nurse.

An hour later, a third nurse as well as the previous two came in and tried, to no avail. Then, they called one more nurse. I felt so bad for Maggie because I knew it was painful, but I also knew she needed an IV. The nurses felt absolutely horrible about not being able to get it in. They brought Maggie all sorts of new toys for being so brave. No one was successful in getting in the IV, so they called the resident and explained the situation to them. They decided that as long as Maggie drank some fluids, that she didn't have to have the IV in. This was probably about one o'clock in the morning. So, we started her on some apple juice at night. In the morning, she woke up with a low-grade fever. Not one high enough to be overly concerned about, but enough to keep a close eye on her. She was not drinking very much at this point. She was pretty groggy in the morning. She did not want any of the nurses to come near her; understandably, considering what she went through the night before.

In the mid-morning, she played for a little bit and had a nap. All the while, she was taking a few sips here and there of maybe half an ounce or so. We were monitoring her fluid intake and diapers closely. They wanted to get a stool sample to make sure she didn't swallow too much blood during surgery. All the drool coming out at this point was clear, but there was plenty of it.

Saturday night was much better than the previous. She slept for approximately four hours at a time and even drank five ounces at one point. When she woke up Sunday, her fever was gone. Hallelujah! The residents came in to check on her and said that she could start eating some soft foods. If she did okay with them, we would be able to go home that day. We ordered her breakfast and she did not eat much of it, but she did eat some. She was also drinking much better. Around 11 o'clock, the doctor called and I spoke with him, saying I was comfortable taking her home. He agreed, so he put in the orders for us to go home. I think Maggie knew something about it because she then drank five ounces of juice.

The doctor and the nurses were wonderful. They were not in any rush to make us leave and left it up to me if I was comfortable with it or not. I just wanted to be home with my little girl. Once we got home, she improved just by walking in the door. As soon as she saw her brother and sister, she started to smile and laugh as best as she could with a swollen mouth. With each day that passes, she eats a little bit better and drinks a little bit more.

We have since, started giving her formula again and that has helped. She has been drinking out of little medicine cups and using a rubber tipped spoon for eating. It is slow going but each day improves. We are just happy to have the surgery behind us and we look forward to the recovery process as each day gets a little bit better.

I Wish I'd Known...
about the cleft before she
was born to help prepare
for it.

Charlotte

Country: United States of America
Type of Cleft: Cleft of the Soft Palate
Birthdate: February 1, 2011
Cleft Team: Carilion Roanoke Memorial Hospital
Found Out About Cleft: Day After Birth
Surgery Date: January 4, 2012
Family History of Clefts: No

Our little girl was born with a cleft in her soft palate. If I'm being honest, during my pregnancy, I worried about miscarriage or complications. But, it genuinely never once occurred to me that she might have any birth defects.

When she came out, she had the most gigantic, horrific looking nose I had ever seen. It was ghastly. In fact, I think I gasped. I remember thinking, "Oh, my, what on earth?" Before you say, "Oh, I'm sure it wasn't bad," consider that this baby was five pounds and six ounces. That was a big nose on a little face. I fell in love, though. I was so miserable during pregnancy that I was convinced she was going to come out the biggest baby ever. Nope, but at 19 inches, she resembled a green bean. Luckily, her nose was either swollen that day or it was adult size and the rest of her head has grown. It's a perfect little nose now.

It wasn't until the next day that a Lactation Consultant saw her cleft palate. When she said it out loud I was in shock. All these things you prepare for and we were stunned. What did this mean? The short version – it meant a very different first year than we had ever anticipated. Her cleft palate consumed the first year. We saw the cleft palate team in our area, which was comprised of an audiologist, an ENT surgeon, a geneticist, nurse, pediatric dentist/orthodontist, a pediatrician, two plastic surgeons, a psychologist, and a speech pathologist. We also saw her pediatrician, so the first year was rough with doctor visits and prepping for her surgery.

I truly do not know how people get through having a child in the hospital because her surgery was the worst experience of my life. The next few months were consumed with dealing with the surgery fallout. She had a ton of unexpected side effects and we were in survival mode.

Then, just as quickly as our world changed upon hearing the news, it was all over. The cleft team cleared her and said she didn't need to be seen for six months. I felt elated and thankful, while somehow also feeling empty and abandoned.

How was it that a major birth defect that had consumed nearly every thought and every aspect of our lives, could suddenly disappear? Charlotte is now doing remarkably well and we are so proud of her.

I Wish I'd Known... how hard post-op would be.

Isabella

Country: United States of America
Type of Cleft: Microform Cleft Lip and Cleft of the Soft Palate
Birthdate: August 3, 2012
Found Out About Cleft: At One-Day-Old
Surgery Date: January 29, 2013
Family History of Clefts: No

From the moment we found out we were expecting, I knew this baby was going to be special. This pregnancy was nothing like my first two. We were taking frequent trips to the doctor for symptoms of early labor and I was put on a handful of medications. Not once did we imagine that there was anything wrong with our daughter.

I was induced on my due date and everything was perfect. The moment she was born, we noticed that she had what looked like a scar from her nose to her lip, and her nose was misshapen. We really started to worry when she first attempted to feed. She started choking at every feeding. We informed the nurse and it took three nurses later to figure out that our little princess had a cleft soft palate.

We were rushed to Texas Children's Hospital right away. There, we spent ten days running tests, doing echoes, and having a swallow function test done. We, finally, were able to come home.

Isabella has been doing amazingly ever since and her lip repair surgery is planned for January 29th 2013. She has made our family so much stronger. She is a true blessing to us.

I Wish I'd Known...
she was going to be born
with a cleft.

126

Peyton

Country: United States of America
Type of Cleft: Cleft of the Soft Palate
Birthdate: January 26, 2010
Found Out About Cleft: A Few Hours After Birth
Cleft Device: Palatal Appliance
Surgery Date: November 1, 2010
Family History of Clefts: No

Our beautiful baby girl, Peyton Marie, was born January 26th 2010. It was a cold and gloomy Tuesday, but sunshine had come into our lives at 6:42 that evening. With her ten fingers and ten toes, she changed our world forever!

Soon after she was born, nurses brought Peyton to the nursery for her newborn screening tests. During their assessment, they found that she had a cleft of the soft palate. The nurses tried to feed her with a Haberman nipple, but she did not feed well. They took her blood sugar and it was extremely low. They immediately transferred her to the neonatal intensive care unit (NICU) for hypoglycemia. My husband and I did not know there was a problem with Peyton until after her admission.

Early the next morning, we were introduced to staff members in the NICU that were on Peyton's case. We also met our Cleft Palate Team Coordinator, our orthodontist, and plastic surgeon. Our team of doctors determined that a palatal appliance was best for Peyton. It truly was.

At nine-months-old, Peyton had a palatoplasty which completely closed her cleft. We spent only one, very rough night in the hospital. Within a few days, Peyton was back to her lovable self. Before surgery, Peyton was eating stage-two baby food twice a day, having a few bottles and sleeping through the night. After surgery, Peyton would not even stick a spoon in her mouth. So, a few bottles turned into a lot of bottles and middle of the night feedings. Then, we started adding stage two foods and cereal to her bottles to fill her hungry little tummy. One doctor told us to starve her and she would eventually get hungry enough to eat food. Another doctor told us she will eat when she was ready. We took the advice of the second doctor.

Still, at age two, Peyton only ate some stage-two foods and mashed potatoes off a spoon. She still would not eat any finger foods, drink water, or juice. We talked to the cleft team's speech therapist. She told us to keep offering and one day she would catch on.

In March 2012, our pediatrician suggested that we be evaluated by a speech therapist because of Peyton's speech delay (she only said 2-3 words and grunted). We sought out services from Early Intervention. They assigned us to a speech and occupational therapist (because of chewing issues) once a week. They are amazing!

Now, just shy of her third birthday, Peyton is thriving! She eats every food we eat and has a vocabulary of an average three to four-year-old! Peyton is the most unique person I have ever known. She has the most contagious laugh, the funniest faces, brightest eyes, and the most beautiful smile I have ever seen. She is friendly and loving with everyone we meet. She is the best thing that has ever happened to me and our family. We learn something new about Peyton every day. I cannot wait to see what we learn tomorrow!

I Wish I'd Known... that doctors cannot tell me exactly what the future holds for my little girl.

Dear Pregnant Mom,

Be honest with yourself. Whatever you are feeling is okay. You can't control whether or not you are angry, sad, or okay with the cleft. But, it is your responsibility as a parent to deal with these emotions so that you can relate to your baby in a positive way. Your child will benefit more from a parent who has processed emotions, rather than one who has suppressed them. It is okay to mourn for your "perfect" child. No one wants their child to have to deal with adversity or challenges. Your job is to give your child the tools and support they need to overcome the challenges they face, help them become confident, well-adjusted, and happy.

Live in the moment, no matter how rough it gets because it goes by quickly. This is YOUR life and only you get to choose how good or bad it will be. Also, take lots of pictures. Your child will want to see that you were proud of them regardless of how they were born. Finally, just enjoy your little one, they are only little once after all.

With love and hugs.

Not a Big Deal

" *The best way I can describe it is that it is a big deal*

that isn't a big deal. "

Cammie

Country: United States of America
Type of Cleft: Incomplete Unilateral Cleft Lip and Complete Bilateral Palate
Birthdate: January 4, 2012
Cleft Team: Kaiser Permanente Oakland
Found Out About Cleft: At Birth
Cleft Device: Tape and Nasal Spring for 10 weeks
Surgery Dates: April 5, 2012 (Lip repair), November 15, 2012 (Palate repair)
Family History of Clefts: No

From the moment Cammie was born, it has been an emotional roller coaster. I had the easiest labor and delivery. After only pushing for thirteen minutes, she arrived. Before we even had the chance to be excited, the nurse informed us of Cammie's cleft lip and palate. Our excitement immediately turned to confusion. We had no experience with a cleft and had no idea what this meant for her.

As they handed her to me, all I could see was perfection. Yes, there was a split in her lip, but she was so incredibly beautiful. And she wasn't crying, she was talking to me - literally! She kept making these adorable sounds and coos while staring straight into my eyes. It was as if she was telling me that everything was going to be okay. She was comforting me. She was staring at me and talking to me for two straight hours. It was incredible.

The next two days in the hospital were a blur. We saw many specialists that came in to look at Cammie and give us information. My parents brought my older daughter, Cailyn, to meet her little sister. I was nervous about Cailyn's reaction. Cailyn immediately fell in love with her sister and said, "She's cute! Let's go home, my baby's here. Let's go home."

People have asked if we knew from the ultrasounds. No, we weren't given that information. We had more ultrasounds than usual, since they were following this pregnancy closely because I had a miscarriage prior to this pregnancy. They discovered I had some issues that had to be corrected with surgery before we conceived Cammie, so they wanted to make sure this was a viable pregnancy.

Regardless, it really doesn't matter if we would have known beforehand. The only thing it would have done is allow for us to emotionally prepare for what was to come. In actuality, I'm kind of happy I didn't know before. I think I would have panicked if I knew all that would be expected of us after delivery. Since we had no idea, we kind of took on the "we just have to do it" attitude, which is what we have done. It is amazing what you can do when there is no other option.

Facebook has connected me to many people that have helped us through this time with Cammie. I have met people who have put me in contact with resources. We have received many messages from people sending us their well wishes and prayers. This has given us a boost in some of our tougher moments. Being able to update everyone on Cammie's status and receiving support in response has been unbelievably helpful.

The nasal spring has been a huge blessing and a curse. The tape and nasal spring has improved Cammie's nose and lip dramatically. The doctor said we have to clean the spring and change the tape every 12 hours. Every 12 hours is best case scenario. Have you met babies? They love to put their hands in their face, pull nasal springs out, and get saliva all over their faces. In Cammie's case, because of her cleft palate, formula occasionally comes out of her nose. I often change the cleft tape up to six times a day, and she hates it. So, this wonderful invention has caused me a lot of heartache. Imagine having to put your baby through discomfort multiple times a day and not being able to explain that it's for the best. It hurts my heart every time I hear her cry when I have to change her tape and spring. It's my job as her mom to prevent and take away everything that causes her to be uncomfortable, not be the cause of it. I just tell myself that she'll thank me when she's older. It's the only way I can get through it. As she cries and fights it each time, I appreciate how much fight she has in her.

The tape has also been a blessing because it covers her split lip and the spring centers her nose and props her collapsed nostril. When people see her, they're not quite sure why the tape is there. I will admit that I had hesitation to take her in public. Not that I would ever be ashamed of her, but because I don't know how I would handle negative reaction toward her. I know that it is the other person's issue, but my protective "Mama Bear" nature would not handle it well.

I remember checking her in to her first weigh-in, two days after we were discharged, and the receptionist mentioned her visit wasn't a well-baby, because there was "something wrong" with our baby. She actually said the words, "something wrong" twice. It took a lot of restraint to not jump over the counter. It's hard to explain that there is nothing wrong with our baby when there is something wrong with our baby. The best way I can describe it is that it is a big deal that isn't a big deal.

Right now, it's a huge deal. Our baby has surgery in two weeks. She will have two surgeries in her first year of life. She may have to have several more, depending on how her face continues to develop. She may have to have ear tubes and is more prone to ear infections. She will begin speech therapy at six-months-old. Down the road, it isn't such a big deal. Many kids have ear infections, ear tubes, and speech therapy. If all goes well, she'll be exited from speech before she begins kindergarten. Her issues can all be corrected.

There are so many things that make this not such a big deal. Our baby is here, she is healthy and pretty darn cute, too. Her geneticist said that most likely the biggest thing she'll have to worry about when she's a teenager is a little scar below her nose. Being a teacher, I know that kids make fun of other kids for anything and everything. If she didn't have her scar, there would be another reason kids would find to make fun of. I really don't think her cleft is going to emotionally scar her. It's up to us, as parents, to make sure she knows there is absolutely nothing wrong with her. She will never use this as a crutch or excuse, nor will we allow her to.

The range of emotions we have gone through have been incredible. I have had some of the ugliest cries of my life over this. But, I have also had my days brightened beyond belief

132

by her smile. Those that have met her know that she's a pretty amazing baby. She also has a pretty amazing big sister; my sweet, sweet Cailyn. The other morning Cailyn woke up and asked where her daddy was. I told her he was at work and I asked her what Mommy's job was now. I expected a cute reply like, "Being our mommy," but she broke my heart with the matter-of-fact reply, "Surgery."

Sometimes I forget that it isn't just my husband and me going through all of this. We're trying our best to keep life normal for Cailyn, too.

I see Cammie's cleft as a blessing for many reasons. For one thing, because of all the appointments she has had, I haven't had any time to mope around the house with a "why us" or "poor me" mentality. She has forced me to get out of the house, where I may have instead stayed-in out of convenience. She gave us opportunities to look at what is important in life and what we really need to value. She has shown us what we are capable of doing as a family.

My husband and I have been challenged beyond belief and, though, we have had some low moments, I have fallen in love with him all over again through what we have to do for our babies. People have told us how strong we are and sometimes I want to yell back, "I don't want to HAVE to be strong!" Cammie has shown us what it means to be strong. I can't

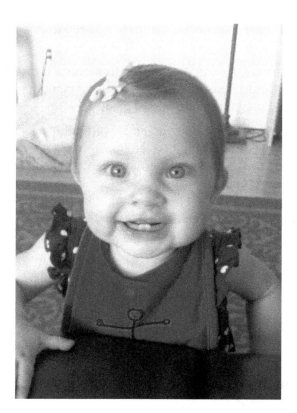

believe what she has to endure and I would take her place in a heartbeat. I'm not excited about her upcoming surgery, because she's already perfect to us. I'm just ready to be done with the "big deal" part of her cleft and move on to the time that "isn't a big deal."

I Wish I'd Known...
how much more my life
would be fulfilled because
of this journey.

Ben

Country: United States of America
Type of Cleft: Incomplete Unilateral Cleft Lip
Birthdate: September 22, 2012
Cleft Team: Children's Hospital of Orange County (CHOC)
Found Out About Cleft: Questionable at 20 Weeks Gestation, Confirmed Upon Delivery
Surgery Date: January 31, 2013
Family History of Clefts: No

I went for my routine 20-week ultrasound and the technologist thought our baby boy might have had a cleft. She was unsure because our boy's hands were covering his face and she could not get a good look at his lip. She told my husband and me not to worry and that everything would be fine.

Well, of course, we worried. We started crying as soon as we got in to the car. All of our friends and family assured us that it was probably nothing since neither of us have a family history of cleft. I immediately started researching clefts and engulfed myself in as much information as possible. After a few days, I felt comfortable with the idea that he may have a cleft lip. I found comfort knowing that his heart looked great and his heartbeat was strong.

A week later, we went to see the perinatologist and she assured us his lip was intact, and that everything looked perfectly normal. My husband and I felt a huge weight off our shoulders and I went through the rest of my pregnancy not worrying about his lip.

At 41 weeks gestation, I went into labor and the on-call doctor delivered the baby. I will never forget my first glimpse of Ben. My eyes went right to his cleft lip. The doctor was nervous; I could see it in his face. He started stuttering and I cut him off and told him that the doctor thought maybe he would have a cleft lip. The baby nurse took him to check his palate and told us his palate was intact. The doctor took a huge sigh of relief. I had done so much research and knew I had a healthy baby. Nothing else mattered to me at that point. All I wanted to do was hold him close.

Now, three months later, we are quickly approaching surgery. He is smiling and cooing and holding his head up and doing all the same things as other babies his age. His lip is such a minor detail compared to all the other milestones in his life.

I Wish I'd Known... how minor the cleft is compared to all the other milestones in a child's development.

Caitlyn

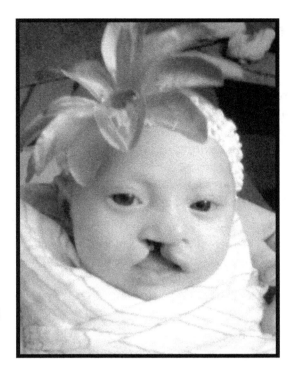

Country: United States of America
Type of Cleft: Complete Unilateral Cleft Lip and Palate
Birthdate: August 14, 2010
Hospital: St. Alexius Medical Center
Found Out About Cleft: 20-Week Ultrasound
Cleft Device: Latham and DynaCleft tape
Surgery Dates: January 3, 2011 (Lip repair), April 18, 2011 (Palate repair)
Family History of Clefts: No

We found out at 20 weeks gestation that Caitlyn had a complete cleft lip and unknown palate involvement. My husband and I were a bit shocked but decided right then and there that we wouldn't let this get us down.

I went home and poured my heart and soul into researching. I spent hours looking at cleft before and after photos and figuring out different bottle combinations. I wanted to be prepared for when I delivered. I purchased every cleft bottle and packed my hospital bag.

Once she was born, we found out she had palate involvement. Oddly enough, instead of feeling overwhelmed, we were at peace once she was born. Her cleft didn't matter to us. What mattered was that she was in our arms.

Now, she is a happy and healthy two-year-old girl who is a total daddy's girl. While we are anxious about future surgeries, we are at ease knowing we have doctors we love and trust.

I Wish I'd Known...
how much I would love her cleft once I saw her. Her cleft doesn't define who she is as a person.

135

Ben

Country: England
Type of Cleft: Cleft of the Hard and Soft Palate
Birthdate: September 28, 2009
Cleft Team: Addenbrooke's Hospital
Found Out About Cleft: At Birth
Cleft Device: NAM
Surgery Date: April 19, 2010
Family History of Clefts: No

My pregnancy with Ben, my third child, was fairly uneventful. However, towards the end, I grew really big and had lots of scans. At birth, Ben was a whopping nine pounds and 13 ounces! We didn't know the sex of the baby, so we were wrapping our heads around having a boy and how big he was when the midwife shocked us even more. "Ooooh, I think he has a cleft palate," she stated.

I was secretly hoping for a girl and with this news on top, I burst into floods of tears. Having breastfed two previous children well into toddlerhood, I knew this was not to be the case for this baby. I stubbornly insisted I would breastfeed. Ben did okay at first, but then struggled. At day five, he had lost 17% of his birth weight and we were back in hospital. Ben was fitted with a NG tube and diagnosed with mild PRS. We stayed in the hospital for a week and I would express breast milk around the clock. Ben put weight on and we were able to go home and enjoy him.

He never became the huge baby he was meant to be, but his weight gain was slow and steady. I was put under huge pressure to formula feed but refused, and expressed all his milk. It is something I am very proud of as it was a huge challenge.

At seven months, Ben was ready for his repair. The operation went well, but Ben did very badly in recovery and was rushed into intensive care. They could not stabilize him and he was put on a ventilator. He stayed in intensive care for nine days. It was a very scary time for us and very humbling to stay in parental accommodation with other parents whose children were on borrowed time. It made me realize Ben's cleft was so minor and how lucky we were to have him.

Since his recovery, Ben has done brilliantly. His speech has come along well and he is now a loving, lively, gorgeous little boy. He loves to follow his brother and sister around like a little shadow. I carried on expressing milk until Ben was 29 months. I am very proud that he actually had breast milk for longer than my first two, after all the upset I felt.

We held a fundraising event to raise money for the Sick Children's Trust, who looked after us whilst Ben was in intensive care. After two children with no clefts, and no clefts in our family history, it was a big shock. But, Ben very quickly went from being "a cleft baby," to simply "Ben," who happened to have a little difference. I'm very proud to tell people about Ben's cleft, it just makes him all the more special.

I Wish I'd Known... that the cleft wouldn't make any difference in the long run.

Dear Pregnant Mom,

It's an up and down journey, especially in the beginning. You hear those words and it feels like your world is crashing in. Know that it does get better and you have to give yourself time to adjust. Take it one day at a time. You will have good and bad days, but don't give up. If you want to cry, then cry. If you want to be mad, then be mad and then get over it. Being the parent of a cleft affected child is not the worst thing in life. It has made me a better person, mother, wife, sister, and leader. I recommend having someone you can talk to whether friend, family, or counselor; someone who will not feel sorry for you. It's more about working through feelings than wallowing in sadness.

Be honest and talk everything through with your partner. Some things just suck. Have a good support system; that's what gets me through each day. Supporting one another is amazing. I felt we had excellent support from family and friends, as well as from others who had walked this path before us.

Breathe, it all works out in the end!

In The Family

" *I wish I'd known how lucky we were to become*

cleft parents – twice! "

Lily & Jack

Country: Canada
Type of Cleft: Soft Palate Only (Lily), Complete Unilateral Cleft Lip and Palate (Jack)
Birthdate: December 9, 2003 (Lily), September 14, 2008 (Jack)
Cleft Team: Children's Hospital of Eastern Ontario (CHEO)
Found Out About Cleft: After birth (Lily), 31-Week Ultrasound (Jack)
Cleft Device: NAM for 6 Months Pre-op (Jack)
Surgery Dates: January 2005 (Lily's palate repair), April 2009 (Jack's lip repair), October 2009 (Jack's palate repair)
Family History of Clefts: Possible history

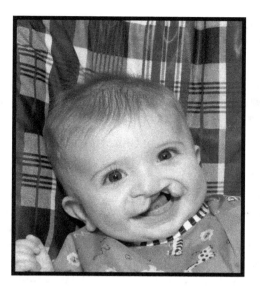

When our daughter, Lily, was born she was our first little miracle. Ten fingers, ten toes; she was perfect, just like we had planned. But, when our early attempts at nursing failed, we discovered that she was born with a cleft of the soft palate. We were confused. As children of the 70's, our thoughts immediately turned to "that kid" we knew in grade school with the crooked nose and the scar on his face. But our daughter didn't look like that, so how could she have a cleft palate? It was the day a critical door swung open on our lives and our journey of understanding and inspiration began.

As a first time mother, I was disappointed that I wouldn't be able to nurse my new baby. We tried everything we could, but in the end, it came down to investing in a good breast pump (which we affectionately refer to as "Bessy") and finding the perfect bottle and nipple combination.

Surprisingly, we weren't disappointed that our daughter was born with a cleft palate. At the time, we still had many questions, so much to learn about the condition, and what to expect over the coming weeks and years. But, when we looked into her beautiful little face, our instincts kicked in and we knew we could handle whatever was in store for us.

Sharing the news with our family was met with overwhelming love and support. We used the opportunity to educate those around us, help everyone understand why it happened, and what came next for Lily.

By the time we had our second child, Sam (born with no cleft anomalies), Lily was two and a half years old. Over a year and a half post-repair, she was doing exceptionally well. Resounding reassurances were that we had been through the worst and came out of it with such a beautiful little girl. "You can't even tell there was a cleft!" some had said.

Two years later, while pregnant with our third child, an ultrasound at 31 weeks revealed our new baby (Jack) was going to be born with a unilateral cleft lip and palate. This time, I was very emotional. We had been down this road before and knew so much about clefts already. We spent the last five years "matter-of-factly" explaining the condition to everyone and anyone who would listen. And yet, I felt as though I was just hit by a truck. I already knew how much love I would feel for this little guy and I was worried for him. In the blink of an eye, I envisioned all of his appointments, his surgeries, his school friends, his girlfriends, his wife, and his kids. I wanted to know that he would be okay and that he would be happy.

In retrospect, we're grateful to have found out about the cleft before Jack was born. It gave us time to accept the situation and prepare ourselves and our family for his arrival. We absorbed every bit of information we could on treatment strategies and I geared up to be reacquainted with "Bessy" for another year.

Finally, our beautiful little boy was born – ten fingers, ten toes, and a cleft lip. He was perfect – just like we had expected. Admittedly, the first year with Jack was challenging. The cleft in his lip made even bottle-feeding tricky and his lip repair surgery was postponed twice due to an annoying chest cold. Weekly trips to the orthodontist for NAM adjustments became part of our new routine and he developed eczema on his cheeks because of the tape used to hold the appliance in place. But, at the end of every appointment, every time he woke up, or ate, or breathed for that matter, he would flash his unbelievable 1000-watt smile. Now, we knew the cleft in his lip made his smile bigger, but there was this profound joy just radiating from his soul. We knew we had a very brave, very happy, little peanut.

Despite my own insecurities, I made a point of taking Jack out with me whenever I could. I braced myself for the strange glances and insensitive comments. Instead, we were greeted with warm smiles and genuine compliments. How touching it was to see an elderly man reach for Jack's little hand and exchange a giggle. I remember waiting for Lily at the hairdresser's one day when a frail, little old lady just spontaneously hobbled over to us. She smiled at Jack, then looked at me and said, "You know he's going to be okay, don't you?" I left that day feeling a little better about the world we live in.

Our family has been through a lot already and we know we have quite a few more miles to go on our journey together. We are extremely grateful for the exceptional Cleft Palate Team at CHEO. Their support and care has meant more to us than words can say. We relish each and every day with our beautiful children; watching how they've grown and imagining what they will become. It has been nothing short of inspirational to see such resilience and bravery in such little people. We are proud to be cleft parents!

I Wish I'd Known…
how lucky we were to
become cleft parents –
twice!

Raymond

Country: Canada
Type of Cleft: Cleft Lip and Palate
Birthdate: November 19, 1955
Cleft Team: Winnipeg Medical Arts Building; Dr. Norman P. Merkely, MD
Found Out About Cleft: After Birth
Surgery Date: 1956 (Lip repair), 1957 (Palate repair)
Family History of Clefts: Yes

Our son was the fourth generation in the family with an open lip and cleft palate. His father's great uncle, aunt, and his youngest sister all had cleft palate. Our surgeon, Dr. Merkely, told us that because he was the fourth generation, he probably would not have cleft palate.

We had a very difficult time feeding him. We made a bigger hole in the nipple which helped quite a bit to feed him a little faster. Raymond was sick a lot with tonsillitis and croup. After the operation, he became allergic to milk. We usually tried to make him blow bubbles, so he would breathe through his mouth instead of his nose. That seemed to help him speak a little more clearly.

He also had a nose lift, when he was about 13 years old. His teeth started to grow but because his palate was open, the teeth came out at the top of the roof of the mouth. He was usually an active child. He was very happy and, I'd say, very "smart."

I Wish I'd Known...
how to feed him.

Chloe

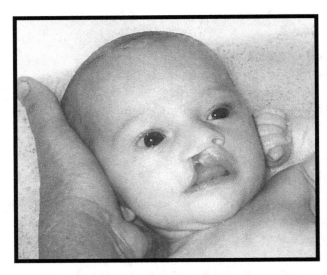

(Half-Sister to 'Sienna' page 144)
Country: Australia
Type of Cleft: Unilateral Cleft Lip and Palate
Birthdate:
November 6, 2001
Cleft Team: Mater Children's Hospital and Royal Children's Hospital
Found Out About Cleft: 18-Week Ultrasound
Cleft Device: Nasal Stent Post-Operatively
Surgery Dates: March 18, 2002; August 9, 2005; May 10, 2007; July 18, 2011
Family History of Clefts: Grandfather on father's side

When I fell pregnant with my first child early in 2001, I was both delighted and worried. My relationship with her father was shaky at best. He was very supportive of me and over the moon to be having a baby with me. Although we had separated, he stayed in the house to help out as I got bigger and more awkward with the pregnancy. He came with me to the 18-week ultrasound. During the ultrasound, we were asked a number of questions about family history including cleft lip and palate. I remember thinking that I didn't even know what that was. My companion jumped in and replied, "Yes, my Dad has that." I did a double take and froze. It's not something we had ever talked about.

We returned to the obstetrician a little bit later. He was quite brash and, in one sentence, told us that the baby had "soft signs" of a syndrome which included, among other things, a unilateral cleft lip and cleft palate. In the same breath he offered a termination, but I needed to make a decision within the next day. I felt that my little girl was very much alive and well, and I wanted to give her the chance to be born.

Chloe Monique came into the world on Melbourne Cup Day in 2001 during the running of the race. A friend of mine held my hand and my mum also helped. I clearly recall someone calling out that the race was now on and calling my midwife away. She called out that the baby was also here and she might just pip them at the post!

Relief and joy washed over me as the doctor declared Chloe well and that her palate was mostly intact. She was beautiful. We had a cuddle and she had a try at breastfeeding, instinctively placing her own pinky finger in her cleft while she drank.

When Chloe was three-weeks-old, I met her paternal grandfather for the first time. I was moved as he held her and told me the story of his own bilateral cleft lip and palate and all the surgeries that he had. In the 1930's, he was thought to be the first child to be operated on to correct his lip. Some professionals felt this was futile and thought it more humane to leave him as he was and allow nature to take course. His mother did not take this lightly and took him to Sydney where he was seen by a doctor who embarked on a series of surgeries for him. His schooling was difficult as his speech was very poor. No one could understand him. He was told that he would never have a speaking profession. Chloe's grandfather was very proud of his career as a minister. He spoke clearly and preached weekly from a pulpit for decades. I was in awe of his experiences and he gave me much hope for the future.

The next weeks and months revolved around Chloe's feeding. She became tired very easily and soon started to refuse her food and became dehydrated in the 35-degree Celsius heat. Chloe was refusing every effort to feed her with formula or breast milk and we were briefly admitted to Mater Children's for failure to thrive. After a day or two, Chloe was given treatment for reflux and immediately began to improve.

Chloe's lip and palate repair was done in one surgery when she was 15-weeks-old. I was prepared for surgery as much as I could be, and yet, still taken aback by the swelling and the sound of her cry as she woke from the anesthetic.

I stayed with her in the hospital for four nights until exhaustion took over. I went home for a sleep and my stepfather stayed with her for the final night. It took three of us to care for her full-time for the next six weeks, as she was a tricky customer with her feeding.

When Chloe was two, I met my husband through my friend who had held my hand during labour. We married in 2005 and Chloe's father attended the wedding with a small group of our friends and family. We returned home from our honeymoon in time for Chloe to have her rhinoplasty surgery for her rather flat nose and remove webbing that had almost closed her nostril on the right side. Some spare teeth were removed, opening up a small fistula to be corrected with an Alveolar Bone Graft later. At five-years-old, this surgery needed to be repeated due to the webbing growing back.

Chloe is a very pretty blue-eyed girl and in all honesty, her scar is minimal. Her personality is bold and bright and seems to more than make up for any other difficulties she has. Even her teachers have not spotted it and asked me why she has so many specialist appointments. She speaks well and is a good student.

Exactly ten years to the day I was told my unborn daughter would be born with a cleft lip and palate, she was to have it repaired. Even with the knowledge the day would come,

we were nervous. We needn't have been so worried.

Chloe recovered completely and is now very proud of the fact she can inflate a balloon, make a bubble with bubble gum, and sip on a thick shake like any other 11-year-old girl. She has more dental work to go, but has said she is happy with her appearance and doesn't want any more surgery.

I Wish I'd Known...
she would inspire me so
much.

Sienna

(Half-Sister to 'Chloe' page 142)
Country: Australia
Type of Cleft: Bilateral Cleft Lip
Birthdate: November 28, 2008
Cleft Team: Royal Children's Hospital
Found Out About Cleft: At Birth
Cleft Device: Post-op Nasal Stent
Surgery Date: April 18, 2009
Family History of Clefts: Half-sister has a
cleft, no other history

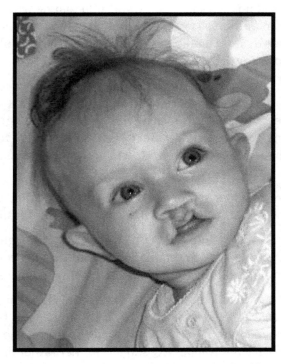

Chloe is my first daughter, she was
born with a cleft and three weeks after
her seventh birthday, we welcomed her
baby sister Sienna Maree. Our 20-week
scan was without any problems. The
sonographer took some time to look
carefully at our baby's face and even gave
us a 4-D picture of our little girl. She looked like her dad. As far as I could see, she had his
lips and the relaxed way they sat when he was sleeping.

On the day Sienna was born, I had a very unsure feeling about her. I told my husband
that I thought there was something wrong. He did his utmost to jolly me along and tell me
not to worry. I went up to the hospital in the morning after my water broke and I delivered
her fairly quickly. I won't say it was easy, but as these things go, it was only a matter of a
few hours before she was born. As soon as I birthed her, the midwife asked me with a
feigned casual tone, "Did the doctors say anything about Sienna having a cleft lip at all?"
My husband and I exchanged a brief glance and I know we were being watched carefully for
our reaction. I just didn't react. I was too tired to care. I just asked to hold her. To me, it
was like finding out the thing you were keeping at home in case of an emergency was just
about to come in handy. In this case, it was my knowledge of cleft lip and palate. I had a
very vivid flashback to seeing Chloe for the first time seven years before.

I apologised to my husband straight away. I felt extremely guilty, but very protective of
Sienna. Once more, I didn't bond with her instantly. It was a familiar feeling, so I wasn't
troubled by not being in love with my baby right away. I just concentrated on looking into
Sienna's eyes and tried to talk to her. She cried an awful lot. I told one nurse that I didn't
expect her to understand how I felt because it's not something that happens to everyone. I
was more concerned about getting home.

I broke the news about Sienna's bilateral cleft lip gently to her sister, Chloe. As she held
Sienna for the first time, she bit her lip and said without taking her eyes off her sister,
"She's like me. We're the same. I know how it feels darling. You and me are just the same.
There's no one like us. I'll help you with everything." It hit me then, that I could no longer
just walk away from our experiences with clefts and surgery and allow them to fade into
the background.

When I told Chloe that she and her sister are two of many children born with this and that they are most definitely not the only ones, her face lit up. It was as though she suddenly felt like she belonged to something and her feelings of being the only one were washed away in that instant. The first time we went to a CleftPALS event, Chloe won the lucky door prize and tugged on my arm saying, "Look, those kids have a scar like mine!"

During this time, Sienna had her first repair. When we took Sienna to her initial appointment, Dr. Thiele stopped in the corridor when he saw Chloe. "I know that face," he declared. She smiled, he smiled, and we chatted. He then noticed Sienna in my arms and we stepped straight into the consult room.

From the first few days of Sienna's life, I trawled the Internet and searched for information about cleft lip and palate. I didn't really learn anything new and I was plagued with feelings of guilt. My husband was adamant that thinking like that was a waste of time. He said it wasn't like that for him. He had accepted Chloe as his daughter, knowing she came with this condition. "Thank God it's not a heart condition or something hidden that could be a time bomb. There are many worse things than this," he said.

My many visits to both Mater and Royal Children's Hospital led me to involvement in the hospitals and the Family Advisory Council at the Royal Children's Hospital. Today, I am the chair of that group and I can honestly say that if it were not for my children's health needs, I would have no place on that committee.

In the midst of Chloe's treatment of her teeth, all of this was going on with Sienna. Chloe was with me when I changed Sienna's stents and she came with me to most of Sienna's appointments. When Sienna had a hearing test, it was Chloe who helped the audiologist reward Sienna's listening with big happy smiles and waving.

In time, Sienna will need some revision on her lip, and orthodontic care. Chloe asked me if she could please stay with Sienna when the time comes for Sienna's bone graft. Out of two difficult situations, at the very least, I am thankful that the girls have each other for support. Our family is quite involved with CleftPALS QLD, organising and holding events for other families to get together. There is nothing my children enjoy more than simply meeting and playing with other children who are like them.

I Wish I'd Known... a cleft can happen to any family.

Misha & Zooey

Country: United States of America
Type of Cleft: Bilateral Cleft Lip and Palate (Misha), Unilateral Cleft Lip and Palate (Zooey)
Birthdate: October 31, 2009
Cleft Team: Primary Children's Medical Center
Found Out About Cleft: 16 Weeks Gestation
Cleft Device: NAM
Surgery Dates: April 20, 2010 (Lip repairs), further surgeries in November and December 2010
Family History of Clefts: Yes

My pregnancy wasn't the normal one-baby and nothing wrong scenario. I found out at nine weeks that I was pregnant with twins. I was not expecting that and went in for the ultrasound. The lady asked, "Are there twins in your families?" "Uhh, no," I replied. She turns the stick and I saw there were two. After looking for a minute, still in shock, she went to get the doctor. The doctor said something about mono-mono twins. I really can't remember much after the word, "twins."

I went back at 12 weeks and they confirmed that they were mono-mono twins. These are twins that share the same sack and have a 50% chance of surviving the pregnancy. I was told a bunch of medical stuff, had ultrasounds every other week and saw the doctor twice a month.

At 16 weeks, instead of finding out genders, we found out about the cleft on both babies. My first thought was, "My girls are going to look like the puppies with a cleft." At 18 weeks, we found out they were identical girls. Horror struck me for a minute, because girls are mean and hurtful. The doctors' visits and monitoring continued and then at 24 weeks, I was admitted into the hospital for constant monitoring. I was there for nine weeks, which included lots of shots, pills, and belly goop.

At 32 weeks, I made the choice to have my girls. I ended up having them via C-section. Misha was born with a bilateral cleft lip and palate. Zooey had a unilateral cleft lip and palate. They had to be on breathing machines for a month. At three-days-old, Dr. Siddiqi came to see them and told the nurses to tape their lips.

They have had eight surgeries in total so far. Some have been hard and they tend to stay in the hospital longer than most. In one surgery, they came out with the new arm restraint that has a band for the waist and arms so that they can move. 15 to 20 minutes after waking up, they were out of them; sneaky little devils.

They learned everything normally, except speech. At three-years-old, they were talking like a one-year-old. There have been mean comments from people that I just cannot handle. But, I think they were given to us because no one else in our family would have helped them. We have lost our house and other things, but we are so much happier where we are now. I also didn't have a lot of family help and still don't from one side. I'm glad they have each other to go through this. I would be lost if only one had it.

I Wish I'd Known... how my heart would break at every mean word spoken, but how strong I have become for my babies.

Dear Pregnant Mom,

Be honest with yourself and with others. You have or will have a baby. Just as you cannot change his or her gender, you cannot change his or her cleft. A cleft is only a tiny part of the person that they are. Don't let the emotions and stress distract you from the fact that you have a perfectly normal and happy child. The first year is all about the cleft and it will still be something that needs attention in the years to come, but you'll be too busy watching your child grow and keeping them out of trouble to think about it much.

Try to stay positive and believe that your baby will have an amazing life filled with love and laughter. You will get through this. It is a blip on the radar. How you treat your cleft affected child is how he will view himself, so treat him no differently than any other child.

Talk to people. Stay open; people want to help. Explain what is going on with you, even if it is just admitting to a stranger in line at the bank that you are having a hard day. You'll find support in unlikely and much-appreciated places.

Find others that are going through the same feelings of being afraid. Don't forget to research; the more you understand, the less scary it is. It has been a little bit of roller coaster, but at the end of the day a child is a blessing, cleft or no cleft.

Wishing you joy in your journey.

A Cleft Doesn't Define

"*Although, he started his life with a cleft lip,*

he is not defined by it."

Emmarie

Country: United States of America
Type of Cleft: Complete Left Unilateral Cleft Lip and Cleft Gum Line
Birthdate: August 27, 2012
Cleft Team: Helen DeVos Children's Hospital; Dr. Mann, MD
Found Out About Cleft: 21 Weeks Gestation
Cleft Device: No
Surgery Date: January 22, 2012
Family History of Clefts: No

There is nothing like it. Nothing like the moment when you are with a doctor and start to catch on that something may be wrong with your child. You wait so long to have a baby. You plan it out. You put all of your hopes and dreams into this little being even before he or she is in existence. I never felt like things were okay with my pregnancy. I kept telling people that things didn't seem right. When we found out that I was carrying twins and one of them wasn't going to make it, you'd think that would be the end of that feeling. It wasn't. That feeling remained. You would think that after our seemingly perfect 20-week ultrasound that my feeling of things being "off" would go away. They didn't.

I left the ultrasound telling a girlfriend that I felt like they spent a lot more time on the face and heart than with my other child. But, they said everything looked great, so I thought I was just being paranoid, as usual. At 21-weeks pregnant, I received a phone call from the ultrasound technician asking me to come back in the next morning. She said everything was great and there was nothing to worry about. We were told that the images "didn't transfer" and they needed to redo the ultrasound. I had my husband go to work as planned and I went in.

It took only minutes for me to realize they were intently focusing on the face and heart again. I asked, "Something's wrong, isn't there?" She responded that she wasn't sure. I immediately followed that up with, "You see a cleft, don't you?" The ultrasound tech responded in a way that every mother fears. She confirmed what she thought was a cleft and began inspecting the heart further as a precaution to locate other problems that can be associated with a cleft. I bawled. I was scared. Before I left, I was referred to a Maternal Fetal Medicine doctor for close monitoring and ultrasounds, as well as a financial advisor from the office to guide me through my options.

When I left, I didn't want to talk about it, so I texted people. Everyone had the same response, "It is just a cleft. It can be fixed. She will be beautiful," and so on. It was all very true. But, that said, it pissed me off. It pissed me off and broke my heart all at the same time. Why couldn't anyone see what else this could mean? She would have trouble eating, trouble gaining weight, she probably couldn't take a normal bottle, she probably couldn't take a pacifier, she probably couldn't breastfeed, may have hearing problems, reflux, ear tubes, speech problems, problems swallowing, teasing, scars, bone grafts, braces, palate expanders, dental implants, nose revisions, financial implications, and surgery risks in general. Everyone seemed to think it would be fixed with one or two surgeries. I wish it was that simple.

More than that, I was heartbroken that I had somehow caused this. Again, everyone said it wasn't genetic, but it didn't matter. I still felt responsible. My anxiety was through the roof the whole pregnancy. I bought every feeder possible so that when she was born, I would have all of my options ready to ensure she could feed like a champ right away. I am a natural 'worrier,' so this was a long 20 weeks.

The doctors measured, examined, and told us so many different things. Everything from it being a wide unilateral complete cleft with no palate involvement, to having palate involvement, to being a bilateral cleft, and then back to being unilateral. At one point, they said she was measuring too small. They even mentioned "short stature" concerns at one point. We also had to tour the NICU just in case. I ended up asking my amazing OB if I needed to keep going. It was making things worse for me, mentally and emotionally. But, because of their small size concerns, we still went.

When the day finally came to meet our baby girl, nerves were high. Thankfully, it was a perfect delivery. She was perfect. I never believed any other cleft moms when they told me that when she was here, I simply wouldn't see the cleft. They were right. I, honestly, only saw my amazingly perfect baby girl. She ended up being seven pounds, two ounces and had no stature issues at all. After all of the worrying, our little Emmie had a complete unilateral cleft lip on the left side with gum line involvement, but no cleft palate at all. To my surprise and delight, our little babe latched right on and went to town nursing! She checked out okay with the NICU team and only had the cleft and a sacral dimple.

Nursing was very slow and I was worried I would have to stop, but after a few lactation consultations, some long nights, and hard work, she continued nursing as any other baby. She was actually much easier to nurse than my son was. The down side was that she hated bottles. But, I got what I wanted and she was nursing. So my husband got to enjoy some extra night-time sleep.

We had met with Dr. Mann a few times to create a plan. Thankfully, I met several local cleft moms during my pregnancy. I knew all about their journeys, all about Dr. Mann, got to see his work first hand, and had an amazing support system with these moms. We meet fairly regularly and that was and is a godsend to me.

We had been told that our surgery would not be until April or May because Dr. Mann was so busy. However, out of the blue we received a call. They had an opening for the following week, so we scheduled right then. I was terrified. I managed to keep her healthy that week and the day was here before I knew it. I took tons of pictures. Before she was born, I thought I would be ready for this day. Since having her, however, the only thing I wanted was to keep her as she was. I didn't want to change her. I didn't want to put her through that.

On a snowy January morning, we checked into the Children's Hospital. She had done great after not eating for several hours and she was being a happy camper. Nothing was going to make it easy, but having her smiley and happy was rough. She had no idea what was coming and that ate me up inside. When we had to hand her off to the anesthesiologist, I thought I would flip out. I was about to, but stopped myself before reaching the lobby which was full of sane, not crying parents. Somehow, I managed to suck it up and not cry until we were alone. She was under for about four hours and in surgery for three and a half hours. Dr. Mann said everything went great. The only setback was that some of the bone in her nose was hardly there. They used surgical foam to build it up and hopefully encourage some bone growth.

My heart broke when I saw her coming out of surgery and off the anesthesia. It was horrible to see her like that. She looked confused, in pain, and sleepy. She was bloody but not really swollen. She had tubes hooked up to her. I was terrified to hold her. Every time she moaned, I tried to give her to my husband. I didn't know what to do for her. It was awful. After we were moved to our room, her blood pressure would shoot up when she fussed. Once that was under control and she was waking up a bit, we were able to feed her. I was able to breastfeed right after. She did fairly well with nursing, but she bled a lot during this part. The blood scared me more. She didn't suck very well for the first few days but other than that, it was fairly seamless. Because the flu was going around so badly in the hospital, they decided to send us home that night rather than keep us overnight as they usually would. We got her some meds and were up with her every few hours all night giving them to her and trying to feed. She did wonderfully.

We now wait for the next surgery in a few months. Until then, we are falling in love with her new smile and enjoying being done with that period of the cleft journey. Someone once told me that everyone has scars; some just wear theirs on the inside. Emmarie is no different; she just shows hers on the outside. We hope to raise her and her brother to be confident, proud of themselves, and ready to help other kids around the world with clefts.

She has the opportunity to make a difference in this world. We hope and pray she will take advantage of that so that we can help her bless others as she herself has been blessed. Family and friends are already donating on behalf of Emmarie to help change other kid's smiles. That's a pretty great impact that Emmarie has been able to have in five short months!

I never knew I could love my children so much. I never knew that this cleft journey would be so bittersweet. I never knew that my newborn baby could teach me so much and make me cherish the imperfections of life way more than the perfections I had previously sought. I never knew how incredibly strong, beautiful, and amazing this baby and I would grow to be. I never knew that this cleft would end up being such a blessing in disguise. I never, ever knew I'd feel this way.

I Wish I'd Known... that a cleft has not defined her and never will define her.

Browen

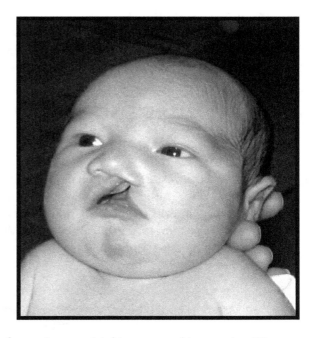

Country: Canada
Type of Cleft: Unilateral Cleft Lip and Palate
Birthdate: February 24, 2011
Cleft Team: Sick Kids Toronto, then Winnipeg Children's Hospital
Found Out About Cleft: 20-Week Ultrasound
Cleft Device: NAM for Nearly 7 Months
Surgery Dates: September 21, 2011 (Lip repair), February 8, 2012 (Palate repair)
Family History of Clefts: No

We were like many couples nowadays. We tried to make sure we did everything right to ensure the ideal pregnancy; eating organic, getting plenty of exercise, no drinking or smoking, and getting rid of all popular cleaning products that we learned are dangerous during pregnancy. All of this, in an effort to achieve the healthiest possible outcome: the perfect baby!

Deep down, my partner and I believed that if we did everything right, that our baby would arrive perfect too! Perhaps, this is why I took the news so hard the day my midwife told us that our baby would be born with a cleft lip and palate. My first thought, and the source of my overwhelming grief, was that I had failed and that somehow we had consciously or unconsciously allowed this to happen. I felt devastated, horrified, and almost furious beyond belief. How could I ever forgive myself? How would I accept my imperfect baby? Would I even be able to look at him without feeling pity, shame, and disgust?

After finally pulling myself together enough to start imagining this beautiful baby still growing inside me, I wish I could say that I immediately came to my senses and accepted his cleft as one aspect that we now know makes up our whole child. The truth is that I experienced every horrible thought and unthinkable emotion imaginable for a mother.

I can tell the truth about these feelings now only because I have a beautiful two-year-old in my arms that has taught me more about love, acceptance, and embracing life's challenges than I ever could have learned on my own. With lots of support from family, friends, and other families of cleft affected kids, notably two of our dearest friends, we navigated the cleft road with both ups and downs. Strangely enough, the hurdles we anticipated and obsessed about during pregnancy ended up being so much easier and manageable than we thought. I worried a lot about how other people would react to seeing my baby in the street and what they might say. As life would have it, I became so good at educating strangers on the subway, in the elevator, and at the bus stop that I actually missed it after the surgeries when people could often no longer tell that he was cleft affected.

153

The surgeries, another huge worry of ours, ended up going smoothly and his pain was very well managed. Sick Kids took impeccable care of us and Browen made a speedy recovery. Thinking back, they were not traumatic events. Yet, seeing him for the first time after the lip repair made me mourn his huge smile that I had loved and kissed for so long.

Although associated with the cleft, some of our biggest challenges were the frequent ear infections and exclusively pumping breast milk for the first year. These things could have been faced by parents of non-affected children as well. Our biggest obstacles were none other than our own thoughts, fears, and anxieties which proved to have been more detrimental than anything the cleft has presented us with. Now that we have entered toddlerhood, words like NAM, tape, and Haberman have been replaced with "Papa," "truck," and "mine." Although, we will never forget or pretend the cleft never existed, the truth is when we look at our boy, we don't even see it. That is, unless of course we are wiping boogers or tomato sauce from his face. We see our entire boy, our mischievous, smart, loveable blessing: Browen.

I Wish I'd Known... that the cleft would only make up a small part of my child, our life and our struggles as parents.

Francine

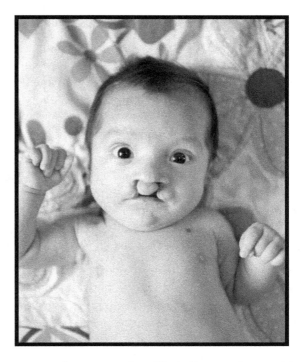

Country: United States of America
Type of Cleft: Bilateral Complete Cleft Lip and Palate
Birthdate: May 17, 2012
Cleft Team: Children's Hospital of Orange County (CHOC)
Found Out About Cleft: At Birth
Surgery Date: September 27, 2012 (Lip repair)
Family History of Clefts: No

I had a fast labor. I almost had the baby in the car! Francine came an hour after I got to the hospital. The doctor delivered her head and said, "There's something wrong with her lip." I had no idea what he meant. The first thought in my mind was, "What, a crumb or something? Wipe it off!" Then they put her on my chest. I was horrified. She was born with a complete bilateral cleft lip and palate. I felt like the whole thing was a living nightmare. It was a whirlwind labor in the middle of the night and then, my baby. I looked at the nurse thinking, "What am I supposed to do with this baby? Put her back and give me the one I'm supposed to have." I thank God I had the sweetest, most compassionate nurses at that hospital.

My husband had called my parents to come to the hospital while I was still in labor. He told them to swing by our house to get the camera. They did, but we never used the camera. I felt so embarrassed, so ashamed, so angry, and cheated. I felt cheated out of that magical moment of seeing my baby for the first time and feeling that overwhelming love for the little miracle before me. I thought my husband would be angry with me for having this un-perfect baby. I looked over at him holding her, swaddled in his arms. He looked down at her with this absolute love in his face and I felt some relief. He adored her, so hopefully I could too.

A specialist doctor came in to examine her for other problems and said she looked perfectly healthy otherwise. He didn't even think she needed to go to the NICU. When we were all wheeled up to our room, I prayed to God for compassion for our baby. I still felt like I didn't like her, let alone love her. "How could she do this to me? How could she be born with this deformity? That's not my identity, the woman with a deformed baby." We were in the hospital for two nights. When family visited and said all these great things about her, I thought they were lying. I knew what they were really thinking, though. This is how I felt for the first couple of weeks. It finally sunk in that people actually did think she was adorable. I quickly started to believe it for myself, too.

While in the hospital, the head of the local children's hospital craniofacial team came to see Francine. She gave us a binder of information and told us to call and make an appointment. They were all informed about us and expected to hear from us. That team was a huge relief for us. They gave us guidance and I knew we were being taken care of.

The first few weeks were all about gaining weight. Our cleft team helped us figure out that the Haberman bottle worked best for Francine. I logged every feeding, which was quite tedious. I wasn't able to nurse Francine because she had no suction, so I exclusively pumped. It was so overwhelming. I cried every day for a few weeks. With time, as my husband and I became more used to the cleft, we went out more and hid her face less. We actually never heard a negative comment.

I broke down when we scheduled lip surgery. I was going to lose this little face that I'd grown to love so much. Surgery was cancelled the first time around due to a minor cough. We had to wait two more weeks for it to happen. When my husband and I saw our little girl in recovery, we bawled. That night in the hospital was brutal. She wouldn't sleep and we couldn't put her down. I had the mindset of having a newborn, which made those first ten days go by a little easier because it wasn't as hard as a newborn.

As I write, we are three weeks post lip repair and totally in love with a new little smile. We still have a long road ahead and sometimes I still feel like it's not fair, but I have a strong baby girl that will grow into a strong woman one day. By that time, the cleft journey will be over and just a memory.

I Wish I'd Known... that cleft affected doesn't mean the baby isn't normal in every other way.

Brennan

Country: Australia
Type of Cleft: Left Incomplete
Unilateral Cleft Lip
Birthdate: August 17, 2012
Cleft Surgeon: Dr. Harry Stalewski,
MD
Found Out About Cleft: 20-Week
Ultrasound
Surgery Date: September 27, 2012
Family History of Clefts: No

"You're a smart girl, you know what you're looking at," my obstetrician said. We both stared at the black line joining my unborn baby's mouth to the left nostril. Strangely, I didn't feel anxious or even worried at that stage, but yes, I knew. The remainder of my pregnancy was uneventful despite several more ultrasounds. Our son continued to thrive, reassuring us at each scan with his steady weight growth and cheeky uncooperativeness.

The most difficult part of our pregnancy was what to do with the knowledge of our baby's cleft. Particularly, how to share this knowledge with others. We felt comfortable that our baby and our lives would be fine. We could handle whatever fate threw at us. We were however, concerned about how our families would react and were quite anxious about our son being treated differently than his brothers. Before our due date, my husband and I wrote a letter to our immediate family members. In it, we stated what we knew about our baby's cleft lip, as well as the possibility of a cleft palate. We also reassured our loved ones that both cleft lips and cleft palates are regularly and successfully 'repaired' by highly skilled surgeons. We included ultrasound images of our son, pointing out the visible cleft as well as information provided to us from CleftPALS. Most importantly, we included our dreams for our unborn baby. We made it clear that a cleft lip had not changed or faded the hopes and dreams that we had for and about our child.

Our beautiful son, Brennan, was born in the middle of August of 2012. He was every bit as perfect as we knew that he would be, despite inheriting his father's ginger locks. We did not need all of the specialist feeding equipment that we'd brought to the hospital, as Brennan had only an incomplete unilateral cleft lip. Having breastfed my two other sons, I was relieved to be able to successfully establish breastfeeding with Brennan as well. After three nights in hospital to ensure that feeding was on track and an examination by our paediatrician, we were able to take Brennan home.

As Brennan grew, feeding became more difficult. When he became distressed and cried, as of course all babies do, his little lips seemed to swell, broadening his cleft. This made attachment more difficult. Although he appeared to feed well, he did not have long feeds and suffered a lot from wind. This in turn, exacerbated the problem. I am a member of the Australian Breastfeeding Association and often referred to their publication *Breastfeeding Babies with Clefts of Lip and/or Palate* (2008) for strategies to help Brennan attach. I was determined to persevere and allowed Brennan to have the many, shorter feeds that he seemed best able to handle. At the time of writing, Brennan is six-months-old and until a few weeks ago when he started on solids, he has been exclusively breastfed.

At six-weeks-old, Brennan had his lip repair operation. His father and I were so sad that our little man would never look the same again. He was a healthy baby who we considered to be perfect in every way. As every parent whose child has had a cleft lip repaired will tell you, the last glimpse of his perfect little face was so hard. When we collected him from recovery, he was the mirror image of his older brother even though he'd looked nothing like him before. His father and I both commented that the resemblance was uncanny. After cradling my drowsy little man for perhaps an hour or so, his face suddenly changed. He looked like Brennan again; perfect little Brennan, just as he does today.

Our reading around cleft lips and palates, as well as our discussions with our paediatrician, surgeon, and CleftPALS Qld had left us very prepared for Brennan's operation. We knew what to expect, how the scar would look and heal, as well as how the surgeon wanted us to feed post operatively. We were not however, prepared for the things unrelated to Brennan's cleft which impacted on his recovery. For example, we were not prepared for him developing a stomach bug in hospital which left him diarrheal for days. Nor were we expecting to deal with pressure wounds and burns from monitors and his cannula, which he sustained as a result of miscommunication between nursing staff.

My own ignorance around the term 'tube feeding' also left me trying to convince the nurses that his distressed screaming every two hours was caused by hunger. The nursing staff used a textbook formula to calculate the amount of expressed breast milk to feed him every three hours. I pleaded with them to feed him a lesser amount every two hours, explaining his smaller more frequent feeds at home. Only one nurse during one very long night shift was able to be convinced. As a result, the three and a half days that Brennan was tube fed were a distressing time for us all. I had also been quite nervous about how Brennan would take to the breast after his repair, especially when I thought about how sore his mending lip would be. When he was finally allowed to have a regular feed, he attached perfectly, fed with gusto, and has never looked back. The poor kid was probably so relieved!

At around the time of Brennan's routine four-month Heath Assessment, it became obvious that he was not turning his head to sounds, including my voice, or startling to loud noises (He had passed his hearing screen at birth). When this was confirmed by our doctor, she explained that in very rare instances, some antibiotics administered post-operatively can cause damage to the cochlea. We did not know of this possible complication. Although, it would not have altered our decision to have his cleft repaired, this was another example of a non-cleft hurdle that we were not expecting. We had further hearing tests completed, but the results were inconclusive so he will need to be re-tested in several months. My mothers' instinct tells me that his hearing is improving, but time will tell.

As we'd anticipated from very early on, the most challenging aspect of our journey has been dealing with other's comments and reactions, including those of family members. That said, fewer people commented on Brennan's cleft than we expected prior to his birth. When I was pregnant, I'd been given the advice to react to other's comments by trying to be as informative as the situation allowed. And that is what I did. Most people were fascinated but also taken aback by my calm, matter-of-fact manner.

One uncomfortable situation with a stranger that I found myself in was at the chemist in the days leading up to his operation. I asked to buy Baby Panadol, explaining that I wanted to have some handy following Brennan's repair. I had Brennan in a sling, sleeping and snuggled into my chest, carrying him as I had my other boys as babies. The well intentioned assistant reassured me that a cleft lip was nothing to be ashamed of and that I shouldn't hide him away from the world. It had been a long day and my other boys were cranky. Although, I should've defended myself by saying that nothing could've been further from the truth, I just nodded, leaving with the Panadol and a burning sense of indignation.

We do not see Brennan as being different to other children and certainly not to his brothers. Brennan's cleft has been repaired and we anticipate that he will need future orthodontic work. We now see his cleft as an obstacle that he started life with, has successfully overcome, and will always have behind him as he looks forward towards new challenges and adventures. Although, he started his life with a cleft lip, he is not defined by it. He has startling blue eyes, a mischievous grin and what I'm sure is a devilish predisposition for harassing his brothers lurking beneath his mellow demeanour. He is perfect. I have always known how much I would love Brennan, long before I ever saw him. Everything else, his brothers and he will teach me. Mary Haskell's quote sums it up, "Nothing you become will disappoint me; I have no preconception that I'd like to see you be or do. I have no desire to foresee you only to discover you. You can't disappoint me."

I Wish I'd Known... how much the people who look at him and only see his lip would be missing out on.

Hannah

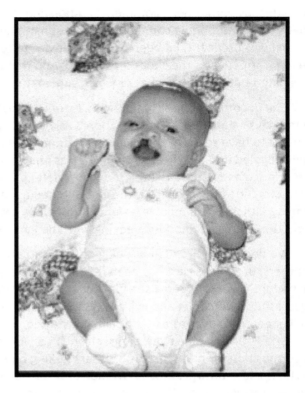

Country: United States of America
Type of Cleft: Complete Unilateral Cleft Lip and Palate
Birthdate: June 7, 2003
Cleft Team: New Mexico Cleft Palate Center
Found Out About Cleft: At Birth
Surgery Dates: September 2003 (Lip repair and ear tubes), March 2004 (Palate repair and ear tubes), October 2010 (Bone graft from hip to gum line), numerous other palate and ear surgeries.
Family History of Clefts: No

Our story can be summed up easily; sometimes the things that we struggle with the most are the very things that later become our biggest strengths.

The world was blessed with Hannah Elaine on June 7, 2003. Hannah was born resilient, happy, incredibly beautiful, and stubborn. She was born two weeks late. Although, we had undergone six ultrasounds throughout my pregnancy, we didn't know she had a complete unilateral cleft lip and palate. Except for feeding complications, Hannah had no other problems or birth defects.

Hannah couldn't suck properly at birth, so she was given a feeding tube in order to be nourished. Little Hannah was stubborn about this feeding tube and pulled it out. Some babies have very good fine motor skills! We spent her first nine days of life trying to get her to swallow more calories than she was used to swallowing. We worked with several feeding specialists provided through the hospital. This has proved to be the biggest challenge of her birth defect. Eventually, through rhythmically dripping milk into her mouth using a modified nipple (and lots of prayer), Hannah was able to slowly start gaining weight and we were able to bring her home.

The next year of Hannah's life was packed full of appointments, surgeries, and meetings regarding her care. Our extraordinary team led by Dr. Cuadros, Dr. Candelaria, and Dr. Horn, repaired her lip and her palate in the first year. They also inserted ear tubes several times in that first year. Hannah proved to be super strong throughout all of this and taught us lessons in trusting others. In that first year, we learned to lean on others for help and to trust our doctors.

The next eight years brought more surgeries, speech therapy, and braces. In each step of the process, Hannah continued to be resilient and exceeded the expectations of all those around us. As a young lady about to turn 10-years-old, she has crystal clear speech, a beautiful smile, and the singing voice of an angel. Academically, she is in the top of her class and she has a very bright future to look forward to. She thrives in musical theater, dance, and piano playing. She loves writing plays, boogie boarding in the ocean, reading, and training our dog. She has lots of friends and is confident in the brilliant, beautiful, and talented person that she is.

We are very thankful to God every day that we get to be her parents. It is a privilege. Hannah's journey has led her to miraculous strength and extraordinary abilities. She is a gift to this world and it is a much brighter place with her in it. The struggles in Hannah's life are the very things that have shaped her into a confident young lady. Sometimes, the ironic things in life are also the most amazing parts of the journey. We have learned to trust ourselves, our medical team, and to lean on others around us. Hannah is stronger than I have ever imagined and she has a bright future with lots of happiness ahead of her!

I Wish I'd Known... that children are resilient beyond words and that we should always trust our medical teams and our own intuition.

Dear Pregnant Mom,

It is hard. Go ahead and resent everything. Mourn the loss of having a "normal" baby. You will go to more doctors' appointments than you ever have in your whole life, all within your baby's first month. Then, look around at the other babies and you'll realize that there is no "normal."

All babies have their struggles. Stick with your gut feeling and question the doctors on anything you think sounds strange. They are there to help you, so make sure you understand everything. Enjoy those little moments; the ones that make you smile and laugh, even when they include unusual noises or faces from your little one.

Surgery will happen faster than you realize and that beautiful wide smile will be gone. So, take in that smile and face while you have a chance because it will soon change and all you will have is pictures as proof of that face you originally fell in love with. And yes, you truly will miss it.

Wishing you strength as you persevere.

Missing the Cleft

" I went from mourning the loss of the 'perfect' baby to

mourning the loss of his beautiful cleft that I loved to kiss. "

Kaeden

Country: Canada
Type of Cleft: Incomplete Unilateral Cleft Lip with Notched Alveolar Ridge
Birthdate: July 7, 2011
Cleft Team: Winnipeg Children's Hospital; Dr. Ross, MD
Found Out About Cleft: At Birth
Cleft Device: Post-op Nasal Stents
Surgery Date: November 2, 2011
Family History of Clefts: No

Pregnancy was a breeze for me. I loved it. There were no red flags that came up at my routine ultrasound. I was feeling good and baby was feeling good too.

On a late summer night, my husband and I were on our way back home from visiting my parent's house, which happens to be near the hospital where we decided to have our baby and two and a half hours from our own house. The plan was to go home one last time to do any last minute preparations for the baby.

Along the way, our car broke down. We watched the sunset together as we waited for the tow truck to arrive. Little did we know, that would be our last sunset before adding another member to our family. After a long ordeal, we arrived home at 11:30 p.m. and a few minutes later I realized my water broke! I quickly contacted a local hospital as well as the hospital where we planned to have our baby. They both said not to worry; the decision of where to go was up to us. Luckily, I had my hospital bag packed and ready to go. We quickly switched all our packed items to our other (working) car, grabbed the hospital bag, car seat, and headed on the two and a half hour trip to the hospital.

Kaeden was born three and a half weeks early. He lay on my chest and I was overwhelmed. I hadn't seen his face yet and soon the doctor took him away and asked the nurse, "Did we know about this?" I tried to stay calm and they quickly explained that our sweet baby boy was born with a cleft lip. I didn't really know what a cleft was at that point and had never seen anyone with a cleft before. During the next 24 hours, I mourned the loss of what I thought was the 'perfect' baby.

During pregnancy, I had this sense like God was telling me our baby was going to be beautiful. I even told my husband, "Our baby is going to be beautiful, I just know it." I didn't realize then what true beauty was. Beauty is not defined by what society deems "perfect." Now, I see that his uniqueness is beautiful and his cleft is exquisite. I wish I had known that then.

I shared a room with another new mom who received many visitors commenting on how absolutely perfect and adorable her baby boy was. People would tell the parents, "Seriously, this is the cutest baby I've ever seen." When people would mention to me how cute Kaeden was, I thought to myself, "Sure, they're just trying to be nice." I loved Kaeden from even before he was born, but for me, the bond took a couple days.

It was day two at the hospital when I was holding Kaeden and he looked into my eyes. Instantly all my worries, anxieties, and fears washed away. In that moment, the peace of God flooded my heart. I burst into tears and had to put him down so I could compose myself. He WAS perfect. He IS perfect. He was created in the image of God. God doesn't make mistakes.

We were in the hospital five days before we were allowed to leave. I was more than ready to leave. I was going a bit stir crazy walking the hall up and down and looking out the window at the people walking around outside. On our way back home I broke down; I cried and cried. I was overwhelmed by being thrown back into all of life's complications, leaving the support of the hospital, and having a precious child to protect. It was a tough day and I was incredibly happy to finally arrive home.

According to the experts and lactation consultants, we should have been able to get breastfeeding to work. We spent many hours trying with tears, frustration, and no luck. It took a good three months of switching from bottle to bottle and attempting breastfeeding in order to find something that worked. We ended up using MAM bottles and MAM soothers.

November 2, 2011, we headed to the hospital early in the morning for Kaeden's first surgery. He was being such a good boy. I'm so glad he was so sleepy because it had been a long time since he had eaten. He was sleeping right up until we handed him off for surgery. During the long two and a half hours of surgery, we tried to get our minds off of what was really going on.

When I got to the recovery room, there was some blood on the sheet. Like never before, my baby was crying in a raspy, weak, little voice. It was heartbreaking as we tried to calm our swollen and bruised baby boy in recovery. I felt so helpless. I didn't know what to do. I carefully picked him up and started rocking him just the way he liked. He wouldn't let me stop; any slowing down in the rocking and he would start fussing again. My first thoughts were, "Why did I put you through this? What have I done? I'm so sorry."

The first night was the worst. I was alone in the hospital caring for Kaeden. He did not want to be put down and he did not want the rocking to stop. I was bouncing on an exercise ball to help me in the rocking, but I was nodding off while holding him. I called the nurses for help, but no one was available to spare their time. I was terrified of collapsing of exhaustion and dropping my poor baby. We eventually made it through the night. That whole night, I had a total of no more than one hour of sleep spread out in five to 10 minute periods.

It was frustrating trying to get him to eat in a new way that he wasn't used to and trying to get him to sleep in a hospital full of noise. I felt like we were force-feeding him as he was learning to eat by syringe. During the first couple of days, he would just cry as we tried to feed him. But, it didn't take long at all and he recovered quickly. He was smiling and talking the morning after the surgery. By a week and a half he was back to his old self, but with a new smile.

When I think of it, the time these cleft children spend in surgery and recovery, is minuscule in comparison to the grand scheme of things. As trying as it was to go through the struggles of feeding and surgery, I would do it all over again because I love him so much. I don't remember the difficulties that well; it's the rewards of the journey that sticks with me. The blessings and joy of a child outweighs the struggles of the journey by far!

Kaeden will be seven this year. I literally feel ill when I think about him having to have a bone graft at the end of the summer. At two and a half years old, he was diagnosed with ADHD. It has affected every aspect of his life. These past five years of no surgery have been more stressful than his first year of life. He has a meltdown when he gets a hangnail or a stuffy nose – how is he going to manage a bone graft? It's hard to be that strong, steady support that he needs all the time. Still, we press on and hope and pray for the best.

People don't notice his scar, instead, he gets many comments about his beautiful eyes and long dark eyelashes. One person told us that he has "prophetic eyes." I like to think that he does too. His beauty goes beyond any outward appearance; it's deep in his spirit where his beauty shines the brightest.

As I think back now, I'm glad Kaeden's cleft was a surprise. This way, I didn't have much time to mourn that "perfect" baby. I was simply thrust into the joy of the parenting journey. I went from mourning the loss of the "perfect" baby to mourning the loss of his beautiful cleft that I loved to kiss. I wish I could see that wide smile again; having been captured forever in photographs; it's just not the same. His face has changed, but he has stayed the same happy, friendly, adorable, loveable, cuddly baby that loves to make people smile and whom I love to love.

I Wish I'd Known... to get professional photos done before lip surgery to capture that beautiful wide smile forever.

Bryson

Country: United States of America
Type of Cleft: Unilateral Cleft Lip
Birthdate: July 12, 2010
Cleft Team: Greenville Hospital System
(GHS) University Medical Group;
Dr. de Brux Jr., MD
Found Out About Cleft: At Birth
Surgery Date: January 3, 2011
Family History of Clefts: No

In November of 2009, I went to the doctor for strep throat and was told that I was pregnant. I was devastated. I had had a miscarriage in July and was already having signs of a miscarriage at this point. Thankfully, after numerous tests and ultrasounds, everything was just fine!

In February, we found out that we were having a baby boy. My husband was ecstatic! I had another ultrasound at 20-weeks that showed our sweet boy was still doing just fine.

Around 33-weeks, we went to have a 3-D ultrasound for fun and to see who our little guy looked like. He was my husband's twin. One of the first things I noticed though, was that his face looked different. Before I realized it, I blurted out, "He has a hare lip!" I was 19-years-old and clueless as to what a cleft lip was. The ultrasound tech said that it was just the umbilical cord and that there was no need to worry. At the same time, my husband told me, "Shut up! There is nothing wrong with him!" It kept popping up from different angles and I would point it out every time I saw it. Again, the tech reassured me that it was nothing and if she saw anything, she would tell me that I needed to speak with my doctor. We left there happy parents and excited to meet our cute little boy in just a few short weeks!

I was admitted into the hospital to be induced on July 11th. By 12 p.m. on July 12th I was fully dilated, but this stubborn little boy wasn't moving. I was rushed to the operating room and had an emergency C-section. At 2:07 p.m., Bryson was born! The doctor held him up and all I could see was his cleft. I started yelling, "What is wrong with my baby?" He was blue and wasn't crying! My husband, who had only seen the non-affected side, kept reassuring me everything was okay and that the doctors were working with him. I tried to tell him that something was wrong with his face, but he wouldn't listen to me. Finally, my doctor told me, "It's just a cleft lip. It's cosmetic and nothing to worry about. It can be repaired." After 10 and a half long minutes my baby was crying. It was the sweetest sound that I had ever heard. The nurse laid him on my chest and I kept telling him how much I loved him. I no longer saw the cleft. He was perfect. He had a unilateral cleft lip and notch of the gum line.

I had planned to nurse before he was born and nothing was going to stop me. At first, he didn't want to latch on and the nurse kept telling me that it would be okay to give him a break. He had a long day and would eat when he was hungry. Shortly after, we tried again and it was a success. He nursed for over an hour. He kept gaining weight like the doctors wanted and we got to go home when he was four days old.

On January 3rd, I walked my five-month-old down the hall to the operating room and handed him off to two ladies that I didn't know. I trusted them to assist Dr. de Brux with my precious baby's surgery and life. The four hour wait in the waiting room was the longest time in my life. I didn't leave once. I sat there waiting very impatiently for the nurses to come get my husband and myself to see our baby. When we finally saw him, I didn't recognize him. He looked so different. This wasn't what I had expected. The face that I loved so much was gone and had been replaced with something that society would accept. I tried to nurse him in the recovery room, but he wouldn't latch on. He was crying. I was crying. We were both clueless as to what was going on. They decided to admit him until he could eat. After a dose of Tylenol, he was eating like a champ. We were discharged later that night.

He is now two-years-old. We haven't had any more surgeries and we shouldn't have to have any more until he is a teen. We are proud of his cleft and wouldn't have him any other way!

I Wish I'd Known... how much I'd miss his wide smile after it was gone.

168

Owen

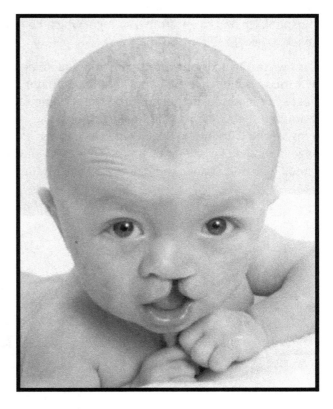

Country: United States of America
Type of Cleft: Complete Unilateral Cleft Lip and Palate
Birthdate: September 17, 2012
Cleft Team: Dartmouth Hitchcock Medical Center
Found Out About Cleft: 5-Month Ultrasound
Cleft Device: NAM
Surgery Date: January 23, 2013 (Lip repair)
Family History of Clefts: No

We found out that our baby was going to have a cleft lip at our five-month ultrasound. I was devastated. I barely made it out of the office, only to break down crying in the parking lot. My husband was so relaxed. He has never been worried or upset throughout this whole process. "They fix them in tents in Africa," he said, "we'll be fine."

I'm a researcher. When I get my mind set on something, I will research it to death. I threw myself into cleft research. I ordered pamphlets, videos, and read other mom's stories online. I also contacted the hospital's cleft team and set up an appointment to meet with them. Eventually, I knew so much that I was going around educating everyone around me.

When Owen was born, I didn't even care about his cleft. He was the most beautiful thing I had ever seen. We instantly fell in love with our little man. My main concern was feeding. I had previously purchased a Haberman feeder and brought that to the hospital. Owen took to the bottle right away. I did try to breast feed, but he could not latch on or form any suction because of his cleft palate. We took Owen home two days later.

At six weeks, he was fitted for his NAM device. At its widest part, the gap in Owen's palate measured 14 mm. Every week, we would drive one hour to have the NAM adjusted. It was a difficult process due to the taping. Owen did get a sore early on, but it healed quickly. Throughout his treatment, Owen's gap moved from 14 mm to three mm. We could have lasted until zero mm, but he stopped tolerating the NAM at four-months-old and would rip it out.

Two weeks after we stopped using the NAM device, we had his lip repair. I dreaded this day. I loved his wide smile and didn't want it to go away. We took him to get professional pictures a week before and I'm so happy we did. On the way to the hospital, every bone in my body wanted to turn the car around and drive away so that I could keep our baby's wide smile forever. Still, we went through with it. I expected him to look so different after surgery, but he didn't. He looked like the same beautiful little boy. Owen spent one night in the hospital. He had to eat from a syringe, which he hated. He was in pain and was cranky, but back to his old self in about a week.

As I write, Owen is one month post-op and doing great. I live to see him change and grow. I miss his old smile every day, but know that it is for his own good. He will have his palate repair in approximately five months. People say things about how great he looks and how amazed they are about his healing. I know they mean well but, to me, there was nothing wrong with him to begin with. He was just as beautiful before. Owen is the strongest person I know and he amazes me every day. He is a smiley, loving, precious little boy and I wouldn't change the journey we are on together for anything.

I Wish I'd Known... how much I would miss his wide smile.

Bryce

Country: United States of America
Type of Cleft: Bilateral Cleft Lip and Palate
Birthdate: November 8, 2011
Cleft Team: Texas Children's Hospital
Found Out About Cleft: After 20-Week Ultrasound
Surgery Dates: April 5, 2012 (Lip repair), August 23, 2012 (Palate repair)
Family History of Clefts: Yes

Being pregnant and finding out your baby would be born into a life of surgeries was hard. Yet, it was not as hard as looking for your baby after his lip repair and not recognizing him when his wide smile had been transformed. I miss his wide smile every day. Sometimes, I look back at old pictures and cry seeing how far he has come in such a small amount of time.

I would never wish the agony of seeing Bryce in pain after surgery on anyone else. But then, I'm so in love with the person he is that I would never ask for anything different. Being a mommy of a cleft affected baby has taught me more about myself than anything before the day he was born.

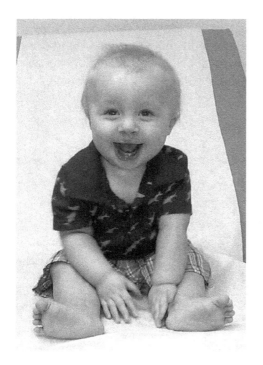

Sometimes, I wish I wouldn't have known about the cleft before he was born because I worried so much while I was pregnant. Learning and being prepared consumed the latter part of my pregnancy and I wish I had enjoyed it more instead of worrying for no reason. I just loved him and his smile so much and so fast. Both surgeries were hard, but they went by fast.

I've never met anyone stronger than my little man. I cried more than he did! Now, Bryce is 14-months-old and the happiest baby I've ever laid eyes on. He loves to crawl and play with his big brothers and is in the 90th percentile for weight at his age.

I Wish I'd Known...
how much I would miss your
cleft when it was gone.

Dear Pregnant Mom,

I went on a roller coaster of emotions during my pregnancy, but once my baby was here, I knew everything was okay and all my worries were gone. Once you see your child for the first time, you realize that nothing else in the world matters and you can get through anything.

There will be difficult days, but it is nothing you can't handle. We are not given circumstances in which we cannot handle. Enjoy loving your baby, take lots of pictures and videos, share your story, and raise your baby like any other. Our cleft babies were God's plan and our purpose.

It really is not as bad as you think it will be. You still get the same joyful giggles that make your knees weak, the same sweet snuggles you look forward to everyday, and the same precious little hands that grasp your finger. Don't worry; it all works out. I worried too much and it was for nothing. We would still be in the same place today had I not worried and I would have enjoyed much more of the road we took to get here.

From a mom who has been there.

All that Worry for Nothing

"
I wasted so much time worrying for nothing. I wish I could

get it all back. I was so disappointed for nothing."

Nikolai

Country: United States of America
Type of Cleft: Cleft of the Soft Palate
Birthdate: January 16, 2012
Cleft Team: Dr. Munson out of Sioux Falls, SD; then Dr. Allen at Childrens in Denver CO
Found Out About Cleft: At Birth
Surgery Date: November 13, 2012
Family History of Clefts: No

My first daughter was born when I was just 15. She had extensive health problems. Finally, at nine months it was confirmed that she had a rare disorder in which she did not produce hormones. The next four years were spent in and out of the hospital. I had an amazing family that was a godsend and helped with everything. She is now 19-years-old and aside for replacement hormones, a healthy young adult.

When she was 13, I met the man of my dreams and we got pregnant, not planned, but we were ok with it. At my 20-week ultrasound, they found a tumor on her (yes, another girl) tail bone. Born on Valentine's Day at 32 weeks, she was in great health aside from the tumor and only being four pounds. At two weeks, they took her into surgery and removed the tumor. She went home a week later and is now a healthy five-year-old.

After our first two princesses, we had talked about more kids. I consulted with the doctor and they could not guarantee me a healthy baby, but they did not see any reason why I would not have one. So, we started trying and got pregnant within a few months.

We had the big ultrasound at 20-weeks and the doctor was there just to make sure everything was good. They told me it was a boy and all the organs looked good. He looked like he was healthy and right on track. I got one front face 3-D picture and every time I looked at I thought, "Wow, he looks like he has a cleft lip." The doctor said it was just the way the picture was and that his lip was fine.

We had planned an early C-section at 37-weeks due to a previous C-section I had. Nikolai was six pounds, two ounces and 17 inches long. I heard him cry, got to kiss him, and see his sweet face. I was sad that I would not get to hold him right away, but told Daddy he was to go with him to the nursery and stay with him till he could bring him to me. The nurse and Daddy brought Nikolai to the nursery while I was stitched up and sent back to my room.

It finally happened, I thought. I had a healthy baby who would get to nurse and come right home with me. I was in heaven on cloud nine and could not wait for Him to be brought to me so I could hold and snuggle him. Now, my husband is not the most medically knowledgeable guy, bless his heart. He came into my room a few minutes after I got in there and I asked, "Where's the baby? Why did you leave him?" He said, still beaming with a smile, "The pediatrician is looking at him. She said something about a cleft palate. I am not real sure." I freaked out and replied, "What? What do you mean? You go back in there and find out what is going on and do not come back till you know!" My nurse got involved and said she would find out and just sit tight. The nurse came back and did inform me that he did have a soft cleft palate and the pediatrician would be in shortly to talk with us.

I was heartbroken and distraught by the news. He was supposed to be my perfect healthy baby with no problems and here we go again. My pediatrician came in to a crying mess of me to tell me, "This is not a big deal." She has been my pediatrician for 19 years and knows my history. She told me, "You can do this! This is cake compared to what you have overcome with your girls." I bucked up and thought, "She is right. He is healthy and perfect; can't nurse, but I pumped breast milk with my girls, so I can do it for him too. Plus, he gets to come home with me!"

Nikolai had trouble gaining weight and getting him to eat a lot. It took us about six weeks to get it down with the help of our occupational therapist, who came once a week. She was wonderful. It has all worked out just like our doctor said it would.

I spent so much of the first seven months worrying if there could be something else wrong, that I was miserable. I eventually just had to let it all go and have been so happy ever since.

Nikolai is now almost 10-months-old, crawling all over the place and getting into everything. He sleeps through the entire night and is the sweetest little thing. I wasted so much time worrying for nothing. I wish I could get it all back. I was so disappointed for nothing. I had hopes for a healthy baby and he is. I know there will be bumps in the road,

but you get that with every baby. I hope any moms out there who get a birthday surprise the same as mine don't make the mistake of all the worrying I did. Enjoy that baby! Whether cleft lip, cleft palate or both; those wide smiles are the best. You can't help but love them.

I Wish I'd Known...
how things worked out just as
my doctor said they would. I
did not need to worry.

Bailey

Country: United States of America
Type of Cleft: Right Unilateral Cleft Lip and Palate
Birthdate: February 19, 2010
Cleft Team: Boy's Town National Research Hospital
Found Out About Cleft: 24-Week Ultrasound
Surgery Dates: May 2010 (Lip repair), November 2010 (Palate repair)
Family History of Clefts: No

I was heartsick when I learned of your cleft. I felt like the joy and excitement of pregnancy were shrinking away before my very own eyes, right there in the ultrasound room. Your father was there with me. He had a different experience. While he didn't cry the tears I cried, he worried too. He worried silently right alongside me. As the weeks went by, I slowly stopped crying whenever I thought of your cleft. I researched. I prepared.

When you came into the world, I thought I was prepared. I wasn't. Nothing could have prepared me for how much I would love you. The next day as I was holding you and

stroking your cheek, I said to your daddy, "Her eyes are so beautiful." He replied, "I know. I knew they would be." When I looked at him for an explanation, he simply said, "I prayed to God that He would give her beautiful eyes so that people would notice them first."

In the coming weeks, strangers would stop me in stores and on the street to tell me how beautiful your eyes were. People still tell us that to this day. Every time I hear it, it makes me smile. Yes, our girl, you truly are beautiful.

I Wish I'd Known... how little the cleft would truly matter

Beckham

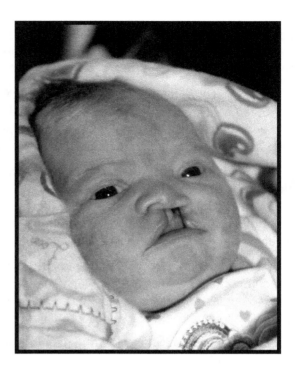

Country: Canada
Type of Cleft: Unilateral Cleft Lip and Palate
Birthdate: February 14, 2012
Cleft Team: Winnipeg Children's Hospital; Dr. Ross, MD
Found Out About Cleft: 24-Week Ultrasound
Cleft Device: DynaCleft
Surgery Date: May 30, 2012 (Lip repair), January 30, 2013 (Palate repair)
Family History of Clefts: Yes

I was born in 1981 with a cleft lip and soft palate cleft. Therefore, we have screened each of my pregnancies for clefts. I have to admit, I was feeling a little bit cocky about it since we already had two perfectly healthy and "normal" babies.

When I was 20-weeks along, my initial ultrasound indicated a potential cleft. We were then referred to a different city to confirm. A few weeks passed between ultrasounds. My husband and I went through a roller coaster of emotions and I was feeling conflicted and having a really tough time. Part of me was sad for her, worried about how she would look, worried what people would say, and sad for what we would have to watch her go through. Another part of me felt guilty for feeling those things because I was born with the same thing and to be upset about her cleft, somehow, was insulting to myself.

When we went to the ultrasound, we left the older two at home with Nana and Grampa. I was so nervous as I lay on the table. I thought I was going to vomit and when the technician casually said, "Yep, there it is," tears streamed down my face. I couldn't control it. I guess I had been holding out hope that it wasn't really there, but we could see it on the ultrasound. We knew for sure it was the lip but they couldn't see the palate. The emotions of the last few weeks built up to that moment. As we left the appointment, I was filled with an intense sense of relief. We now knew it was there. It was just a matter of dealing with it.

The next few weeks were time for us to gather information. I had lots of talks with my mom about what she went through when I was a baby. I had big long conversations with Cindy, the nurse clinician at our craniofacial program. Cindy very patiently explained what the process would be, when surgeries would be, and what each surgery would involve.

Leading up to the confirming ultrasound, we hadn't told anybody that the cleft was suspected. Afterward, we informed our family and closest friends via mass email. I wanted to make sure that all of our closest family and friends heard about it from us and also that they got the correct information. I was worried details would get mixed up as the story was told from one person to another. I felt that it was important to pre-inform everybody about the cleft because when she was born we wanted to focus on the joy of the baby and not have to explain the cleft over and over. I am really glad that we wrote that letter. It allowed the people around us to prepare themselves and when Beckham was born, we were able to fully celebrate her arrival.

I also feel grateful that I was born with a cleft because I had a frame of reference for her outcome. I knew she could be happy and healthy. She could go to school, have friends and be physically active. I think that this entire process would have been a whole lot scarier and more uncertain had I not gone through the same thing.

I thought the doctor had said that, generally, in cases where the mother also had a cleft, the baby's cleft tends to be equal or not as worse than the mother's. My husband interpreted what the doctor said differently, though. I was really hanging onto the hope that it would be equal or better than mine. The biggest thing that I was hoping for was to be able to nurse. My mom successfully nursed me and I really wanted the same.

At 12:17 a.m. on Valentine's Day in 2012, Beckham came into this world. When they lay her on my chest my first thought was, "That's way worse than mine." Through the night, I tried to nurse at the beginning of each feeding, but it was clear that she was not latching and I didn't want her to starve because I was being stubborn.

Early the next morning when the pediatrician checked on us, he explained that she had a complete left cleft which means it affected her nose, lip, gums, hard palate, soft palate, and uvula. Basically, it ran front to back on the left side and there was probably no hope of nursing because she didn't have the ability to suck. However, she took to the special bottles and ate very well right away. I was worried that if I couldn't nurse I would somehow miss out on that special time and bond with my baby, but there was a knack to using those bottles. For the first little while I was the only one who would feed her, so it was still our special time and I felt completely bonded with her.

When I look at her, I see a beautiful face on a sweet girl who has a full life ahead of her. I am thankful that she can grow up to be an intelligent, educated, and kind woman who doesn't have any limitations on what she can experience in her life.

I Wish I'd Known...
that I didn't need to worry so much because everything turned out all right.

Haley

Country: United States of America
Type of Cleft: Bilateral Cleft Lip and Palate
Birthdate: December 14, 2011
Cleft Team: Children's Hospital Los Angeles
Found Out About Cleft: 32-Week Ultrasound
Cleft Device: NAM
Surgery Dates: April 9, 2012 (Lip repair), October 26, 2012 (Palate repair)
Family History of Clefts: No

When I first found out about my daughter having a cleft lip and palate, like many moms, I was very scared and confused. My doctor suspected a cleft lip and possible palate involvement at the 32-week ultrasound. I was referred to a perinatal specialist. My doctor gave me a hug and said, "Plastic surgery does a great job these days. It doesn't necessarily mean other problems if it's an isolated cleft. Let's hope for the best."

I didn't know much about it at that time and felt momentarily numb. As it sank in, I cried and cried for days. The perinatologist confirmed the diagnosis as well as a single umbilical artery, which added to the possibility of chromosomal abnormalities. He said it looked severe, but that it can sometimes look worse than it actually seems. He recommended that I do an amniocentesis. However, I refused given that I was far along in the pregnancy and feared that I would miscarry and lose my precious little girl.

My entire pregnancy was going smoothly up until that point. From then on, I was stressed and worried every day. As I did my research and tried to educate myself, I found a cleft lip and palate forum on BabyCenter.com. I would have been lost without this group. I grew stronger each day with the support of other moms who have been through this. I remember being really excited about my first born, yet terrified of the unknown. I prayed and prayed every minute of the day that God would give me a healthy baby.

My daughter, Haley Francesca, was born on December 14, 2011 at 39 weeks and four days. She came in weighing six pounds and 12 ounces with a bilateral cleft lip and palate. She was the most beautiful little angel I had ever seen. After running many tests throughout our four day hospital stay, I was told that Haley appeared to be healthy and with no chromosomal abnormality. My prayers were answered! I wish I had known not to stress too much for the last couple of weeks. In our eyes, she was born perfect in every way.

We found an amazing cleft team at Children's Hospital Los Angeles. Both of her surgeries (lip and palate repairs) during her first year of life went smoothly with no complications. She has the most beautiful smile!

As I write this story, Haley is now a 14-month-old toddler and is our biggest joy and blessing. She is active, smart, funny, and loves to give us kisses. She is such a sweet girl. We embrace each moment with her and know that we have been given a precious gift. We have been wonderfully blessed to have been chosen to be her parents. Our journey and challenges together as a family has taught us the power of patience, acceptance, gratitude, and love. Our love for her grows more and more each and every day!

I Wish I'd Known... not to stress too much.

Oliver

Country: Canada
Type of Cleft: Incomplete Unilateral Cleft Lip and Bilateral Cleft Palate
Birthdate: November 16, 2012
Cleft Team: McMaster University Cleft Lip & Palate Team
Found Out About Cleft: Elective Ultrasound at 28 Weeks
Cleft Device: Cleft Tape
Surgery Date: February 7, 2013 (Lip repair)
Family History of Clefts: No

Photo by Meg Gallina

We were unbelievably excited about Oliver's arrival and when I was 28 weeks pregnant, we went to see his beautiful face at an entertainment 3-D ultrasound. We did not realize that day would take us on a new path and a new journey with him. A week after we saw his beautiful smile in the 3-D video, we confirmed that he indeed had a cleft lip. The doctors could not confirm any palate involvement until birth. As first time parents with no history of cleft lip and palate on either side, we were shocked. Overall, though, I think we handled it well.

Over the next few weeks, we prepared for Oliver's arrival and had some emotional ups and downs. We were never worried or concerned about what he would look like or what people would say. Our only concern and heartache was for what he would have to endure at such a young age.

Oliver made his grand appearance on November 16, 2012 at 7:34 p.m. We had never felt a love so strong and so pure. The minute we saw him, nothing else mattered. All we saw was our beautiful son and we didn't even see the cleft lip. The doctors were talking, but we weren't listening. All we wanted was to hold him and never give him up. Oliver learned to eat pretty much right away from the Haberman Special Needs bottle and we were released after a few days.

As we settled in our home as a new happy family, we soon realized that Oliver was pretty much like every other baby and, my goodness, he was happy all the time. We will never forget the first time he smiled his gorgeous wide smile and, little did we know, that would be the first of many flirty little smiles to everyone who looked his way.

When Oliver was two and a half months, he was scheduled for his lip repair surgery. A week before surgery, we started stressing out about what to expect. Our biggest concern was how Oliver was going to survive without his beloved 'chooch' (a.k.a. soother). Again, it never crossed our minds about what he would look like. We adored him and were actually going to miss his smile. The morning of surgery, I was a basket case. When we had to hand Oliver over to the surgeon, I cried and cried. I wished I could change places with him. We then waited for the longest two and a half hours of our lives for the surgeon to come out and tell us what we already knew, Oliver was amazing. Just as others said, the surgery was harder on us as parents than it was on Oliver.

The next 24 hours of recovery were tough but by all means, not unbearable. The hospital staff was amazing and the day after surgery Oliver was already flirting with his nurse and trying to smile. The next two weeks flew by and all the things we worried about again didn't seem to matter. Oliver got along with his arm restraints just fine. In fact, he didn't even care. He cried for his chooch a few nights, but nothing some extra cuddling couldn't cure. When we went for post-op and the surgeon gave the okay for his chooch back; Oliver was the happiest kid ever!

We have only started our cleft journey, but we have already learned so much. When we were pregnant, I didn't know anyone with the same issues (or so we thought), so I reached out online to find other parents going through the same thing. There was no local support group here, so we started one. We posted our trials and tribulations on Facebook and found numerous people we know had been going through the same thing and we didn't even realize.

I wish I'd known that all the advice other parents gave us would be exactly right. We look back now and wonder why we worried so much. As we are writing this, Oliver is sitting in his bouncy chair having a nap after filling his belly with milk from a regular bottle and cereal with a regular spoon. He is just like every other baby with a few differences. He is ours and he will be proud of who is and what he has already accomplished in his few months of life. That is what we focus on, not the cleft.

I Wish I'd Known... that all of the things we worried about when we found out about the cleft lip would never really matter.

Farah

Country: United States of America
Type of Cleft: Unilateral Cleft Lip and Bilateral Cleft Palate
Birthdate: February 7, 2011
Cleft Team: University of Virginia Hospital; Dr. Lin, MD
Found Out About Cleft: At Routine Ultrasound
Cleft Device: DynaCleft tape
Surgery Dates: April 9, 2011 (Lip revision), August 26, 2011 (Lip and nose repair), December 9, 2011 (Palate repair)
Family History of Clefts: No (Too far down the line to be considered genetic)

On October 8, 2010, we went for a routine ultrasound. The ultrasound tech told us some unexpected news. Our plans of blue were, in fact, going to be pink. Then, she asked us to wait in the lobby to speak with a doctor. Dr. Gary Helmbrect did a much more extensive ultrasound to reveal that our little girl would be born with a cleft lip. The exact type was unknown. Our baby girl was not keen on having her picture taken, so even after four months and several ultrasounds; no definite conclusion was ever met.

Our baby girl had trouble swallowing in utero, so I carried extra fluid and measured several weeks farther along. During the many ultrasounds over the remaining weeks of the pregnancy, she was measuring very large at an estimated 9.5 pounds for birth. Arm length was in the 90th percentile, head size in the 95th and the nurses all called her a "sumo wrestler." While everything measured quite large, her stomach continued to measure small due to her inability to swallow.

Due to her size, she was due to arrive via induced labor on her due date: February 7, 2011. Baby Girl took her entrance into her own tiny hands and I went into natural labor in the early morning hours of the 7th. Her heart rate was being closely monitored and could be seen dropping with every contraction. Her heart rate continued to plummet with every contraction and an emergency C-section was performed around 7:25 p.m. Farah Cerie arrived at 7:28 p.m. and was quickly examined by the nurses. It wasn't until nearly two hours later when Farah was finally delivered to my arms. The moment she arrived cannot be explained. She was beautiful and I had never loved anyone so fiercely.

Farah was born with a complete unilateral cleft lip and a bilateral cleft palate. She was 20 ¾ inches long and seven pounds, 12 ounces. She was born with a head full of thick blonde and brown hair. She was squishy in all the right places; the number of kisses placed on those chubby cheeks cannot be measured.

Breastfeeding was attempted but impossible due to Farah's inability to suck. Pumping with a hospital grade breast pump began the following day and Farah first ate by dribbling the milk into her mouth via spoon. Hours later, she was successfully using a Haberman feeder and, with assistance, increasing her intake from 10 ounces to 50 ounces within days. Farah lost only about two ounces and by her discharge date two days after she was born, she was already back to birth weight.

We met Dr. Lin with the University of Virginia a few weeks after Farah was born. He told us that Farah had a wide cleft, measuring over 14 mm. He suggested that we try DynaCleft tape to help draw her lip closer together with the hope to do an entire lip and nose repair in one surgery. Farah's cheeks quickly became raw from removing and replacing the tape each day. After some research, we purchased DuoDERM online, trimmed it to size, and put it on her skin before the DynaCleft tape. This dramatically cut down the chaffing and pain involved with the tape.

Farah loved her "Ollie" and even at only a few weeks old could grip his soft body in her hands. Ollie was her Wubbanub pacifier and her favorite possession for a long time.

Dr. Lin would be able to determine that day if she would need one or two surgeries to repair her lip and nose. At nine-weeks-old, Farah was admitted into the University of Virginia hospital for her first surgery. Early in the morning on April 9th, we were informed that surgery would involve a lip revision and a second surgery would occur later in the year for a full lip and nose repair.

After what felt like days, but was really only an hour and a half, we were called to the post-op recovery room. What we had not anticipated was the drastic change in how Farah looked. Her face was very swollen from the anesthesia and her wide smile was gone. Her nose was swollen; she was obviously uncomfortable and out of sorts. It was a very emotional moment for our little family. She spent the night in the Pediatric Acute Care Unit (PACU) and was released late the following morning.

Time passed quickly. She was reaching every milestone any other baby reaches. Before we knew it, her lip and nose repair had arrived on August 26, 2011. This surgery was a bit longer and more extensive. We were called to the post-op recovery room a few hours later and, once again, were greeted by a very swollen and upset baby girl. She was also expected to wear a nasal mold stitched in her nose until her final surgery in December.

This recovery period was much harder than the previous. Three weeks in No-no's was ordered during a very exploratory period for a baby. She was on the cusp of crawling, she loved to move, and she was always bouncing in her bouncer. After the prescribed three weeks and the No-no's came off, she was on the move and began crawling almost immediately.

October and November passed quickly. Her nasal mold began to irritate her in late November and was removed after she rubbed it, tearing out some of the stitches. Her final surgery for 2011 was scheduled for December ninth. Dr. Lin warned us that it would be one to three nights in the Pediatric Intensive Care Unit, followed by three to five nights in Pediatric Acute Care Unit.

Although it was Farah's third surgery, we still felt unprepared and very emotional. We were fully aware of how delicate the palate repair would be. It involved stretching her palate across the cleft and attaching it together with the hopes of no holes developing over time. The anesthesiologist took her into the operating room at 7:30 that morning. We were in for a very long wait. One of the nurses was in constant contact with us, letting us know everything that was happening in the operating room. She was even kind enough to take Farah's stuffed aardvark into the operating room. To this day, it still wears a hospital band around his foot.

Seeing Farah post-op from the first two surgeries wasn't easy, but was mild in comparison to this. Her face and lips were swollen beyond recognition and there was blood all over her lips and mouth. A thread was stitched through her tongue, coiled and taped to her outside cheek in case her tongue swelled and hampered her breathing. Worst of all, she sounded completely different. She was lying face down, asleep, in the hospital crib to allow any blood to drain into the sheets.

Surprisingly, Farah was much more coherent after this surgery when she woke. She was sitting in the crib, playing with toys, and dancing to SpongeBob on TV. Not three hours after surgery was complete, she attempted to smile. Blood, swelling, and thread aside, it was the most beautiful and heart wrenching smile we had ever seen. Farah was letting everyone know that it was going to be okay. Farah's night nurses were two incredible women. They took care of Farah with efficient and knowledgeable movements while being incredibly loving and gentle. They made us feel like she was their only patient.

That following morning, Farah had improved exponentially. After only one night in PICU, she was moved to PACU. It was a challenge keeping up with her. She wanted to play. She napped sporadically and ate very little. She was very unhappy about not using a bottle and was opposed to using a cup. Finally, we tried a Mead Johnson bottle and squeezed fluid into her mouth. It worked, but she lost interest quickly.

Farah spent much of the afternoon and evening in the hospital playroom. That night, Farah and I sat in the dark playroom overlooking our town twinkling with Christmas lights and snuggled while watching *Polar Express*. The next morning, Daddy arrived with the

nurse to tell us we were being discharged after only two nights. Everyone was very pleased with how quickly she was recovering.

As her doctor promised, by Farah's first birthday her wide smile was nothing but a cherished memory. Each day Farah reminds us how lucky we are. She smiles and frowns, giggles and shrieks, makes us proud, and drives us crazy. We wouldn't trade a day of this journey. Not only has she shown us how strong she is, but we found strength within ourselves. We learned that the scary things aren't so scary when you can tackle them together.

I Wish I'd Known...
not to worry so much! All of her smiles bring light into the world!

Thank God

"*God gave him to you because you can handle it.*"

Jesse

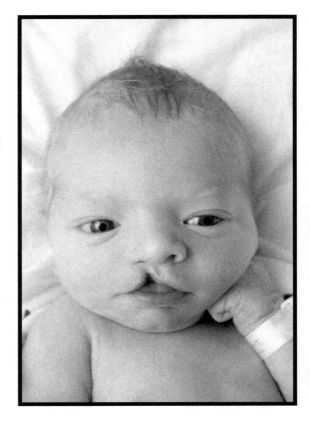

Country: United States of America
Type of Cleft: Unilateral Cleft Lip and Cleft of the Soft Palate
Birthdate: March 31, 2010
Cleft Team: Children's Facial Center at Edward Hospital
Found Out About Cleft: At Birth
Surgery Dates: June 30, 2010 (Lip and nose repair, ear tubes), February 16, 2011 (Soft palate repair)
Family History of Clefts: No

Jesse is my first and only child. When I got pregnant, I had a lot to learn. I was 34-years-old and certainly felt mature enough. I knew I had to start having kids before it got too late. I read my week-by-week pregnancy book. I visited the baby websites daily and signed up for the emails. I was very excited to start on this new adventure in life.

My pregnancy was totally normal, in fact, I enjoyed every second of it. I think, I was most at peace in my life when I was pregnant. I had a blood test done early in my pregnancy to check for things like Down Syndrome and Spina Bifida. Everything came back normal. All my ultrasounds and heartbeat checks were normal.

I was a little scared about the whole childbirth thing, but I told myself that millions of people give birth all the time since the beginning of time. I can do this, too. My husband and I got to the hospital bright and early for my induction. Labor and delivery was slow that day and most of the rooms were empty, so things got started right away. I was hooked up to the monitors, put on IV and they soon injected me with Pitocin. I finally delivered at 7:45 p.m.

They put him on my belly and my husband cut the cord. They took him to examine him, clean him off a little and take his measurements. I was so exhausted after 12 hours of labor and over two hours pushing. I am not really sure when I heard it, but during all this I heard the word "cleft" and "his palate is intact." I honestly didn't know what those things meant. I started getting worried. I started thinking something was terribly wrong. They finally handed him to me and I saw his face, I instantly put the pieces together. He had a cleft lip. I kept my emotions hidden, but I looked at him. He wasn't the child I was expecting. Honestly, I was devastated. I told myself, "Okay, you can handle this, it's just a little lip thing."

I spent some time with him and tried breastfeeding, but had no luck. A few hours later, the nurses took him away to be bathed, sent me to my room and told me he would be joining me within the hour. That hour came and went, and he hadn't come back. Almost two hours later a doctor came in. He informed us that our son not only had a cleft lip, but also a cleft soft palate as well as a heart murmur. He was in the NICU and we could see him in an hour. When I finally got to see him, I held him and just cried. I was in shock that my baby was in the NICU and that he wasn't "perfect." I don't think I even slept that night. I cried, a lot. The following morning was hard. I didn't have my baby there by my side.

Around 11 a.m. I was told he would be released from the NICU shortly and the heart murmur had healed itself. They brought him in and I was finally able to feed him myself. Soon, a social worker came in. She was also born with a cleft and she gave us a lot of information. My mind was more at ease after her visit because I was very uneducated about clefts. Later that day a plastic surgeon came to visit. She explained a little about clefts, her cleft team, and the surgeries involved. A weight was lifted after that and I was able to see my son's face in a whole new light. I knew it wasn't going to be easy, but at least I understood what we were facing.

The next day we were released and went home to start our new life as a family. I was much more relaxed. I was able to take deep breaths and I was finally able to sleep. We had some visitors in the first few days, one being my aunt. I will never forget what she told me, "God gave him to you because you can handle it." I will never forget those words. At first, I wasn't so sure I could handle it but looking back now, she was right.

The first few months he was alive I had a lot of fears, anxiety, guilt, and self-consciousness. I thought people would judge me, like I did something to cause this. I felt a lot of guilt because I really thought I did something to cause this. I still hadn't realized how common clefts were and I felt the need to explain it when people looked at him. I felt very alone. My husband didn't even understand what I was going through.

Feeding was challenging. Since he never nursed, I chose to pump. I knew he'd be having surgery and needed as many antibodies as possible, so I felt that breast milk was best for him. We did not use any special bottle. I just used a red preemie nipple with an X cut. He was eating, but it took a long time. He was burning a lot of calories just to replenish those calories used for eating. He had some weight gain, but it wasn't dangerously low. He was small but healthy. We kept a journal of his feedings so we would know how many ounces he consumed in a day. We could then share the information with his doctors.

At 6-weeks-old, we scheduled a surgery date for when he would be 3 months. All would go as planned, as long as he continued to gain weight. Aside from the eating issues, he had some minor breathing problems. He couldn't sleep on his back, or he would choke. He slept in his swing for the first few months, then found out he was able to sleep in his crib on a positioning wedge, on his side. I discovered this when I had him on the couch one day. I placed him on his side and he fell right to sleep, so I figured I'd give it a try in the crib that night. It worked wonders!

The time came for his first surgery. They would be repairing his lip, nose, and inserting ear tubes (He had fluid in his ears since shortly after birth). Needless-to-say, I was a wreck. A lot of fear and anxiety ran through me. I felt as if I was going crazy, but when he needed me to be his advocate, I was there for him. I was strong and did everything I needed to do. It wasn't easy watching him get taken away into surgery, but I knew it was best for him. I sat anxiously in the waiting room for the doctor to come out and tell me the surgery was a success and I could go see him. After a few long hours, I was able to go see him. I was so sad to see him in pain, but it was the start of a new beginning.

Within days, my little boy was smiling again, eating well, and getting back to his old happy self. At 4-months-old, he just did not seem satisfied with the formula (I had stopped pumping breast milk before surgery). I decided to let him try some cereal. He loved it from the beginning and started packing on the pounds. This is what he needed - real food. A few weeks later, he was eating pureed fruits, then vegetables.

By 8-months-old, he was not a little boy anymore. He was in the 90th percentile for his weight. He was eating all sorts of food, even table food. We did have some challenges, like sneezing because food would get up into his nasal cavity. Then, of course, it would come out his nose which could not have been a pleasant experience. But, he managed to get through it. I think it was because a full belly was worth it.

When it came time for his soft palate surgery at 10-months-old, there was no doubt he'd be healthy enough. Of course, I had the anxiety and fear just like the first surgery. When it came down to it, I was strong like I needed to be for him and for myself. Recovery was much harder and longer this time around but once again, we managed to get through it. After the worst part of recovery was over, things changed. He was making new sounds, he didn't sneeze when he ate, and food didn't come out his nose. The surgery worked! Within a few months he started sucking and by 15-months-old he could drink from a straw.

I now have a happy, healthy little boy. It's amazing to look back and see how far we've come. I am proud of him and I am proud of myself. I remember my aunt's words again, "God gave him to you because you can handle it." I CAN handle it. Instead of being ashamed of having a child with a cleft, I now share it and educate people about it. I have put myself out there to help people who feel the way I felt when I saw my child for the first time. I've turned negative feelings and experiences into good by helping, educating, inspiring, and sharing our story.

I Wish I'd Known... more about clefts before my son was born.

Dwane

Country: South Africa
Type of Cleft: Complete Bilateral Cleft Lip and Palate
Birthdate: December 6, 2011
Cleft Surgeons: Daleen du Plessis, Hester van den Berg, and Professor K.W. Bütow
Found Out About Cleft: 21 Weeks Gestation
Surgery Dates: June 18, 2012 (Lip repair), August 20, 2012 (Palate repair), September 20, 2012
Family History of Clefts: No

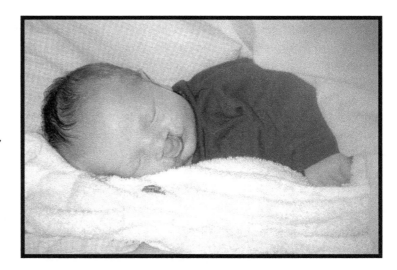

We fell pregnant unexpectedly after two years of attempting to conceive our third baby. The excitement was greater than any feeling in the entire world. The Downs tests were done and they came back negative. There was no sign whatsoever that our little gift from God would be born with any problem.

The night before my 21st week sonar, I had the strangest dream that robbed me of my sleep. I dreamt that there was something wrong with my baby angel's mouth. The next morning, I went for my sonar and the gynaecologist said he was a big, strong, healthy little boy! With my dream weighing heavily on my heart, I asked her to show me his mouth. She went back on with the sonar and became silent. The gynaecologist said that she couldn't get a top lip which meant a cleft lip. My heart was broken. I knew nothing much about clefts but what I did know was that it was a long road ahead.

At 37 weeks gestation, I had to have a C-section due to my high blood pressure. After months and months of praying, the big day had arrived. It was the scariest feeling we have ever been through. We were excited, but worried that our little baby would have more issues than simply a cleft lip. On the 6th of December in 2011, Dwane was born! He was such a big and healthy baby boy, weighing 3.8 kg and perfect in his mom's and dad's eyes.

Then our tough road began. The following day, our little gift from God was taken with one of the ICU sisters to have a special plate fitted. He is such a brave little boy. He was in the ICU for 2 weeks and finally, he was home in time for Christmas. This was the best Christmas present we could ever have asked for.

Then came his first operation. We were so scared of this long awaited operation to start the repair of his cleft lip and palate. I have never cried so much in my life before. The operation was a huge success but then came the healing. Dwane was slow to start healing but eventually healed perfectly. The second operation was much easier. He cried less and was just a happy baby for the entire stay in the hospital.

As I write, we are now 3 and a half weeks away from his third and final operation for this year. We feel more prepared and we know that Our Heavenly Father will continue to work through Prof. Butow's hands and complete the final step in our precious baby boy's repair.

I always said that I would never be able to handle a baby with a deformity. Yet, here I stand with a gorgeous little boy and we made it. "When God solves your problems, you have faith in HIS abilities. When God doesn't solve your problems, HE has faith in your abilities" (author unknown). All the glory be to God for carrying us through each and every step of this journey. Our entire family loves and adores Dwane. He is our miracle baby. We cannot imagine our lives without Dwane in it. He completes us all. Parents of a child born with a cleft, stay on your knees and praise God because the repair will be done and you will be left with a gorgeous baby who will bring nothing but pleasure in your lives.

I Wish I'd Known... how much this entire experience would humble us and ground us in our faith.

Corban

Country: United States of America
Type of Cleft: Unilateral Cleft Lip with Complete Cleft Palate
Birthdate: January 14, 2009
Cleft Team: University of North Carolina at Chapel Hill
Found Out About Cleft: 20-Week Ultrasound
Surgery Dates: March 2009 (Lip repair and ear tubes), September 2009 (Palate repair), November 2009 (Ear tubes replaced), 2010 (Ear tubes replaced), February 4, 2013 (Z-plasty, ear tubes replaced and P-Flap surgery)
Cleft Device: Post-op Nasal Stents
Family History of Clefts: No

My husband and I went in for my 20-week ultrasound hoping pink was the answer to all our guessing. I knew deep down inside that the answer was blue. The tech began her work and we saw his cute face. "Awww, he or she is smiling," I said. Then, it was gender time and as she asked me what I thought it was. I looked at the screen and said a boy. I was right, blue was the answer. She kept looking at his face and taking pictures. All I could say is that he just kept smiling, not thinking anything of it. She left the room to get another doctor. It seemed like forever that she was gone. The other doctor finally came in and put his hand on my knee and said, "We found something on your ultrasound, but it's not the end of the world."

Immediately I began thinking, "Oh my gosh, my baby has cancer or something." He asked us if we had heard of a cleft lip. To which we replied, "Yes." He said it appeared our unborn little boy had a cleft. They were unsure if the palate was involved yet. It wasn't until months later that an ultrasound proved the palate was indeed affected, but you never know the extent until after the child is born.

I remember going home and just crying, "Why? Why my kids?" We had just found out about possibilities of our daughter never walking or possible muscular dystrophy. I overheard my husband reading the Bible to the kids. He was reading about the lame man and the man walking with Jesus asked who had sinned, his mother or father? "Neither this man, nor his parents sinned," said Jesus, "but this happened so that the work of God might be displayed in his life" (John 9:3). Immediately, I felt comfort and peace.

January 14, 2009, Corban was born weighing six pounds, eight ounces and 19 inches long. He was the cutest thing ever. After examination, it was confirmed he had a unilateral cleft lip on the left side and a complete cleft palate. Our other children came into the room to see their new baby brother. His brother, Haiden, saw him and said, "Oh Mommy, he's broked!"

Corban started to feed very well with a pigeon bottle at 3-days-old. I wanted to breastfeed so bad, but it was virtually impossible. Therefore, I pumped and pumped and pumped until he was 1-year-old! Corban had his first lip repair when he was 2-months-old and his soft palate repair when he was 8-months-old.

He is such a strong little boy. Each surgery breaks my heart to see what he goes through, but I know that in it all, God has His hands on him. Right now, Corban is a vibrant 4-year-old boy with a big personality. I would never change the fact that he was born with a cleft. Everything in life is a learning lesson and He has a special plan. I don't just see a scar on his face, I see a story!

I Wish I'd Known... how proud I would be to be a cleft mommy!

Foster

Country: United States of America
Type of Cleft: Bilateral Cleft Lip and Palate
Birthdate: January 21, 2013
Cleft Team: Shands Health Care
Found Out About Cleft: 20 Weeks Gestation
Cleft Device: NAM
Surgery Date: May 28, 2013
Family History of Clefts: No

 This pregnancy was nothing like my last and it soon became even more true. It was just supposed to be a routine OB visit. I knew they would do an ultrasound to monitor the hematoma but since I hadn't had any bleeding in over a month, I expected a good report and opted to go by myself and let my husband stay home with our son. It was the first time in seventeen years of practice that my new OB had to make this diagnosis. "I am pretty sure that what I see here is a cleft." That was it. It was one of those turning point moments. I majored in Speech and Language Pathology and took a whole class on clefts in grad school. I immediately knew everything that little five-letter-word had entailed. My heart sank to the floor. "Really?" was all I said. I didn't cry at first, but at the end when he finally said he, "Hated having to tell me such hard news when I didn't have anyone with me," the tears came. I was by myself and I felt really alone in that room.

 Five minutes later I was sitting in my car dialing my mom. She knows clefts too. She's one of the best Speech Pathologists around and works closely with the craniofacial team at Children's in Birmingham. She cried with me. The rest of the day was tough. I had many unanswered questions and felt like I had little reign on my emotions. The thing is, I really do believe that the Lord doesn't lead us where he has not already prepared in advance for us to go. God's goodness was already so apparent in our journey. He made sure we were where we needed to be to provide great care and resources for our baby. If I hadn't had the hematoma, they may not have done the ultrasound which caught the cleft. This is our family that God is forming and it is something to rejoice about. When I look back at my life, it is the hard and seemingly yucky stuff that I wouldn't change because that's when I've experienced the Lord the most. What I really want isn't for our family (or my life) to be "pretty" or bump free. What I want is for it to glorify the Lord and bless people. In those hours after that appointment, I kept being reminded of truth and of the bigger picture. All I wanted to do was to rest in those things that day and the days to come. But, my flesh was at war with the Spirit. I battled through all the "what if" thoughts. Some of them were reasonable, but most of them were unmerited and even an attempt to take the control away from God.

I left the doctor's appointment only knowing one thing; our little boy had some kind of a cleft. I was referred to see a specialist three long weeks later. Through my mother, I was able to talk to a few people and get us worked in the following week for a high resolution sonogram and a meeting with the surgeon and geneticist. Even though this meant driving around seven hours, it also meant waiting 2 less weeks to get a better idea of what we were dealing with.

During the sonogram, they checked organs, measured every body part and were able to tell that, physically, everything else looked healthy and normal. This was a huge sigh of relief because it ruled out some syndromes that can sometimes be associated with clefts.

They examined the face and showed us some 4-D pictures so we could see the cleft better. At first, the tech just spotted the obvious cleft on the left side, but said she kept seeing something suspicious on the right. We saw what she was talking about too. Sometimes it looked like there was a cleft there and then other times, depending on where she moved the transducer, it seemed to disappear. Ultimately, she determined that it indeed was on both sides but that the right side seemed to be less severe. This new diagnosis meant there would be more surgeries, guaranteed feeding difficulty, more ear infections, speech problems, major dental work, a higher likely-hood of jaw problems later on, and a more challenging road ahead of us.

The next day, we met with the surgeon. He walked us through the surgeries we were looking at with the diagnosis. I sat there looking at pictures and hearing details of what each procedure would entail and all I could think was, "I'm not strong enough for this." I know I will continue to doubt myself, but I am certain of one thing; the Lord is always with us, always before us, and we can count it as joy that we are called to walk through this, having our faith tested in a way that produces steadfastness. There is One who is working all things together, perfectly and purposefully.

While we were at an event one day, we randomly ran into a family that had a baby boy who was one day post lip surgery. They were honest about the hard stuff but at one point the dad said, "We feel like we're the lucky ones because we get to fall in love with our son's smile twice."

Next, we had an appointment with the Cleft and Craniofacial team at Shands Hospital. It was the last step in this process before our baby boy would be born. The team at Shands is highly respected. The Cleft Clinical Coordinator for the whole state of Florida is the Coordinator of this team, simply because she believes it's the best. People travel long distances to see them. The majority of patients that are treated at this clinic live out of town and it's common for people to drive five or more hours one way every week for their appointment.

During our appointment we got to sit down individually with 8 of the different specialists who make up the Craniofacial team: the Social Worker, ENT, Orthodontist, Pediatrician, Genetics counselor, Speech & Language Pathologist, Pediatric Dentist, and the Plastic Surgeon. Some of them will be working with Foster more closely than others for longer periods of time, but I left feeling convinced that all of them were ready to care for us and love Foster as well. God specifically led us to this team. There was a time when our options were either China or Gainesville. We knew nothing of Gainesville at the time. For so long we couldn't make sense of why we were brought here, but it has opened our eyes to God's hand on us in a new way.

Waiting for Foster to arrive gave me time to process through all the "what if's" and there were a lot of them. But, the bottom line is that the Lord allows "what if's" in our life for a reason. We have a choice of what we'll do with them before we know whether or not they will come to fruition. The reality is that I know I can trust God with my worst "what if." If I can trust Him with my worst, then surely I can trust Him in the "what if's" about Foster. Not only has the Lord gone before us but, "It is the Lord your God who goes with you. He will not leave you or forsake you" (Deuteronomy 31:6). How can I be anxious when that is the truth?

On a Monday, I called at four a.m. to make sure there was a bed open. By 7:30 a.m., I was dressed in that less than flattering gown and hooked up to an IV. During the 24 hours prior to Monday morning I felt my body preparing itself and fast. Irregular contractions as well as other signs, let me know labor was close. By one p.m., I was fully dilated and fully effaced. My midwife, Ronnie Jo, rushed in to get changed and I started pushing. After four contractions, there he was. Time stood still. My whole world changed in an instant. All I could do was cry. Every anticipation, every fear, and every question was evaporated and swallowed up in that single moment by a love for this tiny being that overwhelmed me to my core. Nothing else mattered.

Everything about the birth and right after was so normal. I was able to do skin to skin for as long as I wanted before they took his stats and cleaned him up. I had prayed for months in advance for grace in feeding times - for me and for Foster. I knew it would take both of us working together but if we could tackle feeding, then we'd be a step ahead. The Lord chose to answer our prayers. It was a little bit of a learning curve but things were going great.

By his appointment two days later, he was already gaining weight. I have been exclusively pumping and using Mead Johnson bottles. Without the ability to create suction, Foster is left to use the movement of his tongue on the bottle nipple to work the milk out. As he does this, I put pressure on the bottle to help squeeze some of the milk into his mouth and down his throat. Coordinating when to squeeze, how much to squeeze, and how long to squeeze before he needs to stop and take a breath is the tough part. If I squeeze too hard he'll kind of choke or not be able to catch his breath, and is more likely to spit up. If I don't squeeze enough he gets frustrated because he isn't getting much and it takes a long time to get just a couple ounces down. I'm learning what works best for him and it's very rewarding.

Our doctor, Dr. Abi. (Dr. Abimbola O Adewumi), is amazing at what she does. She cares deeply about our boy. She lets me cry and she has the coolest accent. She made an impression of Foster's palate to create his NAM device. We started taping the cleft which will also be done alongside the NAM. We weren't expecting to start it that day, but after looking at Foster's cleft, Dr. Abi decided that he would benefit from intervention as soon as possible. Plus, this way he can get used to a little at a time. The tape is put on with adhesive glue and stretches the lips together. The taping by itself isn't so bad and doesn't seem to bother Foster too much once it's on.

The fitting appointment for the NAM was a long one. Foster hated (almost) every second of it. Dr. Abi had to take the device in and out about 10 times to make adjustments or trim it down so it would fit his mouth and nose just perfectly. We both practiced with it until we were confident we could do it on our own. Foster will wear this 24 hours a day with the exception of three to four times a day that we are cleaning it. This is our new normal until his first surgery on May 28th, 2013.

As I write, we are on day three of the NAM and even though there's been an adjustment period (mainly with him re-learning how to take a bottle), Foster is doing really well. The taping and NAM have been a huge commitment on our part, physically and emotionally, but we know it's best for Foster. I don't mind shedding some tears if it means helping our sweet boy. I remind myself, that the NAM device is a process. The Lord is making Foster whole and as I watch what's happening on the outside, my heart prays that it's happening on the inside too.

My husband reminded me earlier today that God enjoys a process, a story. It's in them that the Gospel works, spilling out the glory of the Lord in a beautiful way. I want that, and I don't want to miss the lessons and the growth that come from the process either. Writing down our journey has been therapeutic for me. I want to be able to trace back to the

beginning the things that God was choosing to teach me through this temporary trial. Honestly, this journey has not been as hard or overwhelming as we were prepared for. It's been all grace, I'm certain of it. My precious child, I love you so.

I Wish I'd Known...
how special his cleft
makes him!

Lilian

Country: United States of America
Type of Cleft: Bilateral Cleft Lip
Birthdate: May 17, 2012
Cleft Team: Children's Mercy Hospital
Found Out About Cleft: 20-Week Anatomy Scan
Cleft Device: NAM
Surgery Date: October 24, 2012
Family History of Clefts: Yes

We knew before we had children that it was possible to have a child with a cleft because of our family history. We had our first child in 2008 and he was not cleft affected, so I just figured we were good. When we went in at our 20-week scan, I knew something was wrong. They were really looking over the face. They kept saying she had her hands in front of her face. I knew in my heart that something was wrong. We were told a few days later that they thought they detected a cleft.

I was sent for a level two scan and it was there that we were told our daughter had a bilateral cleft lip and we would not know about palate involvement until birth. Of course, we were devastated. We went through all of the grieving emotions: anger, denial, fear, worry, everything.

A few weeks later, we chose to pull ourselves together and make plans. I am a strong Christian woman and this is the biggest trial I have ever faced. I thought at first, "Why is God punishing me?" I now know that He was never punishing my family nor myself. God was giving me a trial to see how I would react and I needed to lean on him. That is exactly what I did. We prayed for her multiple times a day. We prayed that her palate would be intact. We prayed that she would have great surgical results and that she would only have minimal surgeries.

We were preparing for our daughter and five weeks before her due date, Lilian decided it was time. We were shocked it was happening. She was delivered and crying and beautiful! My husband went over while they were checking her out and he yelled over to me, "Her palate is intact!" I burst into tears and praised Jesus right there. She nursed a little, but couldn't get a good seal. Bottle-feeding worked great, though.

Lilian began wearing the NAM at five weeks of age. I wanted to protect my daughter and didn't take her out much because I could not handle the stares and comments. This is something I very much regret. She was so beautiful with her little NAM.

At five months and two weeks of age, she was ready for her first surgery. Her lip and nose repair was done. I was a nervous wreck up until two days before surgery. Then, God gave me such a sense of calming that cannot be explained. I kissed her little lips and handed her off. I knew she was in great hands surgically and even better hands with God. She came out of surgery tired and groggy. We used Tylenol for about one week. Lilian wore arm restraints and had nasal stents, which were in for two weeks.

Lilian is now nine months and doing amazing! We are so in love with her. We pray for her (and her brother) daily. We are so blessed!

I Wish I'd Known... how much I would fall in love with my daughter's wide smile.

Penelope

Country: Canada
Type of Cleft: Unilateral Cleft Lip and Palate
Birthdate: October 29, 2012
Cleft Team: Alberta Children's Hospital
Found Out About Cleft: 18-Week Ultrasound
Surgery Date: February 19, 2013
Family History of Clefts: No

As I ponder over the last few months, I start to feel quite nostalgic. Our little one has just had her first surgery this past week. Leading up to her surgery I would have described it as bittersweet. On one hand, I knew she needed the lip repair. On the other hand, to me and our family, she was perfect. I went through a roller coaster of emotions and had to resist cancelling her surgery. It was scary, intense, and overwhelming all at once, still we made it through. Our sweet baby was stronger than ever. I am simply thankful and blessed beyond measure to have such a joy in my life! She did remarkably well and has been recovering even better than I had imagined. Her new smile is priceless!

We had decided on two names before she was born, John for a boy and Penelope for a girl. I was so eager to find out whether I was having another girl or boy that I booked my routine 20-week ultrasound two weeks early. The next day, I could hardly wait and eagerly answered the phone when the doctor's office called. The nurse on the other line told me everything looked fine, baby was healthy, she confirmed my dates, told me "no twins," that our baby's gender was undetermined (much to my disappointment), and that our baby had a cleft. I thanked her and hung up the phone. I headed for the kitchen and stopped dead in my tracks. "Wait! Did she say cleft?" I was stunned. It took me a couple of minutes to process. I had never really seen a cleft lip and didn't know much about it other than what I'd seen in magazine ads. The nurse had mentioned it so casually. Curious and not knowing what else to do, I Googled "cleft lip." Over the next few hours, I read page after page and looked at many pictures. Some were extremely sad and disturbing (it is, after all, the Internet) but most was beautiful and dear. I read blog stories, medical pages, and found an online community full of families who had gone before me. My brain was full. That night, I had nightmares and visions of the worst case scenarios. In hindsight, it might not have been a great idea to Google everything all at once.

However, over the next few days I read many encouraging testimonies and, as I told friends and family, I was dearly blessed by how supportive and loving everyone was in response. When we told our children, the first thing they said was that it didn't matter – she'd be cute and beautiful no matter what. I knew it was going to be okay. God had given my husband and me an incredible peace and we knew without a doubt that God would bring good of it all and that His glory would be seen in our little one's life. I was already in love with my sweet baby and I felt fiercely protective of her.

That same week, we booked another ultrasound privately and found out we were having another girl (our sixth daughter, seven children total!). I looked up the meaning for 'Penelope' and found that it meant 'weaver' or 'she with a web over her face.' I was so surprised at these two meanings and pondered them in my heart. Later that same week, a dear friend of mine who is interested in names and their meanings, excitedly sent me a text asking if I knew the meaning of 'Penelope.' She shared that she believed our choosing Penelope was prophetic as I had picked the name long before I even conceived. She shared with me that 'weaver' or the 'web over her face' definition might relate to stitches or something woven together. She had a vision of a faint scar; a piece of the web.

She shared scripture from John 9 that says, "As he went along, he saw a man blind from birth. His disciples asked him, 'Rabbi, who sinned, this man or his parents, that he was born blind?' 'Neither this man nor his parents sinned,' said Jesus, 'but this happened so that the works of God might be displayed in him.'" I was blown away. I was amazed and thankful that the Lord had used my dear friend to confirm that He did have this situation under His control and that His glory would indeed be seen in her life. I just knew that He would use her cleft journey for good and that He had a purpose for her or all of us in this. Romans 8:28 says, "And we know that in all things God works for the good of those who love Him, who have been called according to His purpose." God is so good!

I committed myself to learn as much as I could and to be as prepared as I could be. I was sad that nursing wasn't going to be a possibility with a cleft palate, which we discovered in a subsequent ultrasound. Still, I was determined to make the best of it. In all honesty, I thought about the cleft constantly and many of my decisions and conversations were based on our little one having a cleft. I wanted to make sure I had my head wrapped around everything. Feeding was my top concern.

Near the end of my pregnancy, I had the opportunity to see our little one via 3-D ultrasound. I will never forget that day. The ultrasound tech, bless her heart, was cooing over my little one and making remarks about how sweet and darling she was. It was then that I first saw passed her cleft. There was a switch in my thinking and I saw first, my daughter. I fell in love all over again and, suddenly, her being cleft affected really didn't matter. It was a reality for sure, but no longer was my pregnancy or my daughter solely defined by her cleft. I could see distinct features; she looked so dainty and lovely. She even frowned a few times. She played with her hands and put them in her mouth. I could see that she looked so much like one of my other daughters as well.

It always amazes me how the Lord faithfully draws me closer when I lose focus. Near the end of my pregnancy, I became a bit restless and started to worry. "What if she can't breathe? What if they take her away from me? What if I can't pump? What if I can't feed her properly?" But, a dear friend prayed for me and all the joy and blessings the Lord had shown me throughout my pregnancy came flooding back.

She was born a few days later, a full ten days late. She weighed in at a healthy nine pounds, three ounces. The days that followed were full of getting to know our beautiful baby, love, picture taking, baby sharing, bonding, and it seemed our days revolved around feeding. I was determined to feed Penelope breast milk and, as such, I was pumping around the clock. We used the Haberman feeder which took us a good six weeks to finally feel we were using right. It was a learning curve for sure. Looking back, the hardest thing in those early weeks was the lack of sleep. I had to give up one of my middle-of-the-night pumps; otherwise I would have gone crazy. Here we are, four months later and I am so glad to have persevered.

My other children, my husband, and I are over-the-moon in love with our newest family member. We definitely consider ourselves blessed beyond measure. If I had to describe how I felt about having a little one with a cleft I would say that I'm thankful, blessed, and humbled. I'm thankful and humbled, that the Lord chose us to care for this little one, knowing that He will provide the strength and grace needed to get through the trials. I'm thankful and blessed, that our children get to experience loving and caring for someone with special needs and a facial difference. I'm blessed beyond words in hearing and seeing our other children love Penelope just the way she is, wishing even, that she could keep her cleft. I'll admit, I had to agree with them that her clefted smile was one of the most beautiful I've ever seen. I'll always miss it.

I'm thankful for a community of families who have gone through the same experiences and who are passionate advocates for their little ones. I'm thankful and humbled to have the healthcare system we do and that surgeries, special feeders, pumps, a whole cleft team, and so much more are available to us. I'm thankful, blessed, and humbled for our church, our friends, and family as they have all gathered around us in full support, love, acceptance, and in prayers offered. Our cleft story is far from finished. It is full of emotion, trust in God, and learning to take it one day at a time. We move forward, knowing and resting in God's faithfulness.

I Wish I'd Known...
how much I'd miss
that little lip.

Faith

Country: United States of America
Type of Cleft: Unilateral Cleft Lip and Bilateral Cleft Palate
Birthdate: April 11, 2012
Cleft Team: OHSU Doernbecher Children's Hospital
Found Out About Cleft: 20-Week Scan
Cleft Device: NAM and Nose Stents
Surgery Date: October 9, 2012
Family History of Clefts: No (Too distant to be considered genetic)

©2012 | Amanda Richelle | Lifestyle Photographer |

Ever since I can remember I, like many little girls, began planning my future way before I could ever really know what "plan" God had waiting for me around the corner. That dream began to turn into reality when I met the man of my dreams in 2004. We eventually became pregnant and had a baby boy, Elijah, in April of 2010. After seven years together, on May 1st, 2011, we decided to make a bigger commitment to each other and go before God and join together in holy matrimony. Months went by and everything was going just as planned, or so we thought. All of a sudden, we were thrown a curve ball. I realized that my period was late. I began to worry because I wasn't sure if we could handle this so soon. Our son was one and a half, still a baby to me, and we weren't very stable financially. My husband would just tell me, "Have faith. We can do this. God wouldn't put us through anything we could not handle."

I'll never forget going to the doctors, hearing the first heartbeat and being given the due date of April 16, 2012. It made it so real. I was in love again and we finally felt that we could share the news with our family and friends. The time drew closer to our 20-week scan and I would count down the days to when the gender would finally be revealed. I remember waking up that day anxious and excited. Everything was going great when she asked, "Would you like to know the gender?" We responded, "Of course!" She then said, "It's a girl." We were so excited. It was such a great moment. We were given some pictures of our little girl and we were sent to the exam room for a follow-up appointment with my doctor.

We were waiting there, overjoyed that everything was going great. Then, our doctor walked in and I felt something I can't explain. It was just an awkward feeling when our eyes met and I felt as if she had a look of concern on her face. Still, I was so happy that it didn't fully register right away. She began to speak, "Your scan was good and your daughter is healthy, but did the ultrasound tech say anything to you while you were in there?" We responded that it was a girl and everything seemed healthy. She then said the words that would continuously ring in the back of my head for weeks after our appointment. "Your baby is suspected to have a cleft lip, but we are unsure because she had her hand in front of her face." I fought back any and every feeling and held in my tears. I never thought I would hear the words 'cleft lip' and 'your baby' in the same sentence. The moment we left and were in the car, I broke down. I cried and cried. I didn't know why this was happening to our daughter.

The next week, I was scheduled for an ultrasound to confirm the cleft. They told us lots of interesting facts and information about clefts. They told us how certain clefts can be related to bigger problems and offered for us to have an amniocentesis if the cleft was confirmed. I then asked, "Why would I be offered an amnio? It's a high risk procedure." They basically said, "So that if there are other problems, you can be given the chance to terminate your pregnancy." I responded right away letting them know they were crazy to even offer it and I didn't care what was suspected. I would never put my baby through that and would never terminate a pregnancy.

Following that, we had the ultrasound where they confirmed that our baby had a unilateral cleft lip and possible palate. I found myself mourning the loss of the "perfect" baby girl I thought we would have. My husband was my rock, time and again, reminding me to have faith. Having faith truly seemed to be the theme of our pregnancy.

We finally came up with the perfect name for her. Since my husband was always telling me to have faith, I asked him what he thought about me literally having "Faith." Naming her 'Faith' fit all too perfectly. He was constantly telling me to have Faith and little did we know, we had Faith with us the whole time.

In the early morning on April 11, 2012, I wasn't able to sleep and felt like I had to constantly sit on the toilet and pee. My husband had to work early that morning. Leaving around 5:15 a.m., he asked if he should stay home. I told him, "No," reassuring him that I would be fine and that I had a doctor's appointment that afternoon. Once he left, the pain became instant. My son was asleep and I couldn't leave the toilet because I was so uncomfortable. My mother-in-law stayed with my son and my mom had to coax me out of the house as I was trying to finish any last minute things. Since her due date wasn't for another five days, I wasn't quite fully prepared. Once she got me in the car, we raced to the hospital where I ran straight to the bathroom to my best friend, the toilet. My husband had met me at the hospital.

They rushed me up to a room where they discovered Faith was almost ready to make her appearance. I was already eight centimeters dilated. Faith came into this world at 9:23 a.m., screaming and crying. It was one of the best moments of my life. The moment she was raised up, put onto my chest and our eyes locked, my heart melted. I was looking at the most beautiful girl in the whole world and she was all ours! She had the most beautiful, big smile with beautiful, big eyes, the most adorable chubby cheeks, and a little bit of golden hair like a goddess. That moment was so eye-opening. It was like the cleft didn't matter. She was perfect. From that moment on, it was never about her cleft. It was just about her, and I wish I'd known that.

In the first few days, we had rough spots with feeding. We just had to figure out which bottle and what position worked best for Faith. We tried the Pigeon bottle, but ultimately decided on the Haberman. When Faith was five days old, we drove two hours to Doernbecher Children's Hospital where she had her first appointment with her cleft team. We went up and met with the pediatrician, her surgeon and team. We also had her hearing screened. It was quite a long day because it was filled with so much information. It was a lot to take in on the first appointment day. They decided to start taping that day and we also decided on doing the NAM. I was heartbroken. I didn't want to tape my daughters face up. I felt as if it would hurt her and cover up her beauty. But I just had to remind myself that it was for the best and beginning the process so we could be prepared for surgery.

Taping was really hard at first. She would cry and fuss while putting it on, but once it was on, it wasn't as bad. We had to relearn how to feed her as the tape kind of got in the way of how we did it at first. Faith is such a trooper and she just took right to it. We continued to do the taping for a couple weeks and then it was time to start the NAM process. Our first appointment entailed Faith being taken back without me, to have an impression of her mouth done so the doctor could make the NAM. She was gone for less than five minutes, but it already felt like forever. We went back the next week to have her NAM fitted and we were taught how to put it in and take it out.

She hated it and we, once again, had to relearn how to eat with this denture-like plate in her mouth. The first few days were the hardest. She had a difficulty eating, was fussy a lot, and uncomfortable. I felt like giving up several times that week and just throwing in the towel. In fact, there were times we just would have it out if she wasn't eating because she was taking it out all the time by herself. After that first week or two, things began to get a little easier. Of course, we had our hard times as NAM can be a difficult process, but the results we began seeing made it well worth it.

We went to the Doernbecher Children's Hospital for Faith's NAM appointments weekly for checkup, measurements, and adjustments. It was a two hour drive, but we would do anything to give Faith the best possible care. Faith's NAM started at 14mm, and by the first week it was at 12mm. Now, every week isn't like that. Sometimes there is little to no movement but every millimeter counts. We would celebrate those weeks it moved and know we were one step closer to getting the surgery over with. During the whole NAM process, we would learn little tricks to make things easier like pre-making the tapes and using Fixodent to hold it in place.

One of our hardest struggles was Faith's diagnosis of acid reflux. She would have multiple episodes a day where she seemed in so much pain. She would be arching her back and she had trouble eating. She would even have really bad reactions where she would stop breathing for a minute, which was very scary! We finally found out she had acid reflux and we were given medicine to help. It made such a difference. She was back to eating her bottles like a champ.

During the whole process, one of my worries about Faith, besides everything she will have to endure, was if she would get rude remarks or stares. I'm happy to say that almost everyone would stop and say how beautiful she is and what a gorgeous smile she has. There were always those few people that would say the wrong thing by accident, or on purpose, and as much as it would hurt me, I tried not to take it the wrong way. Instead, I took it as a chance to educate them and spread awareness. One time someone said, "I bet she's going to be so beautiful after surgery." I replied with, "Yeah, thanks, but I couldn't imagine her any more beautiful then she already is."

As time went on, we were getting closer and closer measurements with the NAM, which meant surgery too was that much closer. When August came around, we finally reached the 5mm mark. This meant that Faith was ready to get her nose stent added on. This was a big milestone because it meant surgery was right around the corner. The next few months flew by. Faith was and has always been a happy baby even through everything she has been enduring. Her smile is contagious and could make even the maddest person stop and smile.

Finally, the day came when we were given the date; the date that would change all of our lives forever, Faith's surgery date. On October 9, 2012 at 7:00 a.m., we would have to hand our little baby girl over to complete strangers so she could undergo this major surgery. All of a sudden, I dreaded this surgery. She was perfect and there was nothing wrong with her. I just wanted to run away so we could just enjoy this smile forever. I also know that, in the long run, it gives her the best life in all aspects. Looking on the bright side, we are very blessed that we are given two first smiles to fall in love with. Her first smile will always be in my heart, captured forever in the many pictures we took.

On surgery day, we drove over to the hospital, began the check-in process, went up to the waiting room, and waited for them to call us back. When we were called, she got her first hospital gown. It was the tiniest hospital gown ever. Then we sat and went over a few instructions, we prayed, said our goodbyes, and handed her off to the surgical team. It was hard to hand our little baby off, but we just had to keep in mind that she was in great hands. God was watching over her and she'd be back in our arms soon.

It was the longest four hours of our lives. Finally, we were called back to talk with the surgeon where she reassured us everything went great. She then proceeded to show us the first pic of Faith after surgery. It was a little shocking to me at first, but I believe that was a mix of all the swelling and also just such a dramatic change. She looked just as beautiful as she did before and we were both very pleased with how the surgery went. We were finally allowed to see her and the nurse laid her in my arms. It was such a great feeling to hold her after missing her for what felt like eternity. She was swollen, her voice raspy, she had dried blood on her, and just seemed uncomfortable. We sat there for a few minutes and then were transferred to our room where she could begin recovery. While we got settled, we tried giving her the first bottle. This was something I was always worried about because she got used to feeding with the NAM in and would always refuse to eat without it. She once again showed us how tough she is and how she is such a trooper. She downed two ounces of glucose water and we were thrilled.

Overall, as hard as it was to hand her over, have her go through surgery and see her in pain, it wasn't as bad as I had imagined it. She even showed off her new smile the night we came home. Boy, was that new smile gorgeous; just as gorgeous as her first, but different.

When we look back, we feel blessed to be given the chance to be parents to both of our beautiful children and would never change a thing about Faith. We love her and everything about her. I would never change any of our treatment plans. NAM was tough and definitely is not for everybody but it worked well for us. Today, Faith is still the happiest baby ever. She is constantly showing off her gorgeous smile and laughing at anything and everything. Our little girl is amazing and can tackle any obstacle thrown at her.

We are now preparing for her second surgery which will be closing her palate. These first 11 months on our journey with Faith has been full of ups and some downs, but I would never change it for anything. We thank God daily for our little perfect princess and prince. She is truly a blessing and has made us better people. She has taught us much about life, love, compassion, and FAITH. I wish I'd known all this before I allowed myself to mourn the loss of what I thought was a perfect baby, because we truly were given the most perfect baby.

I Wish I'd Known...
how much I'd love
everything about
you.

Afterword

"   "
Hope rebuilds.

Samuel

Country: United States of America
Type of Cleft: Bilateral Cleft Lip and Palate
Birthdate: January 29, 2012
Cleft Team: UC Davis Children's Hospital
Found Out About Cleft: At Birth
Cleft Device: Cleft Tape
Surgery Dates: July 16, 2012 (Lip repair), January 17, 2013 (Palate repair)

This is how my special baby has taught me to live....

It was numbness at first. The distinct absence of emotion as if capability to feel anything fled the moment I gave birth to my fourth son, Samuel, and recognized something different. He had a bilateral cleft lip and palate. I held my son, stared at him, and begged to feel anything. The feelings, tears, and grief came soon enough. By evening, I was curled up with my special boy, friends and family at my side, crying those gasping for hope sobs.

HOPE: That's really what it's all about. We hope our unborn children will grow healthy and their birth will be a victorious celebration. We hope that our children will be loved, accepted, and recognized for every bit of potential they hold. We hope our families will be safe and free from heartache. We hope that siblings will hold a close, endearing bond. We hope all the dreams we have for our future and our children's future will have no limitations. Although in the moment I found out my son had a cleft, I felt as if my world had come crashing down, it was really my hope that took a blow. But, hope rebuilds.

Many of my initial fears have been replaced with the glorious reality that having a child with special needs is not the end of the world. It is rather the beginning of an inspiring experience. Through connecting with families in the special-needs community, we learned of so many inspiring stories and have seen the promises of what Samuel's bright future holds.

And the bonus gift? TRANSFORMATION. I have changed. I have been enlightened of the power of perspective and learned to recognize that beauty comes in many different forms. I discovered strengths I didn't realize I possessed. I tapped into hidden potential to make a difference in the world in new ways. More than anything, I know never to doubt the power of my love for my children. It's my constant anchor, my unfailing support.

I Wish I'd Known... how much he would change my life for the better.

Appendices

Survey Results

In the making of this book, a survey was conducted. 108 anonymous participants responded and the following includes the results of the inquiry. These participants vary greatly by country, with the majority residing in the United States of America. The responses collected are of cleft affected children from varying stages of their cleft journey. Therefore, for the most part, those that have selected "not applicable" for a particular question simply have not reached that part of the cleft journey yet to be able to answer.

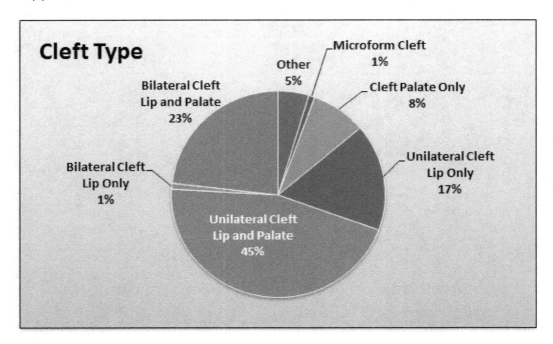

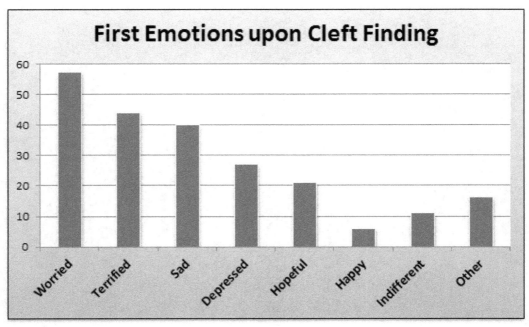

Family Medical History of a Cleft
> *History* – 18%
> *No History* – 71%
> *Unknown* – 11%

Most Popular Feeding System Based on Cleft Type
> *Unilateral Cleft Lip Only* – Direct Breastfeeding
> *Unilateral Cleft Lip and Palate* – Medela Special Needs Nurser
> *Bilateral Cleft Lip Only* – Mead Johnson Bottle
> *Bilateral Cleft Lip and Palate* – Mead Johnson Bottle
> *Cleft Palate Only* – Pigeon Bottle

Most Popular Pacifier Based on Cleft Type
The most popular response in each category was 'no pacifier used.' The information below shows the highest preferred pacifier brands.
> *Unilateral Cleft Lip Only* –Soothie
> *Unilateral Cleft Lip and Palate* –Soothie and Wubbanub
> *Bilateral Cleft Lip* – None
> *Bilateral Cleft Lip and Palate* – Soothie and Wubbanub
> *Cleft Palate Only* – Nuk and Sofie the Giraffe

Direct Breastfeeding
> *Unilateral Cleft Lip Only* – 80% were successful with breastfeeding and 20% attempted breastfeeding and were unsuccessful
> *Unilateral Cleft Lip and Palate* – 53% attempted breastfeeding and were unsuccessful, 39% did not attempt breastfeeding and 8% were successful with breastfeeding.
> *Bilateral Cleft Lip* – 100% did not attempt breastfeeding.
> *Bilateral Cleft Lip and Palate* – 55% attempted breastfeeding and were unsuccessful, 45% did not attempt breastfeeding.
> *Cleft Palate Only* – 78% attempted breastfeeding and were unsuccessful, 11% did not attempt breastfeeding and 11% were successful with breastfeeding.

When Asked if Their Child Would Need or Has Had Speech Therapy...
> *Unilateral Cleft Lip Only* – 47% said 'Not Applicable,' 40% said 'No,' and 13% replied 'yes'
> *Unilateral Cleft Lip and Palate* – 62% said 'yes,' 27% was 'Not Applicable' and 11% said 'No'
> *Bilateral Cleft Lip* – 89% replied 'yes,' and 11% said 'Not Applicable'
> *Bilateral Cleft Lip and Palate* – 59% replied 'yes,' 36% said 'Not Applicable,' and 5% said 'No'
> *Cleft Palate Only* – 100% said 'Not Applicable'

Estimated Number of Total Surgeries Needed

> *Unilateral Cleft Lip Only* – 93% responded '1-3' and 7% said '4-6'
> *Unilateral Cleft Lip and Palate* – 41% said '4-6,' 33% marked '1-3,' 20% replied '7-9,' and 6% said '10+'
> *Bilateral Cleft Lip* – 100% responded '4-6'
> *Bilateral Cleft Lip and Palate* –30% said '4-6,' 26% marked '7-9,' 26% said '10+,' and 18% replied '1-3'
> *Cleft Palate Only* – 72% replied '1-3,' 27% said '4-6,' and 1% responded '10+'

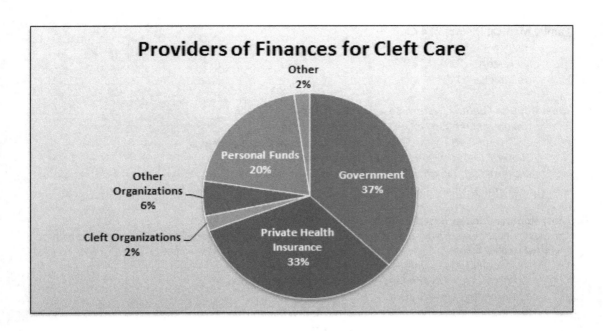

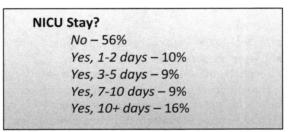

NICU Stay?
No – 56%
Yes, 1-2 days – 10%
Yes, 3-5 days – 9%
Yes, 7-10 days – 9%
Yes, 10+ days – 16%

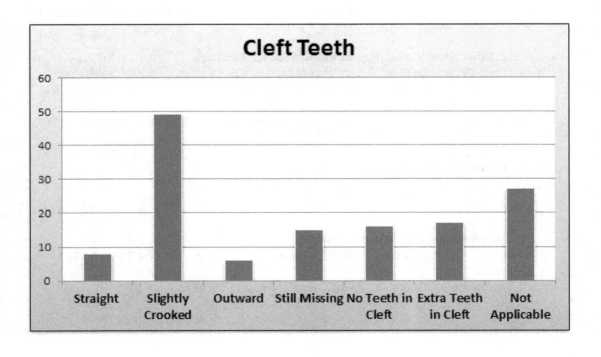

Did You Bond Instantly With Your Child?

As with any newborn, a parent may or may not bond instantly with their child; sometimes it may come with time.

Yes – 82%
No – 18%

How Long Did it Take to Bond With Your Child?

For those that did not bond instantly with their child, the following results shows the time it took to experience that bond.

1-7 days – 62%
1-4 weeks – 24%
4-10 weeks – 5%
10+ weeks – 9%

How Long Did it Take to Find a Suitable Feeding System for Your Cleft Child?

Many caretakers attempt various feeding devices to find the one that fits and works the best with a child's cleft. This can include direct breastfeeding, various bottles, spoon feeding, or tube feeding.

0-7 days – 55%
1-4 weeks – 27%
1-3 months – 7%
3-6 months – 7%
6+ months – 4%

What Post-Surgery Supplies Were Used During Recovery?

The recommendations for post-surgery care vary by surgeon, cleft type, and surgical procedure.

Arm Restraints – 44%
Nose Stents – 21%
Surgical Tape – 19%
Other – 7%
None – 5%
Not Applicable – 4%

What Post-Surgery Feeding System was Used During Recovery?

The recommendations for post-surgery care vary per surgeon, cleft type, and surgical procedure.

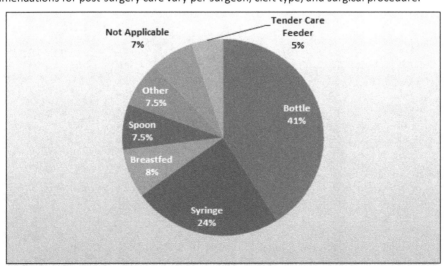

Questions of the Journey

The following questions were asked of survey participants regarding their cleft journey as parents. Most questions are summarized and are followed by responses of actual survey participants.

The Most Rewarding Part of Your Cleft Journey

Having a child with a cleft will transform your life. You will be changed for the better after enduring the trials of the cleft journey. Most often, your family will be drawn closer in the process. Those who reach out to others in the cleft community will be blessed beyond words with new friendships and cleft education. Parents of a cleft affected child are blessed to enjoy the different smiles in their child. A cleft child is like any other child and watching them grow and achieve is a blessing in itself.

"Waking up each morning to a beautiful little girl with a wonderful heartwarming smile."

"We were given a gift! We were able to fall in love with our angel's smile twice."

"The transformation my son has showed me. Beauty comes in many forms. Never judge another because you don't know their story."

"That my little man is AWESOME, strong, and can do anything he puts his mind to."

"I have learned so much about my own strength as a mother, as well as, the strength of my relationship with my husband. I feel that our bond with our baby is very strong through the trials we have endured with her."

"The most rewarding is seeing his beautiful smile every day. Most parents only get to see their baby's first smile one time. We were lucky enough to see three first smiles; one wide smile, one partially repaired, and one completely repaired. They were and are equally beautiful to me."

"The people I've met. I'll be honest; I lost some friends after my son was born. But, the new ones I've gained have been some of the truest, most genuine people I've ever had the pleasure to meet."

"Meeting new people in the same situation from all over the world, realizing a cause to support, and having the most beautiful boy ever!"

"Watching her grow into such a strong and resilient and brave person. Her cleft doesn't define her. She is talented and funny. We've all become more aware that people have differences whether or not you can see them."

"My child's smile!"

"His wonderful, caring cleft surgery team."

"He is amazing. He has taught us so much about life and love. He is our reward. The cleft has been my most bittersweet journey. He is the strongest little guy I know. The growth is an amazing and inspiring thing!"

"It has made us closer as a family and me a much stronger person. We have such a special bond with our brave little boy."

The Most Difficult Part of Your Cleft Journey

The most common response for the greatest aspect of difficulty in the cleft journey was surgery. The worry and stress of the parents and the pain and suffering of the child were the second most common responses.

"The two weeks after surgery. It was hard watching him be uncomfortable. It was also hard when they took him back for surgery."

"Family not wanting to be around them until they were 'fixed.'"

"Wow… all of it! Feeding was a nightmare at first. She kept losing weight and was diagnosed failure to thrive. Then, you have tons of doctor appointments on top of therapies."

"The hardest part of my cleft journey is trying to get my friends or family to understand what I am going through mentally. Even my boyfriend doesn't really understand."

"The hardest part for me is immediately after surgery and the days following. Seeing him in pain breaks my heart. This will get easier as he gets older, but as an infant, it was awful."

"That we have to 'fix' how God made him."

"I am a grandmother raising her cleft afflicted granddaughter. The hardest part was watching her parents struggle to accept the cleft, having to take responsibility for her medical needs, and realizing I was to become the advocate for her life."

"The surgeries and having very little support."

"Feeling like people stared and judged before her first surgery."

"Finding a feeding rhythm and method that works."

"Almost losing him during his fifth surgery."

"Time demands; having to fit all medical appointments into life and work."

"To be honest, the greatest difficulty was keeping my husband encouraged when he was worried about how everything would evolve, how others would see her, how this would affect her in school, etc. The other big challenge was keeping my energy up for pumping and feeding every two hours."

"Not knowing how having a cleft will affect her in the future."

"Post-op was horrible. She refused all fluids for seven weeks (ten jars a day of baby food) and has never again had milk or formula."

"Weight gaining issues and handing her to the surgeon for her surgery."

"Initially, the fear; then, it was the waiting time until surgery. Then, it was letting him go for surgery. Then, the sleep problems he had for several weeks after each surgery."

"Telling family who had previously made very unkind comments about children with clefts."

"The first 24 hours after his surgery were awful. All he did was cry if you weren't bouncing him up and down. I was alone with him in the hospital overnight bouncing all night long minus five or ten minutes here and there. The nurses were too busy to help me. I'm just thankful I didn't pass out of exhaustion."

When/How Did you Tell Others About the Cleft Diagnosis?

If you are trying to decide when and how to tell others about a cleft diagnosis, simply go with your heart. Tell others however and whenever you are comfortable. For some people, the news may be too difficult to share initially. However, telling others is a step that often helps get through the difficulties of the cleft journey.

"As soon as I told my family the news they looked relieved. I was crying so hard that they thought something was wrong with the baby. In my mind, something was wrong with the baby, but my family felt otherwise. This was something that could be repaired. As far as they were concerned, the baby was perfectly fine. It turns out, they were absolutely right!"

"We told everyone right away. We were proud of her and we knew we needed to get the word out about the struggles she was facing. We asked everyone we knew to pray for her."

"We told our close friends and family in person. Everyone else we told by email and included pictures and offered to answer any questions they had."

"We shared the news right away with family and friends. We sought support from a few friends whose children had clefts. We also met with our area's craniofacial team for a prenatal appointment. There were some tears, but also relief that the only visible issue was a cleft lip and possible palate, rather than any more severe concern. We were determined that this would not define our daughter."

"We started telling everyone right away. We cried the first few times we told the news, but it got easier every time. Before I knew it, I was telling anyone who asked me about my pregnancy."

"Others were told as needed. We were somber."

"We waited until our daughter was a few days old when we had more information before we told anyone other than parents and three close friends."

"While still pregnant, we told people straightforward. We always added that, either way, the Lord is good and that His glory would be seen in her life."

"We just outright told them that we received bad news at our ultrasound appointment."

"We wrote a detailed letter to immediate family (including links to CleftPALS)."

"We told them immediately and they all were very loving and supportive."

"We found the cleft the same day we found out we were having a boy. We posted the ultrasound picture on Facebook and announced it at the same time as his gender. We didn't want to make a big deal out of it."

"After his birth, we informed others over the phone due to being in the hospital."

"After we learned more info at the 3-D/4-D ultrasound, we let people know."

"I explained to them when I was 20-weeks pregnant that my little guy would have a cleft lip and possible cleft palate. I told them not to be sorry because I was not sorry. I loved my baby no matter what. I showed my other children what a cleft looked like via the internet. My niece was born with a cleft lip so my kids kind of had an idea."

"I wasn't sure how to break the news. We found out at birth, so with family it was one of the first things I mentioned. I felt like I was 'warning' them. It didn't take long for myself to be comfortable with his cleft and share with others."

Emotional Advice

The cleft journey will take you on an emotional roller coaster. It is important to know that you are not alone and there are people out there who can and will support you, give you advice, and help you along the way. There is a lot of emotional advice infused in this book; below, in the stories, and written in the 'dear pregnant mom' letters.

"When you start the journey with your baby, don't be anxious or worried. It goes by faster than you think and before you know it, it's all over. Your precious gift from God will be as happy and normal as all the other babies around you. The only difference is that they have a fantastic story to be able to tell someday."

"It's perfectly normal to feel what you're feeling. What's not normal is letting it consume your life. Find someone to confide in and don't keep things bottled up."

"It's okay to be scared, but more than likely the second you lay eyes on your beautiful, perfect baby you'll be in love."

"You are NOT alone. When my son was born, I thought I was. Social networking sites have brought me into groups with other cleft parents and they are a big support system for me."

"The unknown while you are pregnant is HARD, but don't let it take over everything. You are still creating a beautiful life and deserve to enjoy every second of it."

"My best advice is to try and enjoy the pregnancy and to not stress about "what if's" and worries. I lost so much time worrying! I compromised my physical and mental health due to my intense worry. Once our daughter was born, all the worry just faded away and I truly wish I could have those months back that I wasted worrying!"

"This too shall pass. All the worry will fade as soon as you see their beautiful face!"

"Take it one day at a time. Find support; support from the right sources is vital."

"It really helps to have someone to talk to when things get rough. I also wish I had someone to help me out when I felt overwhelmed."

"See if you can find another cleft mom to walk the road with. I found a woman who has a son that is about a year ahead of my son. She has been an amazing resource and helped me prepare for the surgeries and the days after."

"Cry if you need to. Talk to others who have gone through it. Don't hide away at home. Be proud of your baby!"

"Take photos and never be ashamed of how your baby looks."

"It's very hard to hand your little ones over to the doctor, but just know that it is for the best. You will miss that wide smile you looked at and loved, but they will have a new and equally wonderful smile when they heal."

"The first surgery to repair the lip is the most emotional because it is the first visual change. You want to keep the "crooked lip" because it is what you become attached to. Seeing it gone and then adjusting to the new lip is a bit overwhelming."

"The strangest thing is that you don't think about how you will feel when you see your baby out of surgery. It's actually quite a shock to see your cleft baby without a cleft. We were not expecting that."

Does Your Baby Have Other Medical Issues?

The Center for Disease Control estimates one in every 33 babies will be born with a birth defect. 30% of all orofacial clefts are not isolated and encompass one or more further medical issues. Some of the more common medical issues of cleft children include ear problems, acid reflux, and weight gain. The answers below describe some of the more rare diagnoses that have come alongside a cleft. These may or may not be genetically related.

"Possible CHARGE syndrome."

"Yes, a pit on his spine, hearing loss, hernia, sensory disorder."

"Possible brain condition."

"He was born with a heart murmur, but it healed shortly after birth."

"He was born premature and has developmental delays. He had an oral aversion and has a G-tube, plagiocephaly, torticollis, serious acid reflux, slight hearing loss and ear tubes."

"Clubfoot and fused together kidneys in his left side."

"Van der Woude syndrome."

"Coloboma (key whole in the eye), heart murmur."

"Yes, our son has Stickler Syndrome along with Pierre Robin Sequence."

"At birth, Renee was tongue-tied. This was repaired during her lip repair surgery at six months. Our daughter now has mild asthma, but is in good health otherwise."

"He was born 12 weeks premature, so he has preemie issues as well as some other medical needs. His heart is located in the middle of his chest, he has extra skin in his throat that causes a stridor, he has some hormonal issues, and kidney issues that we are diagnosing."

"Wears hearing aids for glue ear and glasses for squint."

"Craniosynostosis and a small hole in her heart."

"She was born with a Tracheoesophageal fistula as well. She also now has hearing difficulties, vision problems, asthma, and epilepsy."

"As a result of antibiotics administered post lip repair, our son may have some hearing loss. We are still waiting on further testing now at seven-months-old."

"Sensory processing disorder, oppositional defiant disorder, separation anxiety, post-traumatic stress disorder."

"Asperger's syndrome, sensory processing disorder, PTSD, some loss of hearing, auditory processing, possibly ADHD."

"Craniosynostosis. He had reconstructive surgery at eight and a half months of age."

"Yes, my son had a tracheostomy, NG tube, and an underlying syndrome."

"Hypothyroidism, tethered spinal cord."

"Bicuspid Aortic Valve, PDA, Pierre Robin, Acid Reflux."

"Toe syndactyly, severe ear canal stenosis, shallow eye sockets and small stature."

Advice on Medical Issues

Common cleft related health matters can include various palate or cleft devices, ear infections, speech, and dental problems. Always contact your cleft team and/or doctor about any medical concerns you may have. Always follow your doctors' recommendations for treatment.

"Always write down questions you want to ask before appointments. That way you don't forget any of them."

"If you have difficulty in feeding, you can consult a speech therapist for feeding therapy."

"If using the NAM, use it all the time, for feeding and everything. It is way easier in the long run. Have a 'tape-making' night to get tons of extra tapes made so that when you are in a rush you have lots of extra. Using aloe vera under the tape worked best for our son."

"If your team is not doing a good job, you can get a second opinion. It's okay. Do your research; you are your child's best advocate."

"Try to keep the medical side of things as natural (only necessary medications) as possible to avoid other issues (reactions from medications)."

"Be aware of things you think may be making your baby uncomfortable. Ask the doctors a lot of questions. Be persistent."

"Ear tubes don't take long to feel better, so don't worry if your child has to have them. If your child has reflux, get them on a medicine that works for them. There is more than one type. If you don't feel your pediatrician is doing a thing right, it is okay to get a second opinion or a referral to a specialist. Do not hesitate!"

"We were so lucky that our team includes a fantastic ear surgeon. Our daughter failed her hearing tests at birth and struggled with ear infections for years, but with four sets of ear tubes and lots of checkups, she now has perfect hearing. Our plastic surgeon and ear surgeon always worked together so they could do two surgeries at once."

"Our son had a slightly misshapen head. He was treated by a Chiropractor qualified in Cranial Adjusting Turner Style instead of having to wear a helmet 23 hours a day."

"Do speech therapy. Make sure you're having his or her hearing checked."

"As my son grew older, I've researched and learned that there are many things we could do to prevent ear infections from even occurring. Probiotics is a huge factor in getting rid of recurring infections and getting rid of the actual infection by giving him other alternative medicine."

"The best advice we got was from our occupational therapist. She taught us infant massage. It made our fussy, gassy baby so much happier!"

"Follow your doctors' advice and don't be scared to ask questions."

"YOU are the one that is ultimately responsible for all medical decisions affecting your child. Doctors and therapists will all tell you what should be done. You will decide what WILL be done. Listen to your gut."

"Every child is different. You can't go by everything that others tell you."

Comments From Others About the Cleft

The majority of cleft children and parents of a cleft child are met with positive and encouraging comments from the people around them. However, some still experience the negativity of a stranger, family, friends, or religious groups. The comments below display the variety of comments parents have received.

Negative

"I have had dirty looks and one lady called him a mongol child who shouldn't live."

"200 years ago, your child would have been left on the edge of a cliff to die."

"Someday she will be embarrassed of her baby pictures with her cleft."

"Someone asked my husband why he would punch our baby and split his lip open."

"When our son was wearing his arm splints post-surgery, someone in the street said, 'Look at that baby, he must have broken his arms.' I was horrified to think someone thought I had possibly been neglectful to my baby that he could have broken his arms. I was so taken aback though, that I didn't respond."

"Someone said, 'Don't worry, they'll fix your nose one day and then you'll be beautiful.'"

"One relative told me that he wasn't too hideous after all."

"My niece pointed at my son's cleft and laughed. She was only a little over a year, so she didn't understand, but it still hurt."

"The hardest part for me was taking her to church for the first time. I guess not everyone had heard and one lady stood over my shoulder, staring, and not saying anything. Another lady felt the need to come pray for us so that 'we would love our baby.' I was furious and we left."

"Someone said to me that I must have been devastated when my son was born."

"At dinner with my family, a lady at the table behind us asked me to put my daughter away because it was making her lose her appetite."

"We adopted our son at birth and we have had some very interesting comments; some really sweet and some very inconsiderate. Examples: 'Did his birth mom place him for adoption because of his cleft?' 'Wow! You guys saved him!' 'Will he be able to talk?'"

"Peter was our second child who was cleft affected and many people told us that we should stop having children (Note that we just welcomed our third child, and he is cleft free!)."

Funny

"'You know what's so cool? He can still breathe when his mouth is closed!' said a seven-year-old boy."

"As we left the hospital after my son's lip surgery, his lip and nose were stitched, and he was a little bloody and bruised. A woman said, 'Oh my goodness, is your baby okay? What happened?' My husband quickly replied, 'He will be okay. You should see the other guy!'"

"A friend asked my son why he had a scar on his lip. 'I'm from Mars,' was his reply."

"There's a hole in his face! You better fix that!"

"'Have you decided if you'll tell him?' (That he was born with a cleft)."

"Our daughter told her Kindergarten class that her baby brother 'has a hole in his throat.' Other parents thought it was a funny invented malady she came up with on her own because our son has no visible markers."

"When my two-year-old saw our cleft affected child for the first time he said, 'Momma, I think he needs a tissue.'"

"People after the surgery said that she looked so much better. It was a soft palate cleft, so you could never see it anyway!"

"I was seeing a hand surgeon (subspecialty of plastics) and had my daughter with me. He looked at her and said, 'Oh, she's had some work done.'"

"My best friend said, 'After his surgery he is going to have lips like Angelina Jolie!'"

"When taking my son to urgent care about two years after his cleft repair, the doctor asked me about his medical history and after stating 'cleft lip,' she rudely said, 'No. What is his medical history?' She thought I was speaking of a family history because she had no idea his lip had been repaired by first glance."

"Wow, you must have had some bike wreck."

Positive

"We only had positive interactions with people. They would smile, play with her, and then question about her mouth. Nothing we couldn't handle!"

"All the best people are born with clefts."

"A plastic surgery resident at the hospital was shining a light into her scar, 'It looks so good I wasn't sure she had a cleft!'"

"'Your daughter had three surgeries in 2011? What on earth for?' asked another daycare parent. She had seen her every day for a year before she knew about her cleft."

"I teach kindergarten and my class absolutely adores our son. They see right past his cleft and focus on him as the beautiful and fun baby that he is!"

"Everyone loves on our little boy. They tell us how special he is, how blessed we are, and that he is adorable. We think so too!"

"One wonderful thing that my sister-in-law said when her son asked about our child's extra wide smile was, 'Her mouth hasn't finished growing yet and the doctor will soon help it to finish growing.'"

"We met a family while Christmas shopping that came up to us and told us how beautiful our son was. They said it brought back memories. I didn't even notice that their young daughter had had a cleft lip. They gave us so much hope and made us feel so good!"

"A friend of our older, non-clefted son asked him what was wrong with his baby brother's mouth and his reply was, 'Nothing, that's how The Dear Lord made him.'"

"We never heard a rude comment. I don't know if it was because of his cleft or not, but people always gushed over him."

Advice on Comments From Others About the Cleft

Cleft children and parents of cleft affected children will experience a variety of comments or responses to the cleft. It is helpful to be prepared in how to properly respond to these possibly negative or positive comments. Most importantly, one needs to be educated on the basics of the cleft, cleft care, and repair in order to properly answer any questions others may have.

"Most people just don't know what to say when they meet someone with a facial (or any other) difference. Give them a chance. All of these experiences are opportunities to educate others about facial differences. You'll be amazed how empathetic people can be."

"Every human being has an issue that some person will have a comment about. We can't control what other people say or do, but we can surround our children with love and give them lots of opportunities to gain self-confidence."

"You have to keep strong. Sometimes it's just better not to answer some people's comments because, in the end, most people who don't know you don't really care one way or the other. They just want to be heard."

"Ignore someone if they are being rude. They probably don't know anything about a cleft. People are curious and most people I came across were positive rather than negative."

"Try not to take anything too personally. Use other people's ignorance as a chance to share your experience and educate them."

"Remember that it's your child they are talking about. This sweet, precious child did not do anything that led to the cleft. You do not have to answer their questions if you feel they are being too intrusive."

"Keep in mind that while clefts are common, there are still a lot of people who don't know what it is. If you get someone rude, walk away. If you get someone genuinely concerned, explain to them what it is. Above all, be polite and show them why you are the mother of the baby and not them."

"Know that you love your baby. Your baby is adorable and perfect in his or her own way. Try your best to ignore anyone who says differently."

"Just answer questions. They are curious and don't know what to say. When you smile and are positive, people will warm up. Try to understand and show nothing but love for your little one."

"Avoid using terms like 'fix' or 'repair.' Your baby is perfect the way they are."

"If they have first-hand experience then it may well be useful advice. Otherwise, it may not be; however well-intentioned they might be."

"There are always going to be thoughtless people out there. There is absolutely nothing wrong with your child and you have to remember that. People say things that may bother you, but they are usually just genuinely trying to help."

"Most of the time, I think, people just get awkward around the unfamiliar and then stupid things pop out of their mouth."

"Worrying does not take away tomorrow's troubles; it takes away today's PEACE. Take it one day at a time and listen to the advice given. Use what works for you and forget the rest."

Responses to Comments From Others About the Cleft

"Since they cannot see the cleft palate, because it is so far back, I found myself explaining it to people to justify his frequent and noisy breastfeeding."

"I try not to take offence to most people's comments. Some people don't fully understand, so I correct them."

"I am not as sensitive as some other moms when people use such words as 'defect' or 'deformity.' It is what it is."

"I try to help inform and educate everyone that I meet about my sons cleft. I usually do not wait for someone else to bring it up."

"For children, including my older son, I explained that when he was in my tummy his lip didn't fully close, that the doctors would be repairing it, and life will go on. He wasn't hurt and it wasn't a boo-boo."

"I'm a nurse, so I know how far even the smallest amount of education can go. That was my main goal, to educate people. There were a few times I wanted to go full mother-bear on people, but that wouldn't help anyone in the long run."

"I try to explain and educate people who ask. Education is key because some people just have no idea about clefts, what can cause them, and they are simply curious."

"Especially when responding to children, our standard response was, 'Feel the bump on your upper lip with your finger. When Clare was growing in the special spot inside of my belly, the two parts of her lip did not touch like yours did. It doesn't hurt Clare, and soon she will have surgery which will help her eat and speak better.'"

"I was so well informed and prepared before the birth that I became a walking expert in the street on clefts. I answered questions, stares, and comments in the Subway, in the park, at the bus stop, and in elevators. After his surgery, I missed talking to others."

"We live in a large building with an elevator, so avoiding people is quite difficult. I dreaded elevator rides with strangers, so I would often pre-empt comments by telling people about his cleft and the upcoming surgery. Most were very positive, and he would win them over with his big eyes and wide smile."

"I respond matter-of-factly. I need to model what my son will need to do when he is asked questions."

"My quick response to any questions is, 'He was born with angels kisses.'"

"We tried to have compassion with people who seemed to be reaching out with concern and not intending on hurting our feelings. We had to fight the urge to be defensive or take things to heart."

"I assure children that everyone is different, but should be accepted as they are created."

"It depends on the day and my mood. When he was younger, I think I was holding in some repressed emotions I went through having had a cleft myself, so I wouldn't hold back my comments to people. Now that the kids are older, I'm better at shutting my mouth, since I have impressionable children around me."

"God made him that way."

What to Bring to Surgery

The key to preparing what to bring for surgery is to bring anything your child needs to feel at home. Call the hospital to see what gear they may provide. Often, baby essentials will be available, but be mindful if your child is only able to use a specific type of something (e.g. diapers). Know what your surgeon recommends for post-op feeding and be sure to bring along supplies for that or confirm if supplies will be provided by the hospital.

- Zipper sleepers or button-up clothes (those that don't pull over the head)
- A new toy (one with lights and music)
- A favorite stuffed animal or blanket, favorite toy and/or book
- Feeding Supplies: know what your surgeon recommends post-surgery and bring accordingly. This may or may not include bottles (a variety as the surgery may change the way your child feeds most comfortably), pumping supplies, syringes (may be supplied by hospital) or Tender Care Feeder, a bottle brush to clean if using bottles, the same formula you use at home (if using)
- Electronics can be used to keep you occupied during the surgery, keeping your hurting child entertained, as well as providing white noise in a noisy hospital. This may include phones, music devices, portable DVD player, or laptop (And don't forget the chargers!)
- Tissues
- Snacks or change for a vending machine
- Support. It is beneficial to have support from family and friends and take turns caring for your child.
- Bring a change of clothes for everyone. Wear clothes that are fine to get dirty, as there may be blood. Comfy clothes and shoes
- Your own pillow, blanket, slippers, sweater and toiletries
- Whatever comforts your child in the worst of times: bouncy chair or rocker
- Something to keep you busy: crotchet/knitting, cards, phone, electronic games, magazines, books
- Medications (if needed)
- Non-spill adult cups for hot drinks
- A journal to write your experiences down
- A swaddling blanket (helps keep hands away from surgery site), Boppy pillow
- Bubbles, I-Spy book or bottle, balloons, My Pal Scout/Violet toy by LeapFrog
- Diapers, wipes, etc. (See what your hospital provides and go from there) as well as anything else needed for a regular trip away from home.
- Contacts of those you want to update
- Socks with the toes cut off to put overtop of the arm restraints to keep them on
- Camera: take lots of pictures. It may be difficult, but can be helpful to someone or your child in the long run
- Patience
- Remember to take care of yourself also
- The thing your child will want most of all is your loving arms and lots of love and cuddles

Cleft Books

Bristow, L. & Bristow, S. (2007). *Making faces.* Toronto, ON: Pulsus Group Incorporated.

Brown, I. B. (2011). *Before the Lark.* TX: Texas Tech University Press

Cleft New Zealand Inc. (2003). *The Blue Book: A Handbook for parents of children born with cleft lip/palate.* NZ: Cleft New Zealand Inc. (available to order for New Zealand residents only)

Cwir, J. M. (2017). *I Wish I'd Known Clefts Create Courage.* CreateSpace Independent Publishing Platform.

Gaynor, K. (2008). *First Place.* Ireland: Special Stories Publishing

Gilbert, M. & written by Peckinpah, S. L. (2008). *Rosey... The Imperfect Angel* [CD-ROM]. Alden Records

Gore, B. & Gore, Z. (2011). *Zoe, a Cool Cleft Kid.* FL: Sekel House

Graham, J. (2006). *A Special Smile.* IN: Trafford Publishing

Green, J. (2006). *Lippy the Lion.* Canada: Saga Books

Green, J. (2008). *The Story of Thumper the Cleft-Affected Bunny.* Canada: Saga Books

Gruman-Trinkner, C. T. (2001). *The Cleft Affected Child .* CA: Hunter House

Isles, K. (2011). *I Love you Now, I Loved you Then.* CreateSpace Independent Publishing Platform

Jenkins, J. (2012). *Girl Perfect.* CreateSpace Independent Publishing Platform

Kranowitz, C. S. (2006). *The Out of Sync Child.* NY: Perigee Trade

Lipman, B. & Lipman, K. (2000). *My Puzzling Smile.* OH: Self Published

Lipman, K. (2000). *Don't Despair, Cleft Repair.* ND: Legacy Productions

Maus, J. (2003). *Jessie's Blessing.* Toronto, ON: Self Published.

Peckinpah, S. L. (1993). *Rosey... The Imperfect Angel.* Dasan Productions (Currently not in print)

Priddy, R. (2005) *First 100 Words (Bright Baby Series).* NY: Priddy Books; Board edition

Reedy, T. (2011). *Words in the Dust.* NY: Arthur A. Levine Books

Scarry, R. (1995). *A Big Operation.* NY: Aladdin Paperbacks

Simon, P. A. (2017). *Simon and the Buddy Branch.* Lulu publishing platform.

Vermeylen-Nuyts, M. (2011). *Katie's Dream.* Belgium: Bai NV

Wilde, Amy Jo. (2013) *White Bees.* Self Published: Amazon

Helpful Websites

Many of the websites below fit into more than one category. The category that best suited the website was chosen. There is a plethora of websites available for cleft information and support on the web. Our collection displays some that our book participants found useful in their journey.

Cleft Organizations

http://www.aboutface.ca/ For 25 years, AboutFace has aided individuals with a facial disfigurement to experience personal enrichment and growth.

http://www.acpa-cpf.org/ **The American Cleft Palate-Craniofacial Association (ACPA)** is an international non-profit medical society of health care professionals who treat and/or perform research on birth defects of the head and face.

http://www.allianceforsmiles.org/ Alliance for Smiles, Inc. provides free reconstructive surgery and dental treatment to children with cleft lip and palate anomalies in developing countries. They work to establish comprehensive cleft treatment centers and foster cleft awareness.

http://www.changingfaces.org.uk/Home A charity for people and families whose lives are affected by conditions, marks, or scars that alter their appearance.

http://www.clapa.com/ CLAPA is the only UK-wide voluntary organization specifically helping those with, and affected by, cleft lip and palate.

http://www.cleftadvocate.org/ CleftAdvocate and its volunteers strive to teach individuals, families, and the general public about cleft lip and palate and other craniofacial anomalies, what to expect, what to research, and what to ask their team of specialists.

http://www.cleftcareofarkansas.org/ A non-profit, charitable organization that provides travel expense funding for children and their families that are seeking cleft lip and/or palate treatment.

http://www.cleftline.org A non-profit organization whose mission is to enhance the quality of life for individuals affected by cleft lip and palate and other craniofacial birth defects.

http://www.cleftopedia.com A non-profit organization that provides a website for cleft parents. It's a go-to resource to research feeding option, surgical techniques as well as cleft care teams.

http://www.cleftsmile.org/ Cleft Smile educates and brings awareness to others around the world whose lives are touched by cleft lip and/or palate and other craniofacial anomalies by providing support, education, advocacy, and research.

http://www.facetofacecolorado.org/ An organization that seeks to foster an empowered and connected community of people affected by cleft lip and/or cleft palate across the state of Colorado.

http://www.interfacekids.org/ A volunteer group of plastic surgeons and other reconstructive surgeons that give their time and expertise in Mexico.

http://www.operationrainbowcanada.com/ Operation Rainbow provides free reconstructive surgery and related health care for cleft lip and cleft palate deformities to needy children and young adults in developing countries.

http://www.operationsmile.org/ Operation Smile provides free surgeries to repair cleft lip, cleft palate, and other facial deformities for children around the globe.

http://www.projectharar.org/ This organization helps rural children across Ethiopia access medical care so they can eat, speak, and smile like everyone else.

http://www.smilefoundationsa.org/ This organization assists by putting the smile back onto children's faces with free corrective facial reconstructive surgery and treatments.

http://www.surgicalfriends.org/ Surgical Friends provides free reconstructive surgery and post-operative care to young adults living with physical deformities.

http://www.transformingfaces.org Transforming Faces provides free, local, and ongoing multi-disciplinary cleft care for children and adults in developing countries.

Cleft Support

http://www.ameriface.org Ameriface brings support to families whose lives have been touched by cleft lip and palate and other craniofacial anomalies, including acquired facial differences. They connect parents of affected children and provide many resources including USA state based information.

http://www.ccakids.org/ The Children's Craniofacial Association empowers and gives hope to individuals and families affected by facial differences. Also, read their blog page http://www.ccakidsblog.org/

http://www.cleftbeforeafter.com/ A site providing guidance during the confusing time after you find out the difficult news of a cleft anomaly. Also, the site includes many photos of clefts before and after surgery.

http://www.cleftfriends.co.za/ Cleft Friends has been able to train parents in Gauteng, Eastern Cape, and Western Cape to support other cleft parents in their immediate areas.

http://www.cleftkids.org/ Cleft Kids works on connecting families with others who have been affected by clefts.

http://www.cleftsupport.yolasite.com/ This website was created to provide information about cleft lip and palate, to provide a place for parents to ask questions, and seek support.

http://www.cleftys.org/ To bring awareness to clefts and cleft related issues.

http://www.community.babycenter.com/groups/a56125/cleft_lipcleft_palate This Cleft Lip and Palate group forum is a place where parents of cleft children can share their emotional journeys, receive support, and share advice.

http://www.easysite.com/smilefestnm Smile Fest provides cleft support in New Mexico and is dedicated to those who have been blessed with a cleft lip and/or palate.

http://www.faceit.org.nz/ A community for all groups interested in the outcomes for people born with clefts.

http://homepage.powerup.com.au/~cleftpal/index.htm A national, voluntary group comprising parents, relatives, and professionals interested in the welfare of children born with cleft related conditions.

http://www.kidswithcleftsutah.blogspot.ca/ A place to learn and share for parents and families of children with clefts.

Cleft Information

http://www.birthdefects.org/ Birth Defect Research for Children, Inc. (BDRC) is a 501(c) (3) non-profit organization that provides parents and expectant parents with information about birth defects and support services for their children.

http://www.cincinnatichildrens.org/service/c/craniofacial/resources/ Learn more about managing and treating craniofacial malformations through videos, online, and print resources.

http://www.cleftadvocate.org/feeders.html Descriptions of various bottles, nipples, and post-op feeding alternatives for cleft lip and palate patients.

http://www.cleftawareness.org/ This website offers cleft resources, stories, insurance tips, and other essential information for people looking for answers.

http://www.cleftline.org/parents-individuals/feeding-your-baby/ This webpage will give you the facts you need to feed a baby with a cleft.

http://www.cleftline.org/parents-individuals/information-request/ Order your Complimentary hard copies of information on cleft lip and palates here.

http://www.cleftsmile.org/childrens-story-books/ A list of cleft related books for children.

http://www.cleftstories.com/ Stories about kids with cleft lip and palate.

http://www.marchofdimes.com/baby/birthdefects_cleftpalate.html Basic facts about cleft lip and palates.

http://www.micleft.com/home.htm MiCleft offers the information, resources, and guidance you need to become your child's best advocate.

http://www.smilesforkids.missouri.edu/common_conditions/clp.php Basic information about clefts, along with information for the hospital.

Cleft Merchandise

http://www.cuddlycleftlambs.co.uk/ Personalized cleft lip and palate lambs.

http://www.montesbearsforclefts.org/ It is their mission to create a bear with a matching scar to bring happiness to children while undergoing multiple surgeries and procedures as well as to promote cleft awareness.

http://www.tinywidesmiles.com/ Tiny Wide Smiles designs specially made cleft dolls and animals. "We believe everybody deserves a buddy who looks just like they do!"

Cleft Research

http://www.cdc.gov/ncbddd/birthdefects/cleftlip.html?mobile=nocontent The Center For Disease Control provides facts and information regarding health and safety, including cleft lip and cleft palate.

http://www.cleft.org.uk/ A charity which aims to research the unanswered problems in improving care for children born with cleft lip and palate.

http://www.cleftcollective.org.uk/ The Cleft Collective is the world's largest cleft lip and palate research program and founded by the Healing Foundation.

http://www.ecoonline.org/ The European Cleft Organization is a non-profit organization promoting the advancement of medical expertise and standards of care in the treatment of cleft lip and palate in Europe.

Facebook

There are many cleft groups and pages ran by various organizations, companies, non-profit groups, and individuals. Use the Facebook search function if you are looking for something or an organization in particular. Below are some that our story participants have found helpful:

https://www.facebook.com/gracefulgowns?fref=ts **Graceful Gowns**

https://www.facebook.com/groups/319680591449248/ **Clefty's~ Bringing Wide Smiles Wide Open**

https://www.facebook.com/groups/cleftadvocate/ **Cleft Advocate**

https://www.facebook.com/groups/cleftconnection/ **Cleft and Craniofacial Connection**

https://www.facebook.com/groups/Smiles2009/ **Cleft Lip and Palate Foundation of Smiles**

https://www.facebook.com/MontesBearsforClefts?fref=ts **Montes Bears for Clefts**

https://www.facebook.com/pages/Andis-Smile-Page/121154257897704 **Andi's Smile Page**

https://www.facebook.com/pages/CleftPALS-QLD-Inc/118154044887163?fref=ts **CleftPals Queensland**

https://www.facebook.com/pages/Socks-4-Surgery/166232706836715 **Socks 4 Surgery**

https://www.facebook.com/QuiltsByMamaKateforExtraordinaryKids?fref=ts **Quilts by Mama Kate for Extraordinary Kids**

https://www.facebook.com/groups/cleftmomsupport/ **Cleft Mom Support**

https://www.facebook.com/groups/cleftmommies/ **Cleft Mommies**

https://www.facebook.com/1in700/?ref=br_rs **1 in 700**

Cleft Blogs

http://anthonysjourney.weebly.com/ A blog written about a boy, Anthony's, cleft journey. Features cleft information and awareness.

http://ashleyannphotography.com/blog/ A mom and photographer writes about photography, her family, and adopting their little girl born with a cleft.

http://beentheremom.wordpress.com/ Read about a mom of four boys and her experience with healthy living and frugal living, ADD, sensory integration disorder, and her son, Clayton's, cleft journey.

http://caldersworld.com/ A blog written from the perspective of a beautiful little boy named Calder. He was born with a bilateral cleft lip/palate. Features NAM materials and maintenance.

http://christianbuchanan.blogspot.com/ This blog is from a family whose son, Christian, was born with a Tessier cleft and almost completely blind. It is the story of his life, the joys they share, and the challenges they encounter together.

http://ckhofmann.blogspot.com/ This blog is about a boy named Hudson who was born with a cleft lip and palate. Read about his surgeries and cleft progress.

http://coopersmile.blogspot.com/ This blog is from a mom of a boy named Cooper born with a cleft and lip and palate. She explains his journey with a focus on faith.

http://crazylifeofayoungmom.wordpress.com A mom whose son, Declan, was born with bilateral cleft lip and palate.

http://cupidsrosebud.blogspot.com This blog is devoted to Paige, a little girl's journey after being born with a right unilateral cleft lip and palate. Features ear tubes, insurance issues, nasal stents, and taping.

http://jakescleftstory.blogspot.com/ This blog is from a mom whose son was born with a cleft lip and palate. Features NAM, pre and post-op care.

http://kaydees-life.blogspot.com/ Read about Easton's life and cleft story.

http://lifebetweentheclefts.blogspot.com/ This blog is devoted to a family's journey through their son, Gabriel's life with bilateral cleft lip and palate. He has had many complications along the way.

http://littlemanscleftjourney.blogspot.com/ A mom created this blog for family and friends who want to follow their sweet River's journey and to create awareness and compassion for those affected by clefts.

http://littlepumpkinsjourney.blogspot.com Read about Ryland, a little girl born with unilateral incomplete cleft lip and a notch in her alveolar ridge.

http://mehubsandchubs.blogspot.com/ A blog written by a mom featuring her insights on food, recipes, and her daughter, Lucy's, cleft story.

http://mrsnewell.blogspot.com/ A blog about the busy life of a family whose little girl, Ivy, was born with a cleft lip and palate.

http://northofdelaware.wordpress.com This blog is from two mommies whose daughter, Kestrel, was born with a cleft lip.

http://ourluckycharmpatrick.wordpress.com This blog is devoted to Patrick's journey. He was born with an incomplete unilateral cleft lip with a gum-line notch.

http://riapavia.wordpress.com/ A blog about a young adult female born with a cleft lip and palate. She writes about her experience growing up with a cleft.

http://ruthschultz.blogspot.com/ A blog from a mom of a little girl who has a rare chromosomal depletion, panhypopituitarism, a cleft lip and palate, and congenital heart defects.

http://savsjourney.blogspot.com/ This blog is about Savannah who was born with Pierre Robin Sequence. Features her progress with PRS, surgical, and medical experience.

http://solkoblessednest.blogspot.com/ A mom of three writes about her family including her daughter, Bailey, who was born with a right unilateral cleft lip and palate.

http://thejourneyofasmile.weebly.com/ Written by a teenager named Emily, born with a cleft lip and palate. Her blog is devoted to sharing her journey from a teenage perspective and spreading cleft awareness.

http://thekayleehopemonster.blogspot.com/ This blog is from a mom whose daughter, Kaylee, was born with a cleft lip and palate as a birthday surprise. She explains her journey from NAM, surgery, and beyond.

http://themusgroves.blogspot.com/ Read Foster's cleft journey; born with a bilateral cleft lip and palate.

http://theserthedaysofourlives.blogspot.com/ This blog is written from a mom whose son was born with an incomplete cleft lip and palate. Her son also seems to present with high functioning Asperger's syndrome.

http://www.addysonssmile.blogspot.com/ Follow along with Addyson's smile transformation.

http://www.adleycleft.blogspot.com A blog devoted to the journey a family is taking with their daughter, Adley's, bilateral cleft lip and palate.

http://www.aidenssmile.blogspot.com/ This blog is from the mom of Aiden who was born as a preemie with a cleft lip and palate.

http://www.Bunchbabies.blogspot.com An award winning blog from a mom of triplets. One of her boys was born with a cleft lip and all of the children needed to wear helmets due to plagiocephaly.

http://www.captainjacobjames.blogspot.com Jacob was born with a cleft lip, follow his cleft jouney.

http://www.cleftstory.blogspot.com Wyatt was born with a complete unilateral cleft lip and palate. This blog chronicles his journey.

http://www.controlfreakbaby.blogspot.com This blog is from a mom whose baby, Sy, was born with a cleft lip and palate.

http://www.Hope4Hunter.blogspot.com Hunter was born with a complete cleft lip and palate on the right and an incomplete cleft lip and palate on the left. Featuring NAM and surgical procedures.

http://www.jenningsjabber.blogspot.com This blog is for a mom's little boy Calder. He was born with a cleft lip and palate, and her goal is to chronicle their journey.

http://www.lilyscleftjourney.blogspot.com Follow along with Lily's cleft journey. Features NAM.

http://www.littledudesg.blogspot.com This blog is from a family whose son, Simon, was born with a complete unilateral cleft lip and palate.

http://www.livingouthislove.com/ This family adopted a little girl from China born with a cleft lip and palate.

http://www.loveandalens.blogspot.com This blog is from Nikki, a 26-year-old Army wife and first time mom to a beautiful little girl born with a unilateral cleft lip and palate.

http://www.Moreno-Madness.blogspot.com A blog written by mommy of Mia who was born with a bilateral cleft lip and palate.

http://www.parra.ca Read about Aidan who was born with a unilateral cleft lip and palate. His parents share cleft information and support through their blog.

http://www.thecleftofthematter.blogspot.com This blog is from a mom whose daughter was born with an isolated cleft of the soft palate.

http://www.thelackymom.com/the-little-jerk-2/ A mom writes about life in general, including her daughter born with a cleft palate.

http://www.thestraightenedpath.com/ Read the cleft story of Clayton as his mom writes about marriage between best friends, adventures with children, and what the Lord is teaching her along the way.

https://www.facebook.com/pages/Aidens-Smile/136760986389458 Follow Aiden's journey to the perfect smile on Facebook, as his family raises awareness of cleft lip and palate.

https://www.facebook.com/pages/Ivys-Update-Page/295662997133463 This is a Facebook page about Ivy who was born with a bilateral cleft lip and palate and has a feeding tube.

https://www.facebook.com/HopeForHaiden?ref=hl 'Like' the Hope for Haiden page on Facebook and read about Haiden's cleft journey.

Glossary

Acid Reflux: Happens when the lower esophageal sphincter does not close all the way. This results in acid, produced by the stomach, moving up into the esophagus.

Acupuncture: A collection of procedures which involves the stimulation of points on the body using a variety of techniques; such as penetrating the skin with needles that are then manipulated manually or by electrical stimulation.

ADHD or Attention Deficit Hyperactivity Disorder: One of the most common childhood disorders and can continue through adolescence and adulthood. Symptoms include difficulty staying focused and paying attention, difficulty controlling behavior, and hyperactivity (over-activity).

Alveolar Ridge or Alveolus: The boney upper gum that contains teeth.

Amniocentesis: A medical procedure used in prenatal diagnosis of chromosomal abnormalities and fetal infections.

Anesthesiologist: A specially trained medical professional that administers anesthesia.

Anesthetic: Controls pain and maintains vital functions during surgery or other medical procedures.

Antibiotics: Types of medications that destroy or slow down the growth of bacteria.

Antibodies: These are large Y-shaped protein produced by B-cells that is used by the immune system to identify and neutralize foreign objects such as bacteria and viruses.

Apgar Scores: APGAR is a quick test performed on a baby at one and five minutes after birth. The one-minute score determines how well the baby tolerated the birthing process. The five-minute score tells the doctor how well the baby is doing outside the mother's womb.

Apnea Monitor: A device that measures how well you breathe.

APNO or All-Purpose Nipple Ointment: Used to heal nipples and to prevent nipple infection.

Asperger's Syndrome: An autism spectrum disorder (ASD), one of a distinct group of complex neurodevelopment disorders characterized by social impairment, communication difficulties, and restrictive, repetitive, and stereotyped patterns of behavior.

Aspirate: To suck in, accidentally drawing material into the lungs.

Audiologist: A specialist in communication disorders stemming from a hearing impairment will assess and monitor hearing.

Audiology: The study of hearing and hearing related disorders.

Autism: A brain disorder that limits a person's ability to communicate and relate to other people.

Bicornuate Uterus: A uterus that has two horns and a heart shape. It is the most common congenital uterine anomaly and can impact a woman's reproductive capabilities.

Bicuspid Aortic Valve: A heart valve with only two leaflets. With this deformity, the valve doesn't function perfectly, but it may function adequately for years without causing symptoms or obvious signs of a problem.

Bilateral Cleft: A cleft that affects both sides of the mouth or lip areas.

Bili Light: A special light bulb used to treat jaundice.

Bone Defect: An abnormality in the bone or marrow.

Bone Graft: In the case of a cleft, this surgical procedure involves taking a small amount of bone from one place (most often the hip) and placing it in the space of the cleft near the teeth.

Boppy Pillow: The original C-Shaped pillow designed for infant feeding and support.

Bronchitis: A respiratory disease in which the mucus membrane in the lungs' bronchial passages becomes inflamed. As the irritated membrane swells and grows thicker, it narrows or shuts off the tiny airways in the lungs, resulting in coughing spells that may be accompanied by phlegm and breathlessness.

Cannula: A flexible tube that is inserted into a body cavity, duct, or vessel to drain fluid or administer a substance such as a medication.

Cardiologist: Doctors who specialize in diagnosing and treating diseases or conditions of the heart and blood vessels.

Chromosomal Abnormalities: Abnormalities caused by errors in the number or structure of chromosomes. Many children with a chromosomal abnormality have mental and/or physical birth defects.

Cleft Lip: A fissure in the upper lip due to fusion failure of the left and right sides of the lip tissue. It can occur on one side only or on both sides.

Cleft Palate: A cleft palate is a split or opening in the roof of the mouth. It can affect the hard and/or soft palate.

Cleftie or Clefty: Slang term for someone with a cleft lip and/or palate.

Clomid, Clomifene or Clomiphene: Medication used to treat infertility in women.

Cochlea: The inner part of the ear responsible for hearing.

Codeine: Narcotic pain medicine used to treat mild to moderate pain.

CPAP or Continuous Positive Airway Pressure: A treatment that uses mild air pressure to keep the airways open, typically used by people who have breathing problems.

Craniofacial: Relating to the cranium and the face.

Craniosynostosis: A birth defect in which one or more of the joints between the bones of the infant's skull close prematurely, before the brain is fully formed.

Croup: An infection of the upper airway, generally in children, which obstructs breathing and causes a characteristic barking cough.

C-section or Cesarean Section Delivery: A surgical procedure used to deliver a baby through an incision in the mother's abdomen and a second incision in the mother's uterus.

Cupid's Bow: An upper lip with two strong curves in it.

CF or Cystic Fibrosis: An inherited chronic disease that affects the lungs and digestive system.

Deformity: A physical blemish or distortion.

Desat (Desaturation): The condition of a low blood oxygen concentration caused by not breathing or not fully breathing.

D&C or Dilation and Curettage: A brief surgical procedure in which the cervix is dilated and a special instrument is used to scrape the uterine lining.

Down Syndrome: Occurs when an individual has a full or partial extra copy of chromosome 21.

Downs Test: A combined test including an ultrasound to measure a specific region on the back of a baby's neck (known as a nuchal translucency screening test) and blood tests that measure levels of pregnancy-associated plasma protein-A (PAPP-A) and a hormone known as human chorionic gonadotropin (HCG).

DynaCleft Tape: Tape that pre-surgically reduces orofacial clefts for best possible surgical results. It gently guides the soft tissue and bone of the cleft lip and palate into better position for repair.

Ear Canal Stenosis: A narrowed ear canal; one in which the eardrum can be viewed, but the canal is more narrow than normal.

Ear Tubes: Tiny cylinders placed through the ear drum to allow air into the middle ear. Often recommended when a person experiences repeated middle ear infection or has hearing loss caused by the persistent presence of middle ear fluid.

Early Intervention: A program designed to improve outcomes for children with disabilities by providing early, appropriate, and intensive interventions.

ENT or Ear, Nose, and Throat Doctor: Physicians trained in the medical and surgical management and treatment of patients with diseases and disorders of the ear, nose, throat, and related structures of the head and neck. (See also 'ORL')

Facial Artery Myomucosal Flaps (FAMM): "An axial oral musculomucosal flap, based on the facial artery, which can line defects of the mouth and nose." [*Plastic Surgery: Volume 3: Craniofacial, Head and Neck Surgery*; edited by Neligan, Rodriguez, & Losee]

Failure to Thrive: Children whose current weight or rate of weight gain is significantly lower than that of other children of similar age and gender.

Feeding Tube: A tube that may be put directly into the stomach through the abdominal skin if a person is having ongoing and serious trouble swallowing and can't get enough food or liquids by mouth. The tube allows enteral feeding to occur by bypassing the mouth and esophagus.

Fistula or Palatal Fistula: A fistula occurs when the palate fails to fully heal and an opening or hole appears in the palate post palate surgery.

Fixodent: Denture adhesive cream; has been used for cleft children to keep a cleft device in place.

Food Aversion: When an infant or child refuses to accept food by mouth or when they are not accepting the developmentally appropriate amount, variety or type of food by mouth.

G-Tube or Gastronomy Tube: A tube placed in the stomach to provide another way to offer food and/or medicines or to vent the stomach for air or drainage.

Gastrostomy: The surgical placement of a feeding tube through the skin and the stomach wall, directly into the stomach.

Gavage: A feeding tube placed through a baby's nose to carry breast milk or formula to the stomach. Used for babies who cannot get enough nutrition by bottle or breast feedings alone.

Genetic Syndromes: When one or more genes or chromosomes are missing, mutated, or if extra are present, the proteins may not get made, may be made incorrectly, or too many may be made causing abnormal development and growth. Sometimes these abnormal genes or chromosomes are passed down from a parent and sometimes they occur spontaneously without reason.

Genetic: The study of genes, their functions, and their effects.

Geneticist: An individual trained in diagnostic and therapeutic procedures for patients with genetically-linked diseases.

Glucose Water: A commercially prepared substance that is mostly water with a small amount of sugar added. The solution is pre-prepared and ready to feed. Many hospital nurseries have glucose water on hand for treatment of hypoglycemia.

Grommets: Tiny tubes that are inserted in the ear to treat trapped fluid in the middle ear that can result in infection and hearing loss.

Haberman Bottle: See 'Medela Special Needs Feeder'

Hard Palate: The bony anterior part of the palate forming the roof of the mouth.

Heart Catheterization: A surgical procedure that involves passing a thin flexible tube into the right or left side of the heart, usually from the groin or the arm. Also known as cardiac catheterization.

Heart Murmur: An extra or unusual sound heard during a heartbeat. Murmurs range from very faint to very loud. They can also be innocent or a sign of a serious heart defect.

Hematoma: Usually, a mass of clotted blood that forms in a tissue, organ, or body space as a result of a broken blood vessel.

High Amniotic Fluid or Polyhydramnios: Too much amniotic fluid surrounding an unborn infant that can occur if the developing baby does not swallow and absorb amniotic fluid in normal amounts.

HSG test or Hysterosalpingogram: An X-ray test that looks at the inside of the uterus and fallopian tubes and the area around them.

Hyperemesis Gravidarum: A condition characterized by severe nausea, vomiting, weight loss, and electrolyte disturbance.

Hypertrophic Scar: An elevated scar that is typically more stiff than the surrounding skin and usually regresses over time.

Hypoglycemia: A condition characterized by an abnormally low level of blood sugar.

Hypothyroidism: A condition in which your thyroid gland doesn't produce enough of certain important hormones.

Ibuprofen: An anti-inflammatory drug used to reduce fever and treat pain or inflammation.

Infinity Feeding Pump: A small, lightweight, portable, and adaptable pump built to simplify enteral feeding. It safely and accurately delivers any nutritional regimen without compromising quality of life.

Insecure Attachment: A disorder in which a person lacks the skills for building meaningful relationships.

ICP or Intrahepatic Cholestasis of Pregnancy: A liver disorder that occurs in pregnant women that impairs the release of a digestive from liver cells causing severe itchiness in the expectant mother.

Intravenous or IV Medications: Solutions administered directly into the venous circulation via syringe or intravenous catheter (tube).

Intubation: The introduction of a tube into a hollow organ (as the trachea or intestine) to keep it open or restore its patency if obstructed.

Italian Ice: Fruit and fruit flavors blended together and frozen.

J-tube or Jejunostomy Tube: A tube inserted through the abdomen and into the jejunum (the middle section of the small intestine) to assist with feeding and to provide nutrition.

238

Lactation Consultant: A health care professional who specializes in the clinical management of breastfeeding and provides information and support to help prevent and manage common concerns.

Laryngomalacia: A congenital softening of the tissues of the larynx (voice box) above the vocal cords.

Latham Device: A device used to maintain or reposition the segments of the palate prior to surgical repair.

Lip Taping: Preoperative taping across a cleft lip causing soft tissue mobilization and alveolar modeling that allows a single stage lip/nasal surgical repair.

Mastitis: An infection of the breast tissue that results in breast pain, swelling, warmth, and redness of the breast.

Maternal Fetal Medicine Specialist or Perinatologist: A doctor experienced in a wide variety of complex maternal-fetal conditions and offer specialized care of pregnant women and their fetuses.

Mead Johnson Bottle: A soft squeeze bottle with long cross cut nipple designed to be pulse-squeezed with baby's suck and swallowing.

Medela Special Needs Feeder: The bottle of choice for much of the cleft lip and palate population. This bottle has a one way valve that helps reduce the amount of air the baby takes in and also has a squeezable teat to help assist the baby in feeding. The teat is squeezed to provide baby with an adequate amount of formula with the least amount of effort. Formerly known as the Haberman bottle.

Mic-Key Button: A feeding tube which enters the stomach through the feeding and medication port in the abdominal wall allowing the intake of nutrients, medication, and water that your body requires.

Microform Cleft: A mild expression of cleft lip, one in which the lip is fully intact, but a scar-like line is seen in the cleft area.

Mono-Mono or Monoamniotic-Monochorionic Twins: A sub-type of monozygotic twins accounting for the minority of monozygotic twin pregnancies and less than 1-2 % of all twin pregnancies. These fetuses are identical and share a single chorionic sac, a single yolk sac and a single amniotic sac.

Motrin: A non-steroidal, anti-inflammatory drug used to reduce fever and treat pain or inflammation by reducing hormones that cause inflammation and pain in the body.

NAM or Nasal Alveolar Molding Device: A nonsurgical method of reshaping the gums, lip, and nostrils before cleft lip and palate surgery, lessening the severity of the cleft.

Nasal Cavity: The vaulted chamber that lies between the floor of the cranium and the roof of the mouth.

Nasal Conformer: Small silicone tube holding the position of the nostril during the healing time after surgery.

Nasal Mold: A cleft device designed to mold and shape the nasal area. (See also 'NAM')

Nasal Spring: A device placed in the nostril prior to surgery in order to reshape the nose for better results.

Nasal Stents: Small, hollow, rubbery tubes that may be stitched or taped into nostrils to give support to the nasal cartilage after surgery so it keeps its new shape and size.

NG or Nasogastric Tube: A flexible, bidirectional tube that is passed through the nose and down through the nasopharynx and esophagus into the stomach. It can be used to remove the contents of the stomach or to put substances into the stomach.

NICU or Neonatal Intensive Care Unit: A section of the hospital with specialized equipment and highly trained doctors and nurses that provide round the clock care to sick or premature infants.

Nipple Shield: A clear, flexible, nipple shaped piece of silicone with holes in the tip that can be held over the breast while a baby nurses.

No-No's: Pediatric arm immobilizers also referred to as pediatric splints or pediatric arm restraints.

OB or Obstetrician: A physician offering a variety of women's health services and trained to manage complications during pregnancy, birth, and postpartum.

OB-GYN: Doctors specialized in obstetrics and gynecology for the care of women to include the preconception period, pregnancy, labor, childbirth, and postpartum period. OB-GYNs are also trained in woman's general health care, hormonal disorders, treatment of infections, and surgery to correct or treat pelvic organ or urinary tract problems.

Obstructive Sleep Apnea: A potentially serious sleep disorder in which breathing repeatedly stops and starts during sleep.

Obtruator: A prosthetic device that closes or blocks up an opening such as a fissure in the palate.

Occupational Therapist: An individual trained to treat patients with injuries, illnesses, or disabilities through the therapeutic use of everyday activities.

Oppositional Defiant Disorder: A pattern of disobedient, hostile, and defiant behavior toward authority figures.

OR or Operating Room: The unit of a hospital where surgical procedures are performed.

Oral Surgeon: The surgical specialists of the dental profession with extensive education and training, surgical expertise, and unparalleled understanding of esthetics and function to uniquely qualify them to treat the conditions, defects, injuries, and esthetic aspects of the mouth, teeth, jaws, and face.

ORL or Otolaryngologist: Diagnose and manage diseases of the ears, nose, sinuses, larynx, mouth, and throat, as well as structures of the neck and face. (See also 'ENT')

Orthodontist: A dentist with advanced training. They can realign crooked teeth into a straight, healthy smile.

Outpatient surgery: Surgery that does not require an overnight hospital stay. Patients may go home after being released following surgery and time spent in the recovery room.

Pablum: A trademark for an infant cereal.

Palatal Appliance: An appliance that fits into the roof of the mouth used to widen the palate to make room for crowded teeth and improve jaw function.

Palatoplasty: A surgical procedure used to correct or reconstruct the palate. The basic goals of this surgery are to close the abnormal opening between the nose and mouth and help the patient to develop normal speech in order to improve swallowing, breathing, and development of associated structures in the mouth.

Panadol: A prescribed or over-the-counter medication used in the treatment of pain.

Paracetamol: A pain reliever and a fever reducer.

PDA or Patent Ductus Arteriosus: A heart problem that affects some babies soon after birth. In PDA, abnormal blood flow occurs between two of the major arteries connected to the heart.

Pediatrician: A child's physician who provides preventive health maintenance for healthy children and medical care for children who are acutely or chronically ill.

PEG or Percutaneous Endoscopic Gastrostomy Tube: A soft, plastic tube that is put into your stomach through your skin.

Perinatal Specialist: A doctor that specializes in the care of both the infant and the mother in the time just before and just after the baby is born. The perinatal period is generally marked at 22 completed weeks of gestation and lasts until seven completed days after birth.

Pharyngeal Flap Surgery or P-Flap Surgery: A surgical procedure to correct or enhance the quality of your child's speech. Muscle tissue is transferred from the back of the throat or pharynx to the palate in order to narrow the nasal opening.

Phillips Screwdriver: A tool which has a head with pointed edges in the shape of a cross, that fits neatly into the cross slots of a Phillips screw.

PICU or Pediatric Intensive Care Unit: A multidisciplinary unit that provides high quality care for critically ill infants, children, and adolescents.

Pierre Robin Sequence or PRS: A combination of birth defects which usually include a small lower jaw, cleft palate, and a tendency for the tongue to "ball up" in the back of the mouth.

Pigeon Nipple: A nipple which can be used with any bottle and works by compression only. A plastic one-way valve fits into the nipple to keep milk in the nipple. When the baby begins to suck, milk flows readily.

Pitocin: A uterine stimulant that causes uterine contractions for inducing labor in women with Rh problems, diabetes, preeclampsia, or when it is in the best interest of the mother or fetus. It is also used to help produce contractions during the third stage of labor and control bleeding after childbirth.

Placenta Previa: Occurs when the placenta partially or totally covers the mother's cervix and can cause severe bleeding before or during delivery.

Plastic Surgeon: A surgeon that manages the repair, reconstruction, or replacement of physical defects of form or function involving the skin, musculoskeletal system, head, and facial structures, hands, extremities, breasts, and trunk as well as cosmetic enhancement of these areas.

Pneumonia: A lung infection caused by bacteria or viruses that can make you very sick. Symptoms include cough, fever, and difficulty breathing.

Pneumothorax: A collapsed lung occurring when air leaks into the space between your lungs and chest wall. This air pushes on the outside of your lung and causes it to collapse.

Polygrip: A denture adhesive which has been used for cleft children to keep a cleft device in place.

Psychologist: A trained individual who studies mental processes and human behavior by observing, interpreting, and recording how people and other animals relate to one another and the environment.

PTSD or Post Traumatic Stress Disorder: An anxiety disorder that some people get after seeing or living through a dangerous or traumatic event.

Pulse Oximeter: A medical device which provides an easy way of partly assessing breathing by measuring the oxygen saturation of arterial blood.

Pulse Oximetry Monitor: Monitors the amount of oxygen in the blood and pulse rate.

Quad Screen: A maternal blood screening test that looks for four specific substances: AFP, HCG, Estriol, and Inhibin-A.

Red Preemie Nipple: An extra soft, shortened nipple for small or weak mouths; no suction needed.

Respiratory Therapist: Practitioners involved in the evaluation and monitoring of heart and lung function as well as giving treatment.

Rhinoplasty: A nose surgery sometimes referred to as "nose reshaping" or a "nose job" which can improve the appearance and proportion of your nose, or correct a breathing problem associated with the nose.

Routine AFP or Alpha- Fetoprotein Test: A blood test which is done when a woman is between 16 and 18 weeks pregnant that is helpful in identifying high risk pregnancies and some types of birth defects.

Sacral Dimple: An indentation present at birth, in the skin on the lower back, just above the crease between the buttocks. Most sacral dimples are harmless and don't require any treatment, however, those that are accompanied by a nearby tuft of hair, skin tag or certain types of skin discoloration are sometimes associated with a serious underlying abnormality of the spine or spinal cord.

Scar Revision: A surgery meant to minimize a scar so that it is more consistent with your surrounding skin tone and texture.

SCBU or Special Care Baby Unit: A unit taking premature and term babies who do not require intensive care, but are unable to be cared for on a regular postnatal ward.

Sensory Processing Disorder: A condition that exists when sensory signals are not organized into appropriate responses which prevents certain parts of the brain from receiving the information needed to interpret sensory information correctly. Motor clumsiness, behavioral problems, anxiety, depression, school failure, and other impacts may result if the disorder is not treated effectively.

Separation Anxiety Disorder: A condition in which a child becomes fearful and nervous when away from home or separated from a loved one (usually a parent or other caregiver) to whom the child is attached.

Short Stature: A person who is significantly below the average height for a person of the same age and sex.

Single Umbilical Artery: The most common malformation of the umbilical cord seen in 0.5% to 7% of all pregnancies. There is only one artery and one vein present in the umbilical instead of the usual two arteries and one vein.

Social Worker: A professional trained to provide a variety of services, ranging from psychotherapy to the administration of health and welfare programs. They help individuals, families, and groups change behaviors, emotions, attitudes, relationships, and social conditions to restore and enhance their capacity to meet their personal and social needs.

Soft Palate: The soft tissue at the back of the hard palate that partially separates the mouth from the pharynx.

Soothies: Gel pads that provide instant, cooling relief to breastfeeding mothers with sore nipples. (Soothie is also a brand of pacifiers)

Speech Therapist: A specialist with training in the diagnosis and treatment of a variety of speech, voice, and language disorders who works with people unable to make speech sounds or who cannot make them clearly.

Speech-Language Pathologist: Diagnose and treat communication and swallowing disorders in patients.

Spina-Bifida: The most common permanently disabling birth defect in the United States that occurs when a baby is in the womb and the spinal column does not close all of the way.

SSRI or Selective Serotonin Reuptake Inhibitors: The most commonly prescribed antidepressants. They can ease symptoms of moderate to severe depression.

Step-Down Unit: A hospital nursing unit providing care intermediate between that of an intensive care unit and a normally-staffed in-patient division.

Sternum or Breastbone: The long, narrow, flat plate that forms the center of the front of the chest.

Stickler Syndrome: A group of hereditary conditions characterized by a distinctive facial appearance, eye abnormalities, hearing loss, and joint problems.

Strep Throat: A bacterial infection in the throat and the tonsils caused by streptococcal bacteria. The throat gets irritated and inflamed, causing a sudden, severe sore throat.

Stridor: An abnormality in the throat which causes a wheezing sound when breathing.

Submucous Palate: The palate appears to be structurally intact, but there are bony and/or muscular abnormalities underlying the skin's surface.

Supraglottoplasty: A microscopic surgical procedure to alter malformed structures of the upper larynx to allow a child with certain conditions to breathe more easily.

Surgical Foam: A latex free, conformable, hypoallergenic, elastic foam tape which stretches to make an ideal dressing for challenging areas and for specialist applications.

Tender Care Feeder (Soft Sipp): A soft, squeezable 90ml bottle for use when syringe or cup feeding is recommended.

Tethered Spinal Cord: A neurological disorder caused by tissue attachments that limit the movement of the spinal cord within the spinal column.

Tetralogy of Fallot: A rare condition caused by a combination of four heart defects that are present at birth. These defects, which affect the structure of the heart, cause oxygen-poor blood to flow out of the heart and into the rest of the body.

Theatre or Operating Theatre: A room where operations are performed.

Toe Syndactyly: A condition in which fingers and/or toes are joined together.

Tonsillitis: Inflammation of the tonsils most commonly caused by viral or bacterial infection.

Tracheoesophageal Fistula: A severe and even fatal complication of an irregular junction of the trachea and esophagus that requires surgery.

Tracheostomy: A surgically created hole through the front of your neck and into your windpipe (trachea).

Transducer: A device which sends sound waves into your body and picks up the echoes of the sound waves as they bounce off internal organs and tissue. A computer transforms these echoes into an image.

Trisomy 13: A chromosomal condition associated with severe intellectual disability and physical abnormalities in many parts of the body. The majority of babies affected by Trisomy 13 do not live passed their first year of life.

Trisomy 18 or Edwards Syndrome: A chromosomal condition associated with abnormalities in many parts of the body which often results in slow growth before birth and a low birth weight. The majority of fetuses with the syndrome do not survive.

T-Tubes or Tympanostomy Tubes: Small tubes inserted into the eardrum in order to keep the middle ear aerated for a prolonged period of time, and to prevent the accumulation of fluid in the middle ear.

Unilateral Cleft: A cleft affecting one side of the face.

Upper Respiratory Infection: Any type of infection of the head and chest that is caused by a virus. It can affect your nose, throat, sinuses, ears, the tube that connects your middle ear and throat, windpipe, voice box, and airways.

Vascular Ring: A rare cardiovascular birth defect involving an unusual formation of the aorta and/or its surrounding blood vessels which frequently causes breathing and digestive problems.

Ventilator: A machine that supports breathing.

Zip n' Squeeze: A squeezable bag with an attached straw to simplify and ease eating and drinking for patients post-jaw surgery, or with head and neck cancer, oral-facial muscle weakness, and wired jaws.

Z-Plasty: A plastic surgery technique that is used to improve the functional and cosmetic appearance of scars.

Disclaimer

We are not responsible for the content or the privacy practices of other websites or resources (books, blogs, etc.). Any mention of doctors, links, books, blogs, organizations, etc. does not constitute an endorsement. We encourage you to examine each resource's privacy policy and make your own decisions regarding the accuracy, reliability, and correctness of material and information found.

The information contained in this book is not intended nor implied to be a substitute for professional medical advice. It is provided for educational purposes only. You assume full responsibility for how you choose to use this information. Please talk to your doctor prior to using any recommendations given.

Always seek the advice of your physician or other qualified healthcare provider before starting any new treatment or discontinuing an existing treatment. Talk with your healthcare provider first about any questions you may have regarding a medical condition. Do not self-diagnose. Proper medical care is critical to good health. If you have a health concern or undiagnosed sign or symptom, please consult a physician or a health care specialist as soon as possible.

The opinions expressed in the stories, advice, survey responses, and letters are solely those of the writers and do not necessarily reflect the views of the editors or any other organization. Some names may have been changed to protect personal privacy. Stories and other submissions may have been edited for clarity, length and/or size.

Tell us Your Story

This book would not have been possible without the amazing help and contributions of the writers and survey participants. We thank them so much for their participation. We couldn't have done it without you!

Please visit our website to see if we are currently accepting new stories for future editions. We thoroughly enjoy reading every single story. On our website, you can also find links to books, blogs, and websites mentioned in the book. Further, you can find us on Facebook, Twitter, and Instagram.

Website: www.iwishidknown.yolasite.com

Facebook: www.facebook.com/IWishIdKnown

Twitter: www.twitter.com/Cleftbook

Instagram: www.instagram.com/iwishidknown

CPSIA information can be obtained
at www.ICGtesting.com
Printed in the USA
LVHW101758170419
614533LV00011B/82/P